Park & Burgess

THE CITY

THE HERITAGE OF SOCIOLOGY
A Series Edited by **Morris Janowitz**

Robert E. Park
Ernest W. Burgess
Roderick D. McKenzie

THE CITY

With an Introduction by
MORRIS JANOWITZ

THE UNIVERSITY OF CHICAGO PRESS
CHICAGO AND LONDON

ISBN: 0-226-64607-6 (clothbound); 0-226-64608-4 (paperbound)

Library of Congress Catalog Card Number: 66-23694

THE UNIVERSITY OF CHICAGO PRESS, CHICAGO 60637
The University of Chicago Press, Ltd., London

Contents

CONTENTS

Introduction

FROM THE period 1915-40, the writings of the Chicago school
of urban sociology were extensive and their impact diverse. The
key figures had a lasting impact on scholarly research into urban
affairs, and raised fundamental issues of social and political policy.
Their efforts even spilled over into the humanistic disciplines.

Their research monographs presented vivid descriptions of urban reality which commanded a wide audience outside academic
circles. These men initiated the tradition of the detailed case-study
approach which has been continued by men such as David Riesman
and Oscar Lewis. The work of the University of Chicago sociologists
became part of the American literary scene through their interaction with those novelists who lived and wrote in the environs of the
campus. These names included James T. Farrell, Richard Wright
and Saul Bellow to mention only three.

The contemporary issues of physical and social redevelopment
in the inner city were raised long before the Great Depression by
these sociologists who had a strong background in the social gospel.
As field workers they did more than describe the social evils of the
big city. They were concerned with comprehensive schemes of social

change and social planning. They were critical of superficial steps aimed at temporary amelioration. The first criticisms of social work, which in the contemporary era have become painfully shrill, were put forth with reasoned understanding as early as 1918 by W. I. Thomas. Efforts to develop new conceptions were embodied in the Department of Sociology's field station, the Chicago area project, which in the 1930's sought to bring "community development" to Chicago's slums of the near North Side. The results produced notions of citizen participation, self help, and the culture of poverty which have been keystone ideas in the "war against poverty."

But the Chicago school of urban sociology was strongly motivated by a drive to view the city as an object of detached sociological analysis. These men were fascinated with the complexities of the urban community and the prospect of discovering patterns of regularity in its apparent confusion. The contemporary rediscovery of the city has only served to enhance the intellectual relevance of their concepts and propositions. They did not produce definitive answers, but they posed crucial questions which still dominate the thinking of urban sociologists. It was inevitable that as their original theoretical formulations diffused they lost their subtlety. Some of the contemporary arguments in urban sociology seem to contribute to such oversimplification because of a failure to confront their original formulations.

Thus the reprinting of *The City* by Robert E. Park, Ernest W. Burgess, and Roderick D. McKenzie, is most appropriate. This volume, published in 1925, is truly a cross-section of the intellectual concerns of the Chicago urban school during the period of its most intense activity. It contains both key theoretical expositions and interpretative essays about the cultural patterns of urban life. What is missing is the detailed descriptive findings which the reader must find in the individual monographic studies.

Robert E. Park's essay on *The City: Suggestions for the Investigation of Human Behavior in the Urban Environment* is a striking contemporary statement of the issues that research must still confront. Ernest Burgess' analysis of urban zones can be read as the genuine effort of an empiricist who sought to create a cognitive map of the unplanned growth patterns of the city; in the current phase of planned social change, the job must be done again. Roderick D. McKenzie's exploration of ecology is likewise an expression of an intellectual aspiration to analyze the city in holistic terms, a goal which has become even more important as the city becomes larger and more complex.

Throughout the volume the intellectual posture of the Chicago school dominates. The city is not an artifact or a residual arrangement. On the contrary, the city embodies the real nature of human nature. It is an expression of mankind in general and specifically of the social relations generated by territoriality. Modern technology has altered but not eliminated territoriality as the city has come to equal civilization.

These men wrote of magic and mentality; they sought to describe myth and intellectuality. They were sociologists who realized that the tradition, custom, and romantic aspirations of city dwellers converted ecological, economic, and industrial factors into a social organization. In their search for objectivity and generality they did not find it necessary to deny a concern with the values that propel human beings. It is for this reason they often used the term social organization; to organize implies that men are creating social values and social goals.

Today the modern city cannot be fully understood or managed with the types and amount of data they had at their disposal. Their efforts to collect information, although heroic by the standards of their day, were primitive by our standards. For example, the contemporary city and contemporary urban sociology cannot operate without the use of computer technology. These Chicago sociologists who gathered their data by hand would bask in the results of contemporary social science facilities. But they would continue, as their students have done, to show their concern with individuality by their attention to the modern equivalent of the hobo and the taxi-hall dancer.

Morris Janowitz

CHAPTER I

THE CITY: SUGGESTIONS FOR THE INVESTI-GATION OF HUMAN BEHAVIOR IN THE URBAN ENVIRONMENT

The city, from the point of view of this paper, is something more than a congeries of individual men and of social conveniences— streets, buildings, electric lights, tramways, and telephones, etc.; something more, also, than a mere constellation of institutions and administrative devices—courts, hospitals, schools, police, and civil functionaries of various sorts. The city is, rather, a state of mind, a body of customs and traditions, and of the organized attitudes and sentiments that inhere in these customs and are transmitted with this tradition. The city is not, in other words, merely a physical mechanism and an artificial construction. It is involved in the vital processes of the people who compose it; it is a product of nature, and particularly of human nature.

The city has, as Oswald Spengler has recently pointed out, its own culture: "What his house is to the peasant, the city is to civilized man. As the house has its household gods, so has the city its protecting Deity, its local saint. The city also, like the peasant's hut, has its roots in the soil."[1]

The city has been studied, in recent times, from the point of view of its geography, and still more recently from the point of view of its ecology. There are forces at work within the limits of the urban community—within the limits of any natural area of human habitation, in fact—which tend to bring about an orderly and typical grouping of its population and institutions. The science which seeks

[1] Oswald Spengler, *Der Untergang des Abendlandes*, IV (München, 1922), 105.

1

to isolate these factors and to describe the typical constellations of persons and institutions which the co-operation of these forces produce, is what we call human, as distinguished from plant and animal, ecology.

Transport & communication = primary factors in ecological organization of city

Transportation and communication, tramways and telephones, newspapers and advertising, steel construction and elevators—all things, in fact, which tend to bring about at once a greater mobility and a greater concentration of the urban populations—are primary factors in the ecological organization of the city.

City = an economic unit—based on division of Labor

The city is not, however, merely a geographical and ecological unit; it is at the same time an economic unit. The economic organization of the city is based on the division of labor. The multiplication of occupations and professions within the limits of the urban population is one of the most striking and least understood aspects of modern city life. From this point of view, we may, if we choose, think of the city, that is to say, the place and the people, with all the machinery and administrative devices that go with them, as organically related; a kind of psychophysical mechanism in and through which private and political interests find not merely a collective but a corporate expression.

Much of what we ordinarily regard as the city—its charters, formal organization, buildings, street railways, and so forth—is, or seems to be, mere artifact. But these things in themselves are utilities, adventitious devices which become part of the living city only when, and in so far as, through use and wont they connect themselves, like a tool in the hand of man, with the vital forces resident in individuals and in the community.

city = the natural habitat of man

The city is, finally, the natural habitat of civilized man. It is for that reason a cultural area characterized by its own peculiar cultural type:

"It is a quite certain, but never fully recognized, fact," says Spengler, "that all great cultures are city-born. The outstanding man of the second generation is a city-building animal. This is the actual criterion of world-history, as distinguished from the history of mankind: world-history is the history of city men. Nations, governments, politics, and religions—all rest on the basic phenomenon of human existence, the city."[1]

Anthropology, the science of man, has been mainly concerned up to the present with the study of primitive peoples. But civilized man is quite as interesting an object of investigation, and at the same time his life is more open to observation and study. Urban life and culture are more varied, subtle, and complicated, but the fundamental motives are in both instances the same. The same patient methods of observation which anthropologists like Boas and Lowie have expended on the study of the life and manners of the North American Indian might be even more fruitfully employed in the investigation of the customs, beliefs, social practices, and general conceptions of life prevalent in Little Italy on the lower North Side in Chicago, or in recording the more sophisticated folkways of the inhabitants of Greenwich Village and the neighborhood of Washington Square, New York.

We are mainly indebted to writers of fiction for our more intimate knowledge of contemporary urban life. But the life of our cities demands a more searching and disinterested study than even Émile Zola has given us in his "experimental" novels and the annals of the Rougon-Macquart family.

We need such studies, if for no other reason than to enable us to read the newspapers intelligently. The reason that the daily chronicle of the newspaper is so shocking, and at the same time so fascinating, to the average reader is because the average reader knows so little about the life of which the newspaper is the record.

The observations which follow are intended to define a point of view and to indicate a program for the study of urban life: its physical organization, its occupations, and its culture.

[1] Oswald Spengler, *Untergang des Abendlandes,* IV, 106.

I. THE CITY PLAN AND LOCAL ORGANIZATION

[margin: Ground-plan of most cities = block]

The city, particularly the modern American city, strikes one at first blush as so little a product of the artless processes of nature and growth, that it is difficult to recognize it as a living entity. The ground plan of most American cities, for example, is a checkerboard. The unit of distance is the block. This geometrical form *[margin: is there a city a purely artificial construct?]* suggests that the city is a purely artificial construction which might conceivably be taken apart and put together again, like a house of blocks.

[margin: Structure of City is rooted in habits of people] The fact is, however, that the city is rooted in the habits and customs of the people who inhabit it. The consequence is that the city possesses a moral as well as a physical organization, and these two mutually interact in characteristic ways to mold and modify one another. It is the structure of the city which first impresses us *[margin: The Then Formed structure imposes self on people]* by its visible vastness and complexity. But this structure has its basis, nevertheless, in human nature, of which it is an expression. On the other hand, this vast organization which has arisen in response to the needs of its inhabitants, once formed, imposes itself upon them as a crude external fact, and forms them, in turn, in accordance with the design and interests which it incorporates. Structure and tradition are but different aspects of a single cultural complex which determines what is characteristic and peculiar to city, as distinguished from village, life and the life of the open *[margin: There are limits to possible modifications of physical & moral orders]* fields.

The city plan.—It is because the city has a life quite its own that there is a limit to the arbitrary modifications which it is possible to make (1) in its physical structure and (2) in its moral order.

The city plan, for example, establishes metes and bounds, fixes in a general way the location and character of the city's constructions, and imposes an orderly arrangement, within the city area, upon the buildings which are erected by private initiative as well as by public authority. Within the limitations prescribed, however, the inevitable processes of human nature proceed to give these regions and these buildings a character which it is less easy to control. Under our system of individual ownership, for instance, it is not possible to determine in advance the extent of concentration of population which is likely to occur in any given area. The city cannot fix land values, and we leave to private enterprise, for the most part, the task of determining the city's limits and the location of its residential and industrial districts. Personal tastes and convenience, vocational and economic interests, infallibly tend to segregate and thus to classify the populations of great cities. In this way the city acquires an organization and distribution of population which is neither designed nor controlled.

The Bell Telephone Company is now making, particularly in New York and Chicago, elaborate investigations, the purpose of which is to determine, in advance of its actual changes, the probable growth and distribution of the urban population within the metropolitan areas. The Sage Foundation, in the course of its city-planning studies, sought to find mathematical formulae that would enable them to predict future expansion and limits of population in New York City. The recent development of chain stores has made the problem of location a matter of concern to different chain-store corporations. The result has been the rise of a new profession.

There is now a class of experts whose sole occupation is to discover and locate, with something like scientific accuracy, taking account of the changes which present tendencies seem likely to bring about, restaurants, cigar stores, drug-stores, and other smaller retail business units whose success depends largely on location. Real-estate men are not infrequently willing to finance a local business of this sort in locations which they believe will be profitable, accepting as their rent a percentage of the profits.

Physical geography, natural advantages and disadvantages, including means of transportation, determine in advance the general outlines of the urban plan. As the city increases in population, the subtler influences of sympathy, rivalry, and economic necessity tend to control the distribution of population. Business and industry seek advantageous locations and draw around them certain portions of the population. There spring up fashionable residence quarters from which the poorer classes are excluded because of the increased value of the land. Then there grow up slums which are inhabited by great numbers of the poorer classes who are unable to defend themselves from association with the derelict and vicious.

In the course of time every section and quarter of the city takes on something of the character and qualities of its inhabitants. Each separate part of the city is inevitably stained with the peculiar sentiments of its population. The effect of this is to convert what was at first a mere geographical expression into a neighborhood, that is to say, a locality with sentiments, traditions, and a history of its own. Within this neighborhood the continuity of the historical processes is somehow maintained. The past imposes itself upon the present, and the life of every locality moves on with a certain momentum of its own, more or less independent of the larger circle of life and interests about it.

The organization of the city, the character of the urban environment and of the discipline which it imposes is finally determined by the size of the population, its concentration and distribution within the city area. For this reason it is important to study the growth of cities, to compare the idiosyncrasies in the distribution of city populations. Some of the first things we want to know about the city, therefore are:

What are the sources of the city's population?

What part of its population growth is normal, i.e., due to excess of births over deaths?

What part is due to migration (a) of native stocks? (b) foreign stocks?

What are the outstanding "natural" areas, i.e., areas of population segregation?

How is distribution of population within the city area affected by (a) economic interest, i.e., land values? (b) by sentimental interest, race? vocation, etc.?

Where within the city is the population declining? Where is it expanding? Where are population growth and the size of families within the different natural areas of the city correlated with births and deaths, with marriages and divorces, with house rents and standards of living?

The neighborhood.—Proximity and neighborly contact are the basis for the simplest and most elementary form of association with which we have to do in the organization of city life. Local interests and associations breed local sentiment, and, under a system which makes residence the basis for participation in the government, the neighborhood becomes the basis of political control. In the social and political organization of the city it is the smallest local unit.

Neighbor-hood = smallest local unit sociologically & politically

It is surely one of the most remarkable of all social facts that, coming down from untold ages, there should be this instinctive understanding that the man who establishes his home beside yours begins to have a claim upon your sense of comradeship. . . . . The neighborhood is a social unit which, by its clear definition of outline, its inner organic completeness, its hair-trigger reactions, may be fairly considered as functioning like a social mind. . . . . The local boss, however autocratic he may be in the larger sphere of the city with the power he gets from the neighborhood, must always be in and of the people; and he is very careful not to try to deceive the local people so far as their local interests are concerned. It is hard to fool a neighborhood about its own affairs.[1]

The neighborhood exists without formal organization. The local improvement society is a structure erected on the basis of the spontaneous neighborhood organization and exists for the purpose of giving expression to the local sentiment in regard to matters of local interest.

Neighbor-hood — No formal Organization

Under the complex influences of the city life, what may be called the normal neighborhood sentiment has undergone many curious and interesting changes, and produced many unusual types of local communities. More than that, there are nascent neighborhood ands neighborhoods in process of dissolution. Consider, for example, Fifth Avenue, New York, which probably never had an improve-

nascent < dissolute neighborhoods

[1] Robert A. Woods, "The Neighborhood in Social Reconstruction," *Papers and Proceedings of the Eighth Annual Meeting of the American Sociological Society, 1913.*

ment association, and compare with it 135th Street in the Bronx (where the Negro population is probably more concentrated than in any other single spot in the world), which is rapidly becoming a very intimate and highly organized community.

In the history of New York the significance of the name Harlem has changed from Dutch to Irish to Jewish to Negro. Of these changes the last has come most swiftly. Throughout colored America, from Massachusetts to Mississippi and across the continent to Los Angeles and Seattle, its name, which as late as fifteen years ago has scarcely been heard, now stands for the Negro metropolis. Harlem is, indeed, the great Mecca for the sight-seer, the pleasure-seeker, the curious, the adventurous, the enterprising, the ambitious, and the talented of the Negro world; for the lure of it has reached down to every island of the Carib Sea and has penetrated even into Africa.[1]

It is important to know what are the forces which tend to break up the tensions, interests, and sentiments which give neighborhoods their individual character. In general these may be said to be anything and everything that tends to render the population unstable, to divide and concentrate attentions upon widely separated objects of interest.

What part of the population is floating?
Of what elements, i.e., races, classes, etc., is this population composed?
How many people live in hotels, apartments, and tenements?
How many people own their own homes?
What proportion of the population consists of nomads, hobos, gypsies?

On the other hand, certain urban neighborhoods suffer from isolation. Efforts have been made at different times to reconstruct and quicken the life of city neighborhoods and to bring them in touch with the larger interests of the community. Such is, in part, the purpose of the social settlements. These organizations and others which are attempting to reconstruct city life have developed certain methods and a technique for stimulating and controlling local communities. We should study, in connection with the investigation of these agencies, these methods and this technique, since it

[1] James Welden Johnson, "The Making of Harlem," *Survey Graphic*, March 1, 1925.

is just the method by which objects are practically controlled that reveals their essential nature, that is to say, their predictable character (*Gesetzmässigkeit*).[1]

In many of the European cities, and to some extent in this country, reconstruction of city life has gone to the length of building garden suburbs, or replacing unhealthful and run-down tenements with model buildings owned and controlled by the municipality.

In American cities the attempt has been made to renovate evil neighborhoods by the construction of playgrounds and the introduction of supervised sports of various kinds, including municipal dances in municipal dance halls. These and other devices which are intended primarily to elevate the moral tone of the segregated populations of great cities should be studied in connection with the investigation of the neighborhood in general. They should be studied, in short, not merely for their own sake, but for what they can reveal to us of human behavior and human nature generally.

Colonies and segregated areas.—In the city environment the neighborhood tends to lose much of the significance which it possessed in simpler and more primitive forms of society. The easy means of communication and of transportation, which enable individuals to distribute their attention and to live at the same time in several different worlds, tend to destroy the permanency and intimacy of the neighborhood. On the other hand, the isolation of the immigrant and racial colonies of the so-called ghettos and areas of population segregation tend to preserve and, where there is racial prejudice, to intensify the intimacies and solidarity of the local and

[1] "Wenn wir daher das Wort [Natur] als einen logischen Terminus in der Wissenschaftslehre gebrauchen wollen, so werden wir sagen dürfen, dass Natur die Wirklichkeit ist mit Rücksicht auf ihren gesetzmässigen Zusammenhang. Diese Bedeutung finden wir z. B. in dem Worte Naturgesetz. Dann aber können wir die Natur der Dinge auch das nennen was in die Begriffe eingeht, oder am kürzesten uns dahin ausdrücken: die Natur ist die Wirklichkeit mit Rücksicht auf das Allgemeine. So gewinnt dann das Wort erst eine logische Bedeutung" (H. Rickert, *Die Grenzen der naturwissenschaftlichen Begriffsbildung*, p. 212).

neighborhood groups. Where individuals of the same race or of the same vocation live together in segregated groups, neighborhood sentiment tends to fuse together with racial antagonisms and class interests.

Physical and sentimental distances reinforce each other, and the influences of local distribution of the population participate with the influences of class and race in the evolution of the social organization. Every great city has its racial colonies, like the Chinatowns of San Francisco and New York, the Little Sicily of Chicago, and various other less pronounced types. In addition to these, most cities have their segregated vice districts, like that which until recently existed in Chicago, their rendezvous for criminals of various sorts. Every large city has its occupational suburbs, like the Stockyards in Chicago, and its residential enclaves, like Brookline in Boston, the so-called "Gold Coast" in Chicago, Greenwich Village in New York, each of which has the size and the character of a complete separate town, village, or city, except that its population is a selected one. Undoubtedly the most remarkable of these cities within cities, of which the most interesting characteristic is that they are composed of persons of the same race, or of persons of different races but of the same social class, is East London, with a population of 2,000,000 laborers.

The people of the original East London have now overflowed and crossed the Lea, and spread themselves over the marshes and meadows beyond. This population has created new towns which were formerly rural villages, West Ham, with a population of nearly 300,000; East Ham, with 90,000; Stratford, with its "daughters," 150,000; and other "hamlets" similarly overgrown. Including these new populations, we have an aggregate of nearly two millions of people. The population is greater than that of Berlin or Vienna, or St. Petersburg, or Philadelphia.

It is a city full of churches and places of worship, yet there are no cathedrals, either Anglican or Roman; it has a sufficient supply of elementary schools, but it has no public or high school, and it has no colleges for the higher education and no university; the people all read newspapers, yet there is no

East London paper except of the smaller and local kind. . . . . In the streets there are never seen any private carriages; there is no fashionable quarter . . . . one meets no ladies in the principal thoroughfares. People, shops, houses, conveyances—all together are stamped with the unmistakable seal of the working class.

Perhaps the strangest thing of all is this: in a city of two millions of people there are no hotels! That means, of course, that there are no visitors.[1]

In the older cities of Europe, where the processes of segregation have gone farther, neighborhood distinctions are likely to be more marked than they are in America. East London is a city of a single class, but within the limits of that city the population is segregated again and again by racial, cultural, and vocational interests. Neighborhood sentiment, deeply rooted in local tradition and in local custom, exercises a decisive selective influence upon the populations of the older European cities and shows itself ultimately in a marked way in the characteristics of the inhabitants.

What we want to know of these neighborhoods, racial communities, and segregated city areas, existing within or on the outer rims of great cities, is what we want to know of all other social groups:

What are the elements of which they are composed?

To what extent are they the product of a selective process?

How do people get in and out of the group thus formed?

What are the relative permanence and stability of their populations?

What about the age, sex, and social condition of the people?

What about the children? How many of them are born, and how many of them remain?

What is the history of the neighborhood? What is there in the subconsciousness—in the forgotten or dimly remembered experiences—of this neighborhood which determines its sentiments and atittudes?

What is there in clear consciousness, i.e., what are its avowed sentiments, doctrines, etc.?

What does it regard as matter of fact? What is news? What is the general run of attention? What models does it imitate and are these within or without the group?

[1] Walter Besant, *East London*, pp. 7–9.

What is the social ritual, i.e., what things must one do in the neighborhood in order to escape being regarded with suspicion or looked upon as peculiar?

Who are the leaders? What interests of the neighborhood do they incorporate in themselves and what is the technique by which they exercise control?

II. INDUSTRIAL ORGANIZATION AND THE MORAL ORDER

Ancient city = fortness

The ancient city was primarily a fortress, a place of refuge in time of war. The modern city, on the contrary, is primarily a convenience of commerce, and owes its existence to the market place around which it sprang up. Industrial competition and the division of labor, which have probably done most to develop the latent powers of mankind, are possible only upon condition of the existence of markets, of money, and other devices for the facilitation of trade and commerce.

Modern city = commerce

[cf J. Jacobs - all cities economic]

Open market " basis for free-man status of midieval town citizen

An old German adage declares that "city air makes men free" (*Stadt Luft macht frei*). This is doubtless a reference to the days when the free cities of Germany enjoyed the patronage of the emperor, and laws made the fugitive serf a free man if he succeeded for a year and a day in breathing city air. Law, of itself, could not, however, have made the craftsman free. An open market in which he might sell the products of his labor was a necessary incident of his freedom, and it was the application of the money economy to the relations of master and man that completed the emancipation of the serf.

Vast array of occupational opportunities in city = basis for personal freedom

Vocational classes and vocational types.—The old adage which describes the city as the natural environment of the free man still holds so far as the individual man finds in the chances, the diversity of interests and tasks, and in the vast unconscious co-operation of city life the opportunity to choose his own vocation and develop his peculiar individual talents. The city offers a market for the special talents of individual men. Personal competition tends to select for each special task the individual who is best suited to perform it.

The difference of natural talents in different men is, in reality, much less than we are aware of; and the very different genius which appears to distinguish men of different professions, when grown up to maturity, is not upon many occasions so much the cause, as the effect of the division of labour. The difference between the most dissimilar characters, between a philosopher and a common street porter, for example, seems to arise not so much from nature, as from habit, custom, and education. When they came into the world, and for the first six or eight years of their existence, they were perhaps very much alike. and neither their parents nor playfellows could perceive any remarkable difference. About that age, or soon after, they come to be employed in different occupations. The difference of talents comes then to be taken notice of, and widens by degrees, till at last the vanity of the philosopher is willing to acknowledge scarce any resemblance. But without the disposition to truck, barter, and exchange, every man must have procured to himself every necessary and conveniency of life which he wanted. All must have had the same duties to perform, and the same work to do, and there could have been no such difference of employment as could alone give occasion to any great difference of talent. . . . ,

As it is the power of exchanging that gives occasion to the division of labour, so the extent of this division must always be limited by the extent of that power, or, in other words, by the extent of the market. . . . . There are some sorts of industry, even of the lowest kind, which can be carried on nowhere but in a great town.[1]

Success, under conditions of personal competition, depends upon concentration upon some single task, and this concentration stimulates the demand for rational methods, technical devices, and exceptional skill. Exceptional skill, while based on natural talent, requires special preparation, and it has called into existence the trade and professional schools, and finally bureaus for vocational guidance. All of these, either directly or indirectly, serve at once to select and emphasize individual differences.

Every device which facilitates trade and industry prepares the way for a further division of labor and so tends further to specialize the tasks in which men find their vocations.

The outcome of this process is to break down or modify the older social and economic organization of society, which was based on family ties, local associations, on culture, caste, and status, and to

[1] Adam Smith, *The Wealth of Nations*, pp. 28–29.

Replaced with organization based on occupation (vocation)

substitute for it an organization based on occupation and vocational interests.

for city every vocation = gets character of profession

In the city every vocation, even that of a beggar, tends to assume the character of a profession and the discipline which success in any vocation imposes, together with the associations that it enforces, emphasizes this tendency—the tendency, namely, not merely to specialize, but to rationalize one's occupation and to develop a specific and conscious technique for carrying it on.

Division of labor produces vocational groupings; neighborhood produces groups based on contiguity & personal association

The effect of the vocations and the division of labor is to produce, in the first instance, not social groups, but vocational types: the actor, the plumber, and the lumber-jack. The organizations, like the trade and labor unions which men of the same trade or profession form, are based on common interests. In this respect they differ from forms of association like the neighborhood, which are based on contiguity, personal association, and the common ties of humanity. The different trades and professions seem disposed to group themselves in classes, that is to say, the artisan, business, and professional classes. But in the modern democratic state the classes have as yet attained no effective organization. Socialism, founded on an effort to create an organization based on "class consciousness," has never succeeded, except, perhaps, in Russia, in creating more than a political party.

The effects of the division of labor as a discipline, i.e., as means of molding character, may therefore be best studied in the vocational types it has produced. Among the types which it would be interesting to study are: the shopgirl, the policeman, the peddler, the cabman, the nightwatchman, the clairvoyant, the vaudeville performer, the quack doctor, the bartender, the ward boss, the strike-breaker, the labor agitator, the school teacher, the reporter, the stockbroker, the pawnbroker; all of these are characteristic products of the conditions of city life; each, with its special experience, insight, and point of view determines for each vocational group and for the city as a whole its individuality.

To what extent is the grade of intelligence represented in the different trades and professions dependent upon natural ability?

To what extent is intelligence determined by the character of the occupation and the conditions under which it is practiced?

To what extent is success in the occupations dependent upon sound judgment and common-sense; to what extent upon technical ability?

Does native ability or special training determine success in the different vocations?

What prestige and what prejudices attach to different trades and professions and why?

Is the choice of the occupation determined by temperamental, by economic, or by sentimental considerations?

In what occupations do men, in what occupations do women, succeed better, and why?

How far is occupation, rather than association, responsible for the mental attitude and moral predilections? Do men in the same profession or trade, but representing different nationalities and different cultural groups, hold characteristic and identical opinions?

To what extent is the social or political creed, that is, socialism, anarchism, syndicalism, etc., determined by occupation? by temperament?

To what extent have social doctrine and social idealism superseded and taken the place of religious faith in the different occupations, and why?

Do social classes tend to assume the character of cultural groups? That is to say, do the classes tend to acquire the exclusiveness and independence of a caste or nationality; or is each class always dependent upon the existence of a corresponding class?

To what extent do children follow the vocations of their parents and why?

To what extent do individuals move from one class to another, and how does this fact modify the character of class relationships?

News and the mobility of the social group.—The division of labor, in making individual success dependent upon concentration upon a special task, has had the effect of increasing the interdependence of the different vocations. A social organization is thus created in which the individual becomes increasingly dependent upon the community of which he is an integral part. The effect, under conditions of personal competition, of this increasing interdependence of the parts is to create in the industrial organization as a whole a certain sort of social solidarity, but a solidarity based, not on sentiment and habit, but on community of interests.

In the sense in which the terms are here used, sentiment is the more concrete, interest the more abstract, term. We may cherish a sentiment for a person, a place, or any object whatsoever. It may be a sentiment of aversion, or a sentiment of possession. But to possess or to be possessed by a sentiment for, or in regard to, anything means that we are incapable of acting toward it in a thoroughly rational way. It means that the object of our sentiment corresponds in some special way to some inherited or acquired disposition. Such a disposition is the affection of a mother for her child, which is instinctive. Or even the feeling she may have for the child's empty cradle, which is acquired.

The existence of a sentimental attitude indicates that there are motives for action of which the individual who is moved by them is not wholly conscious; motives over which he has only a partial control. Every sentiment has a history, either in the experience of the individual, or in the experience of the race, but the person who acts on that sentiment may not be aware of the history.

Interests are directed less toward specific objects than toward the ends which this or that particular object at one time or another embodies. Interests imply, therefore, the existence of means and a consciousness of the distinction between means and ends. Our sentiments are related to our prejudices, and prejudices may attach to anything—persons, races, as well as inanimate things. Prejudices are related also to taboos, and so tend to maintain "social distances" and the existing social organization. Sentiment and prejudice are elementary forms of conservatism. Our interests are rational and mobile, and make for change.

Money is the cardinal device by which values have become rationalized and sentiments have been replaced by interests. It is just because we feel no personal and no sentimental attitude toward our money, such as we do toward, for example, our home, that money becomes a valuable means of exchange. We will be interested in acquiring a certain amount of money in order to achieve a certain purpose, but provided that purpose may be achieved in any other way we are likely to be just as well satisfied. It is only the miser who becomes sentimental about money, and in that case he is likely to prefer one sort of money, say gold, to another, irrespective of its value. In this case the value of gold is determined by personal sentiment rather than by reason.

An organization which is composed of competing individuals and of competing groups of individuals is in a state of unstable equilibrium, and this equilibrium can be maintained only by a process of continuous readjustment. This aspect of social life and this type of social organization are best represented in the world of business which is the special object of investigation of political economy.

competing individuals develope a state of unstable equilibrium ∴ continuous readjustment

The extension of industrial organization, which is based on the impersonal relations defined by money, has gone forward hand in hand with an increasing mobility of the population. The laboring man and the artisan fitted to perform a specific task are compelled, under the conditions created by city life, to move from one region to another in search of the particular kind of employment which they are fitted to perform. The tide of immigration which moves back and forth between Europe and America is to some extent a measure of this same mobility.[1]

mobility of population & impersonal relations defined by money go hand-in-hand

On the other hand, the tradesman, the manufacturer, the professional man, the specialist in every vocation, seeks his clients as the difficulties of travel and communication decrease over an ever widening area of territory. This is another way in which the mobility of the population may be measured. However, mobility in an individual or in a population is measured, not merely by change of location, but rather by the number and variety of the stimulations to which the individual or the population responds. Mobility de-

increased mobility due to increased stimulation (communication) as well as increased opportunity to move (transport)

[1] Walter Bagehot, *The Postulates of Political Economy* (London, 1885), pp. 7–8.

pends, not merely upon transportation, but upon communication. Education and the ability to read, the extension of the money economy to an ever increasing number of the interests of life, in so far as it has tended to depersonalize social relations, has at the same time vastly increased the mobility of modern peoples.

The term "mobility," like its correlative, "isolation," covers a wide range of phenomena. It may represent at the same time a character and a condition. As isolation may be due to the existence of purely physical barriers to communication, or to a peculiarity of temperament and a lack of education, so mobility may be a consequence of the natural means of communication or of an agreeable manner and a college education.

It is now clearly recognized that what we ordinarily call a lack of intelligence in individuals, races, and communities is frequently a result of isolation. On the other hand, the mobility of a population is unquestionably a very large factor in its intellectual development.

There is an intimate connection between the immobility of the primitive man and his so-called inability to use abstract ideas. The knowledge which a peasant ordinarily possesses, from the very nature of his occupation is, concrete and personal. He knows individually and personally every member of the flock he tends. He becomes in the course of years so attached to the land he tills that the mere transposition from the strip of soil on which he has grown up to another with which he is less intimately acquainted is felt by him as a personal loss. For such a man the neighboring valley, or even the strip of land at the other end of the village is in a certain sense alien territory. A large part of the peasant's efficiency as an agricultural laborer depends upon this intimate and personal acquaintance with the idiosyncrasies of a single plot of land to the care of which he has been bred. It is apparent that, under conditions like these, very little of the peasant's practical knowledge will take the abstract form of scientific generalization. He thinks in concrete terms because he knows and needs no other.

On the other hand, the intellectual characteristics of the Jew and his generally recognized interest in abstract and radical ideas are unquestionably connected with the fact that the Jews are, before all else, a city folk. The "Wandering Jew" acquires abstract terms with which to describe the various scenes which he visits. His knowledge of the world is based upon identities and differences, that is to say, on analysis and classification. Reared in intimate association with the bustle and business of the market place, constantly intent on the shrewd and fascinating game of buying and selling, in which he employs hat most interesting of abstractions, money, he has neither opportunity nor nclination to cultivate that intimate attachment to places and persons which s characteristic of the immobile person.[1]

Concentration of populations in cities, the wider markets, the division of labor, the concentration of individuals and groups on special tasks, have continually changed the material conditions of ife, and in doing this have made readjustments to novel conditions ncreasingly necessary. Out of this necessity there have grown up a number of special organizations which exist for the special purpose of facilitating these readjustments. The market which brought the modern city into existence is one of these devices. More interesting, however, are the exchanges, particularly the stock exchange and the board of trade, where prices are constantly being made in response to changes, or rather the reports of changes, in economic conditions all over the world.

These reports, so far as they are calculated to cause readjustments, have the character of what we call news. It is the existence of a critical situation which converts what were otherwise mere information into news. Where there is an issue at stake, where, in short, there is crisis, there information which might affect the outcome one way or another becomes "live matter," as the newspaper men say. Live matter is news; dead matter is mere information.

What is the relation of mobility to suggestion, imitation, etc.?

What are the practical devices by which suggestibility and mobility are increased in a community or in an individual?

Are there pathological conditions in communities corresponding to hysteria in individuals? If so, how are they produced and how controlled?

To what extent is fashion an indication of mobility?

What is the difference in the manner in which fashions and customs are transmitted?

What is social unrest, and what are the conditions under which it manifests itself?

What are the characteristics of a progressive, what the characteristics of a static, community in respect to its resistance to novel suggestions?

[1] Cf. W. I. Thomas, *Source Book of Social Origins*, p. 169.

What mental characteristics of the gypsy, of the hobo, and of the nomad generally can be traced to these nomadic habits?

The stock exchanges and the mob.—The exchanges, upon which we may watch the fluctuation of prices in response to the news of economic conditions in different parts of the world, are typical. Similar readjustments are taking place in every department of social life, where, however, the devices for making these readjustments are not so complete and perfect. For example, the professional and trade papers, which keep the professions and the trades informed in regard to new methods, experiences, and devices, serve to keep the members of these trades and professions abreast of the times, which means that they facilitate readjustments to changing conditions.

There is, however, this important distinction to be made: Competition in the exchanges is more intense; changes are more rapid and, as far as the individuals directly concerned, more momentous. In contrast with such a constellation of forces as we find on the exchanges, where competing dealers meet to buy and sell, so mobile a form of social organization as the crowd and the mob exhibits a relative stability.

It is a commonplace that decisive factors in the movements of crowds, as in the fluctuations of markets, are psychologic. This means that among the individuals who make up the crowd, or who compose the public which participates in the movements reflected in the market, a condition of instability exists which corresponds to what has been defined elsewhere as crisis. It is true of the exchanges, as it is of crowds, that the situation they represent is always critical, that is to say, the tensions are such that a slight cause may precipitate an enormous effect. The current euphemism, "the psychological moment," defines such a critical condition.

Psychological moments may arise in any social situation, but they occur more frequently in a society which has acquired a high state of mobility. They occur more frequently in a society where education is general, where railways, telegraph, and the printing press have become an indispensable part of the social economy. They occur more frequently in cities than in smaller communities. In the crowd and the public every moment may be said to be "psychological."

Crisis may be said to be the normal condition on the exchanges. What are called financial crises are merely an extension of this critical condition to the larger business community. Financial panics which sometimes follow upon financial crises are a precipitate of this critical condition.

The fascinating thing about the study of crises, as of crowds, is that in so far as they are in fact due to psychological causes, that is, in so far as they are the result of the mobility of the communities in which they occur, they can be controlled. The evidence for this is the fact that they can be manipulated, and there is abundant evidence of manipulation in the transactions of the stock market. The evidence for the manipulation of crowds is less accessible. Labor organizations have, however, known how to develop a pretty definite technique for the instigation and control of strikes. The Salvation Army has worked out a book of tactics which is very largely devoted to the handling of street crowds; and professional revivalists, like Billy Sunday, have an elaborate technique for conducting their revivals.

Under the title of collective psychology much has been written in recent years in regard to crowds and kindred phenomena of social life. Most that has been written thus far has been based upon general observation and almost no systematic methods exist for the study of this type of social organization. The practical methods which practical men like the political boss, the labor agitator, the stock-exchange speculator, and others have worked out for the control and manipulation of the public and the crowd furnish a body of materials from which it is possible to make a more detailed, a more intimate study of what may be called, in order to distinguish it from that of more highly organized groups, collective behavior.

The city, and particularly the great city, in which more than elsewhere human relations are likely to be impersonal and rational defined in terms of interest and in terms of cash, is in a very real sense a laboratory for the investigation of collective behavior Strikes and minor revolutionary movements are endemic in the urban environment. Cities, and particularly the great cities, are in unstable equilibrium. The result is that the vast casual and mobile aggregations which constitute our urban populations are in a state of perpetual agitation, swept by every new wind of doctrine, subject to constant alarms, and in consequence the community is in a chronic condition of crisis.

What has been said suggests first of all the importance of a more detailed and fundamental study of collective behavior. The questions which follow will perhaps suggest lines of investigation that could be followed profitably by students of urban life.

What is the psychology of crisis? What is the cycle of events involved in the evolution of a crisis, political or economic?

To what extent may the parliamentary system, including the electoral system, be regarded as an attempt to regularize revolution and to meet and control crises?

To what extent are mob violence, strikes, and radical political movements the results of the same general conditions that provoke financial panics, real estate booms, and mass movements in the population generally?

To what extent are the existing unstable equilibrium and social ferment due to the extent and speed of economic changes as reflected in the stock exchange?

What are the effects of the extension of communication and of news upon fluctuations in the stock market and economic changes generally?

Does the scale of stocks on the exchanges tend to exaggerate the fluctuations in the market, or to stabilize them?

Do the reports in the newspapers, so far as they represent the facts, tend to speed up social changes, or to stabilize a movement already in progress?

What is the effect of propaganda and rumor, in cases where the sources of accurate information are cut off?

To what extent can fluctuations of the stock market be controlled by formal regulation?

To what extent can social changes, strikes, and revolutionary movements be controlled by the censorship?

To what extent can the scientific forecasting of economic and social changes exercise a useful control over the trend of prices and of events?

To what extent can the prices recorded by the stock exchange be compared with public opinion as recorded by the newspaper?

To what extent can the city, which responds more quickly and more decisively to changing events, be regarded as nerve centers of the social organism?

III.   SECONDARY RELATIONS AND SOCIAL CONTROL

Modern methods of urban transportation and communication— the electric railway, the automobile, the telephone, and the radio— have silently and rapidly changed in recent years the social and industrial organization of the modern city. They have been the means of concentrating traffic in the business districts, have changed the whole character of retail trade, multiplying the residence suburbs and making the department store possible. These changes in the industrial organization and in the distribution of population have been accompanied by corresponding changes in the habits, sentiments, and character of the urban population.

The general nature of these changes is indicated by the fact that the growth of cities has been accompanied by the substitution of indirect, "secondary," for direct, face-to-face, "primary" relations in the associations of individuals in the community.

By primary groups I mean those characterized by intimate face-to-face association and co-operation. They are primary in several senses, but chiefly in that they are fundamental in forming the social nature and ideals of the individual. The result of intimate association, psychologically, is a certain fusion of individualities in a common whole, so that one's very self, for many purposes at least, is the common life and purpose of the group. Perhaps the simplest way of describing this wholeness is by saying that it is a "we"; it involves the sort of sympathy and mutual identification for which "we" is the natural expression. One lives in the feeling of the whole and finds the chief aims of his will in that feeling. . . . .[1]

[1] Charles Horton Cooley, *Social Organization*, p. 15.

Touch and sight, physical contact, are the basis for the first and most elementary human relationships. Mother and child, husband and wife, father and son, master and servant, kinsman and neighbor, minister, physician, and teacher—these are the most intimate and real relationships of life, and in the small community they are practically inclusive.

The interactions which take place among the members of a community so constituted are immediate and unreflecting. Intercourse is carried on largely within the region of instinct and feeling. Social control arises, for the most part spontaneously, in direct response to personal influences and public sentiment. It is the result of a personal accommodation, rather than the formulation of a rational and abstract principle.

The church, the school, and the family.—In a great city, where the population is unstable, where parents and children are employed out of the house and often in distant parts of the city, where thousands of people live side by side for years without so much as a bowing acquaintance, these intimate relationships of the primary group are weakened and the moral order which rested upon them is gradually dissolved.

Under the disintegrating influences of city life most of our traditional institutions, the church, the school, and the family, have been greatly modified. The school, for example, has taken over some of the functions of the family. It is around the public school and its solicitude for the moral and physical welfare of the children that something like a new neighborhood and community spirit tends to get itself organized.

The church, on the other hand, which has lost much of its influence since the printed page has so largely taken the place of the pulpit in the interpretation of life, seems at present to be in process of readjustment to the new conditions.

It is important that the church, the school, and the family should be studied from the point of view of this readjustment to the conditions of city life.

What changes have taken place in recent years in the family sentiments? in the attitudes of husbands toward wives? of wives toward husbands? of children toward parents, etc.?

What do the records of the juvenile and morals courts indicate in regard to this matter?

In what regions of social life have the mores on the subject of the family life changed most?

To what extent have these changes taken place in response to the influences of the city environment?

Similarly, investigations might be carried on with reference to the school and the church. Here, too, there is a changed attitude and changed policy in response to a changed environment. This is important because it is, in the last analysis, upon these institutions in which the immediate and vital interests of life find a corporate expression that social organization ultimately rests.

It is probably the breaking down of local attachments and the weakening of the restraints and inhibitions of the primary group, under the influence of the urban environment, which are largely responsible for the increase of vice and crime in great cities. It would be interesting in this connection to determine by investigation how far the increase in crime keeps pace with the increasing mobility of the population and to what extent this mobility is a function of the growth of population. It is from this point of view that we should seek to interpret all those statistics which register the disintegration of the moral order, for example, the statistics of divorce, of truancy, and of crime.

What is the effect of ownership of property, particularly of the home, on truancy, on divorce, and on crime?

In what regions and classes are certain kinds of crime endemic?

In what classes does divorce occur most frequently? What is the difference in this respect between farmers and, say, actors?

To what extent in any given racial group, for example, the Italians in New York or the Poles in Chicago, do parents and children live in the same world, speak the same language, and share the same ideas, and how far do the conditions found account for juvenile delinquency in that particular group?

How far are the home mores responsible for criminal manifestations of an immigrant group?

Crisis and the courts.—It is characteristic of city life that all sorts of people meet and mingle together who never fully comprehend one another. The anarchist and the club man, the priest and the Levite, the actor and the missionary who touch elbows on the street still live in totally different worlds. So complete is the segregation of vocational classes that it is possible within the limits of the city to live in an isolation almost as complete as that of some remote rural community.

Walter Besant tells the following anecdote of his experience as editor of the *People's Palace Journal:*

In that capacity I endeavored to encourage literary effort, in the hope of lighting upon some unknown and latent genius. The readers of the *Journal* were the members of the various classes connected with the educational side of the place. They were young clerks chiefly—some of them very good fellows. They had a debating society which I attended from time to time. Alas! They carried on their debates in an ignorance the most profound, the most unconscious, and the most satisfied. I endeavored to persuade them that it was desirable at least to master the facts of the case before they spoke. In vain. Then I proposed subjects for essays, and offered prizes for verses. I discovered, to my amazement, that among all the thousands of these young people, lads and girls, there was not discoverable the least rudimentary indication of any literary power whatever. In all other towns there are young people who nourish literary ambitions, with some measure of literary ability. How should there be any in this town, where there were no books, no papers, no journals, and, at that time, no free libraries?[1]

In the immigrant colonies which are now well established in every large city, foreign populations live in an isolation which is different from that of the population of East London, but in some respects more complete.

The difference is that each one of these little colonies has a more or less independent political and social organization of its own, and is the center of a more or less vigorous nationalist propaganda. For example, each one of these groups has one or more papers printed in its own language. In New York City there were, a few years ago,

[1] Walter Besant, *East London,* p. 13.

270 publications, most of them supported by the local population, printed in 23 different languages. In Chicago there were 19 daily papers published in 7 foreign languages with a combined daily circulation of 368,000 papers.

Under these conditions the social ritual and the moral order which these immigrants brought with them from their native countries have succeeded in maintaining themselves for a considerable time under the influences of the American environment. Social control, based on the home mores, breaks down, however, in the second generation.

We may express the relation of the city to this fact in general terms by saying that the effect of the urban environment is to intensify all effects of crisis.

The term "crisis" is not to be understood in a violent sense. It is involved in any disturbance of habit. There is a crisis in the boy's life when he leaves home. The emancipation of the Negro and the immigration of the European peasant are group crises. Any strain of crisis involves three possible changes: greater fitness, reduced efficiency, or death. In biological terms, "survival" means successful adjustment to crisis, accompanied typically by a modification of structure. In man it means mental stimulation and greater intelligence, or mental depression, in case of failure.[1]

Under the conditions imposed by city life in which individuals and groups of individuals, widely removed in sympathy and understanding, live together under conditions of interdependence, if not of intimacy, the conditions of social control are greatly altered and the difficulties increased.

The problem thus created is usually characterized as one of "assimilation." It is assumed that the reason for rapid increase of crime in our large cities is due to the fact that the foreign element in our population has not succeeded in assimilating American culture and does not conform to the American mores. This would be

[1] William I. Thomas, "Race Psychology: Standpoint and Questionnaire with Particular Reference to the Immigrant and Negro," *American Journal of Sociology*, XVII (May, 1912), 736.

interesting, if true, but the facts seem to suggest that perhaps the truth must be sought in the opposite direction.

One of the most important facts established by the investigation concerns the American-born children of immigrants—the "second generation." The records of convictions in the New York Court of General Sessions during the period from October 1, 1908, to June 30, 1909, and of all commitments to Massachusetts penal institutions, except those to the state farm, during the year ending September 30, 1909, form the basis of this analysis of the criminal tendencies of the second generation.

From these records it appears that a clear tendency exists on the part of the second generation to differ from the first or immigrant generation in the character of its criminality. It also appears that this difference is much more frequently in the direction of the criminality of the American-born of non-immigrant parentage than it is in the opposite direction. This means that the movement of the second-generation crime is away from the crimes peculiar to immigrants and toward those of the American of native parentage. Sometimes this movement has carried second-generation criminality even beyond that of the native-born of native parentage. Of the second-generation groups submitted to this comparison, one maintains a constant adherence to the general rule above referred to, while all the others at some point fail to follow it. This unique group is the Irish second generation.[1]

What we do observe, as a result of the crisis, is that control that was formerly based on mores was replaced by control based on positive law. This change runs parallel to the movement by which secondary relationships have taken the place of primary relationships in the association of individuals in the city environment.

It is characteristic of the United States that great political changes should be effected experimentally under the pressure of agitation or upon the initiative of small but militant minorities. There is probably no other country in the world in which so many "reforms" are in progress as at the present time in the United States. Reform has, in fact, become a kind of popular "indoor sport." The reforms thus effected, almost without exception, involve some sort of restriction or governmental control over activities that were

[1] *Reports of the United States Immigration Commission*, VI, 14–16.

formerly "free" or controlled only by the mores and public opinion.

The effect of this extension of what is called the police power has been to produce a change, not merely in the fundamental policy of the law, but in the character and standing of the courts.

The juvenile and morals courts illustrate a change which is perhaps taking place elsewhere. In these courts the judges have assumed something of the functions of administrative officers, their duties consisting less in the interpretation of law than in prescribing remedies and administering advice intended to restore delinquents brought before them to their normal place in society.

A similar tendency to give judges a wide discretion and to impose upon them a further responsibility is manifest in those courts which have to deal with the technical affairs of the business world, and in the growth in popularity of commissions in which judicial and administrative functions are combined, for example, the Interstate Commerce Commission.

In order to interpret in a fundamental way the facts in regard to social control it is important to start with a clear conception of the nature of corporate action.

Corporate action begins when there is some sort of communication between individuals who constitute a group. Communication may take place at different levels; that is, suggestions may be given and responded to on the instinctive, senso-motor, or ideo-motor levels. The mechanism of communication is very subtle, so subtle, in fact, that it is often difficult to conceive how suggestions are conveyed from one mind to another. This does not imply that there is any special form of consciousness, any special sense of kinship or consciousness of kind, necessary to explain corporate action.

In fact, it has recently been shown that in the case of certain highly organized and static societies, like that of the well-known ant, probably nothing that we would call communication takes place.

It is a well-known fact that if an ant be removed from a nest and afterward put back it will not be attacked, while almost invariably an ant belonging to

Handwritten marginal note: U.S.A. developed a new system of control in which judicial Administrative functions are combined. *eg. juvenile courts* I.C.C.

another nest will be attacked. It has been customary to use the words memory, enmity, friendship, in describing this fact. Now Bethe made the following experiment. An ant was placed in the liquids (blood and lymph) squeezed out from the bodies of nest companions and was then put back into its nest; it was not attacked. It was then put in the juice taken from the inmates of a "hostile" nest, and was at once attacked and killed.[1]

A further instance of the manner in which ants communicate will illustrate how simple and automatic communication may become on the instinctive level.

An ant, when taking a new direction from the nest for the first time, always returns by the same path. This shows that some trace must be left behind which serves as a guide back to the nest. If an ant returning by this path bears no spoils, Bethe found that no other ants try this direction. But if it bring back honey or sugar, other ants are sure to try the path. Hence something of the substances carried over this path by the ants must remain on the path. These substances must be strong enough to affect the ants chemically.[2]

The important fact is that by means of this comparatively simple device corporate action is made possible.

Individuals not only react upon one another in this reflex way, but they inevitably communicate their sentiments, attitudes, and organic excitements, and in doing so they necessarily react, not merely to what each individual actually does, but to what he intends, desires, or hopes to do. The fact that individuals often betray sentiments and attitudes to others of which they are themselves only dimly conscious makes it possible for individual A, for example, to act upon motives and tensions in B as soon, or even before, B is able to do so. Furthermore, A may act upon the suggestions that emanate from B without himself being clearly conscious of the source from which his motives spring. So subtle and intimate may the reactions be which control individuals who are bound together in a social-psychological process.

It is upon the basis of this sort of instinctive and spontaneous

[1] Jacques Loeb, *Comparative Physiology of the Brain*, pp. 220–21.
[2] *Ibid.*, p. 221.

control that every more formal sort of control must be based in order to be effective.

Changes in the form of social control may for the purposes of investigation be grouped under the general heads:

questions dealing with control by positive law —

1. The substitution of positive law for custom, and the extension of municipal control to activities that were formerly left to individual initiative and discretion.

2. The disposition of judges in municipal and criminal courts to assume administrative function so that the administration of the criminal law ceases to be a mere application of the social ritual and becomes an application of rational and technical methods, requiring expert knowledge or advice, in order to restore the individual to society and repair the injury that his delinquency has caused.

3. Changes and divergencies in the mores among the different isolated and segregated groups in the city. What are the mores, for example, of the shop-girl? the immigrant? the politician? and the labor agitator?

It should be the aim of these investigations to distinguish not merely the causes of these changes, the direction in which they are moving, but also the forces that are likely to minimize and neutralize them. For example, it is important to know whether the motives which are at present multiplying the positive restrictions on the individual will necessarily go as far in this country as they have already done in Germany. Will they eventually bring about a condition approaching socialism?

Commercialized vice and the liquor traffic.—Social control, under the conditions of city life, can, perhaps, be best studied in its attempts to stamp out vice and control the liquor traffic.

The saloon and the vice establishments have come into existence as a means of exploiting appetites and instincts fundamental to human nature. This makes the efforts that have been made to regulate and suppress these forms of exploitation and traffic interesting and important as subjects of investigation.

questions to be used to study vice

Such an investigation should be based upon thorough study: (1) of the human nature upon which the commerce has been erected, (2) of the social conditions which tend to convert normal appetites into social vices, (3) of the practical effects of the efforts to limit,

control, and stamp out the vice traffic and to do away with the use
and sale of liquor.

Among the things that we should desire to know are:

To what extent is the appetite for alcoholic stimulus a prenatal disposition?

To what extent may such an appetite be transferred from one form of
stimulation to another; that is, e.g., from whiskey to cocaine, etc.?

To what extent is it possible to substitute normal and healthful for pathological and vicious stimulations?

What are the social and moral effects of secret drinking?

Where a taboo is established early in life, does it have the effect of idealizing
the delights of indulgence? Does it do this in some cases and not in others?
If so, what are the contributing circumstances? Do men suddenly lose the taste
for liquor and other stimulants? What are the conditions under which this
happens?

Many of these questions can be answered only by a study of individual
experiences. Vices undoubtedly have their natural history, like certain forms
of disease. They may therefore be regarded as independent entities which find
their habitat in human environment, are stimulated by certain conditions,
inhibited by others, but invariably exhibit through all changes a character that
is typical.

In the early days the temperance movement had something of
the character of a religious revival, and the effects were highly picturesque. In recent years the leaders have displayed a more deliberate strategy, but the struggle against the liquor traffic still has all
the characteristics of a big popular movement, a movement which,
having first conquered the rural districts, is now seeking to enforce
itself in the cities.

On the other hand, the vice crusade started with the cities,
where, in fact, commercialized vice is indigenous. The mere discussion of this subject in public has meant an enormous change in
the sex mores. The fact that this movement is everywhere coinci-
dent with the entrance of women into a greater freedom, into
industry, the professions, and party politics, is significant.

There are conditions peculiar to the life of great cities (referred
to under the heading "Mobility of the Population of Great Cities")

why do campaigns to control vice meet with less success in cities?

which make the control of vice especially difficult. For example, crusades and religious movements generally do not have the same success in the city environment that they do in the smaller and less heterogeneous communities. What are the conditions which make this true?

Perhaps the facts most worth studying in connection with the movement for suppression of vice are those which indicate the changes which have taken place in fifty years in sex mores, particularly with reference to what is regarded as modest and immodest in the dress and behavior, and with reference to the freedom with which sexual matters are now discussed by young men and young women.

It seems, in fact, as if we were in the presence of two epoch-making changes, the one which seems destined finally to put intoxicating liquors in the category of poisonous drugs, and the other to lift the taboo which, particularly among Anglo-Saxon peoples, has effectually prevented up to the present time the frank discussion of the facts of sex.

Party politics and publicity.—There is everywhere at present a disposition to increase the power of the executive branch of the government at the expense of the legislative. The influence of state legislatures and of city councils has been diminished in some instances by the introduction of the referendum and the recall. In others they have been largely superseded by the commission form of government. The ostensible reason for these changes is that they offer a means for overthrowing the power of the professional politicians. The real ground seems to me the recognition of the fact that the form of government which had its origin in the town meeting and was well suited to the needs of a small community based on primary relations is not suitable to the government of the changing and heterogeneous populations of cities of three or four millions.

Executive being strengthened at expense of present strength of legislature

(overt reason — ousting boss)

(covert reason — town-meeting ≠ apt from gov large cities)

Much, of course, depends upon the character and size of the population. Where it is of American stock, and the number of voting citizens is not too great for thorough and calm discussion, no better school of politics can be imagined nor any method of managing affairs more certain to prevent jobbery and waste, to stimulate vigilance and breed contentment. When, however, the town meeting has grown to exceed seven or eight hundred persons, and, still more, when any considerable section are strangers, such as Irish or French Canadians, who have latterly poured into New England, the institution works less perfectly because the multitude is too large for debate, factions are likely to spring up, and the immigrants, untrained in self-government, become the prey of wire pullers or petty demagogues.[1]

For one thing, the problems of city government have become, with the growth and organization of city life, so complicated that it is no longer desirable to leave them to the control of men whose only qualification for handling them consists in the fact that they have succeeded in gaining office through the ordinary machinery of ward politics.

Another circumstance which has made the selection of city officials by popular vote impractical under the conditions of city life is the fact that, except in special cases, the voter knows little or nothing about the officials he is voting for; knows little or nothing about the functions of the office to which that official is to be elected; and, besides all the rest, is too busy elsewhere to inform himself about conditions and needs of the city as a whole.

At a recent election in Chicago, for example, voters were called upon to select candidates from a ballot containing 250 names, most of them unknown to the voters. Under these circumstances the citizen who wishes to vote intelligently relies on some more or less interested organization or some more or less interested advisor to tell him how to vote.

To meet this emergency, created primarily by conditions imposed by city life, two types of organization have come into existence for controlling those artificial crises that we call elections. One of these is the organization represented by the political boss and the political machine. The other is that represented by the independent

[1] James Bryce, *The American Commonwealth*, I, 566.

voters' leagues, taxpayers' associations, and organizations like the bureaus of municipal research.

It is an indication of the rather primitive conditions in which our political parties were formed that they sought to govern the country on the principle that the remedy for all sorts of administrative evils was to "turn the rascals out," as the popular phrase expressed it, a change of government. The political machine and the political boss have come into existence in the interest of party politics. The parties were necessarily organized to capture elections. The political machine is merely a technical device invented for the purpose of achieving this end. The boss is the expert who runs the machine. He is as necessary to the winning of an election as a professional coach is necessary to success at football.

It is characteristic of the two types of organization which have grown up for the purpose of controlling the popular vote that the first, the political machine, is based, on the whole, on local, personal, that is to say, primary, relationships. The second, the good-government organizations, make their appeal to the public, and the public, as we ordinarily understand that expression, is a group based on secondary relationships. Members of a public are not as a rule personally acquainted.

The political machine is, in fact, an attempt to maintain, inside the formal administrative organization of the city, the control of a primary group. The organizations thus built up, of which Tammany Hall is the classic illustration, appear to be thoroughly feudal in their character. The relations between the boss and his ward captain seem to be precisely that, of personal loyalty on one side and personal protection on the other, which the feudal relation implies. The virtues which such an organization calls out are the old tribal ones of fidelity, loyalty, and devotion to the interests of the chief and the clan. The people within the organization, their friends and supporters, constitute a "we" group, while the rest of the city is merely the outer world, which is not quite alive and not quite human in the sense in which the members of the "we" group are. We have here something approaching the conditions of primitive society.

The conception of "primitive society" which we ought to form is that of small groups scattered over a territory. The size of the groups is determined by the conditions of the struggle for existence. The internal organization of each group corresponds to its size. A group of groups may have some relation to each other (kin, neighborhood, alliance, *connubium*, and *commercium*) which draws them together and differentiates them from others. Thus a differentiation arises between ourselves, the we-group or in-group, and everybody else or the others-groups, out-groups. The insiders in a we-group are in a relation of peace, order, law, government, and industry, to each other. Their relation to all outsiders, or others-groups, is one of war and plunder, except so far as agreements have modified it.

The relation of comradeship and peace in the we-group and that of hostility and war toward others-groups are correlative to each other. The exigencies of war with outsiders are what make peace inside, lest internal discord should weaken the we-group for war. These exigencies also make government and law in the in-group, in order to prevent quarrels and enforce discipline.[1]

The politics of most great cities offer abundant materials for the study of the type represented by the political boss, as well as the social mechanisms created by and embodied in the political machine. It is necessary, however, that we study them disinterestedly. Some of the questions we should seek to answer are:

What, as a matter of fact, is the political organization at any point within the city? What are the sentiments and attitudes and interests which find expression through it?

What are the practical devices it employs for mobilizing its forces and putting them into action?

What is the character of the party appeal in the different moral regions of which the city is made up?

How much of the interest in politics is practical and how much is mere sport?

What part of the cost of elections is advertising? How much of it can be classed as "educational publicity," and how much is pure graft?

[1] Sumner, *Folkways*, p. 12.

To what extent, under existing conditions, particularly as we find them in great cities, can elections be practically controlled by purely technical devices, card catalogues, torch-light processions, spell binders—machinery?

What effect will the introduction of the referendum and recall have upon present methods of conducting elections in cities?

Advertising and social control.—In contrast with the political machine, which has founded its organized action on the local, personal, and immediate interests represented by the different neighborhoods and localities, the good-government organizations, the bureaus of municipal research, and the like have sought to represent the interests of the city as a whole and have appealed to a sentiment and opinion neither local nor personal. These agencies have sought to secure efficiency and good government by the education of the voter, that is to say, by investigating and publishing the facts regarding the government.

[margin notes: Sundary Relations of "Reform" Groups; 1°—Social control Through Advertising Publicity]

In this way publicity has come to be a recognized form of social control, and advertising—"social advertising"—has become a profession with an elaborate technique supported by a body of special knowledge.

It is one of the characteristic phenomena of city life and of society founded on secondary relationships that advertising should have come to occupy so important a place in its economy.

In recent years every individual and organization which has had to deal with the public, that is to say the public outside the smaller and more intimate communities of the village and small town, has come to have its press agent, who is often less an advertising man than a diplomatic man accredited to the newspapers, and through them to the world at large. Institutions like the Russell Sage Foundation, and to a less extent, the General Education Board have sought to influence public opinion directly through the medium of publicity. The Carnegie Report upon Medical Education, the Pittsburgh Survey, the Russel Sage Foundation Report on Comparative Costs of Public-School Education in the several states, are something more than scientific reports. They are rather a high form of journalism, dealing with existing conditions critically, and seeking through the agency of publicity to bring about radical reforms. The work of the Bureau of Municipal Research in New York has had a similar practical purpose. To these must be added the work accomplished by the child-welfare exhibits, by the social surveys undertaken in different parts of the country, and by similar propaganda in favor of public health.

As a source of social control public opinion becomes important in societies founded on secondary relationships, of which great cities are a type. In the city every social group tends to create its own milieu and, as these conditions become fixed, the mores tend to accommodate themselves to the conditions thus created. In secondary groups and in the city fashion tends to take the place of custom, and public opinion, rather than the mores, becomes the dominant force in social control.

In any attempt to understand the nature of public opinion and its relation to social control it is important to investigate first of all the agencies and devices which have come into practical use in the effort to control, enlighten, and exploit it.

The first and the most important of these is the press, that is, the daily newspaper and other forms of current literature, including books classed as current.[1]

After the newspaper, the bureaus of research which are now springing up in all the large cities are the most interesting and the most promising devices for using publicity as a means of control.

The fruits of these investigations do not reach the public directly, but are disseminated through the medium of the press, the pulpit, and other sources of popular enlightenment.

In addition to these there are the educational campaigns in the interest of better health conditions, the child-welfare exhibits, and the numerous "social advertising" devices which are now employed,

[1] Cf. Bryce, *The American Commonwealth*, p. 267.

sometimes upon the initiative of private societies, sometimes upon that of popular magazines or newspapers, in order to educate the public and enlist the masses of the people in the movement for the improvement of conditions of community life.

The newspaper is the great medium of communication within the city, and it is on the basis of the information which it supplies that public opinion rests. The first function which a newspaper supplies is that which formerly was performed by the village gossip.

In spite, however, of the industry with which newspapers pursue facts of personal intelligence and human interest, they cannot compete with the village gossips as a means of social control. For one thing, the newspaper maintains some reservations not recognized by gossip, in the matters of personal intelligence. For example, until they run for office or commit some other overt act that brings them before the public conspicuously, the private life of individual men or women is a subject that is, for the newspaper, taboo. It is not so with gossip, partly because in a small community no individual is so obscure that his private affairs escape observation and discussion; partly because the field is smaller. In small communities there is a perfectly amazing amount of personal information afloat among the individuals who compose them.

The absence of this in the city is what, in large part, makes the city what it is.

Some of the questions that arise in regard to the nature and function of the newspaper and of publicity generally are:

What is news?

What are the methods and motives of the newspaper man? Are they those of an artist? a historian? or merely those of a merchant?

To what extent does the newspaper control and to what extent is it controlled by public sentiment?

What is a "fake" and why?

What is yellow journalism and why is it yellow?

What would be the effect of making the newspaper a municipal monopoly?

What is the difference between advertising and news?

IV.　TEMPERAMENT AND THE URBAN ENVIRONMENT

Great cities have always been the melting-pots of races and of cultures. Out of the vivid and subtle interactions of which they have been the centers, there have come the newer breeds and the newer social types. The great cities of the United States, for example, have drawn from the isolation of their native villages great masses of the rural populations of Europe and America. Under the shock of the new contacts the latent energies of these primitive peoples have been released, and the subtler processes of interaction have brought into existence not merely vocational, but temperamental, types.

Mobilization of the individual man.—Transportation and communication have effected, among many other silent but far-reaching changes, what I have called the "mobilization of the individual man." They have multiplied the opportunities of the individual man for contact and for association with his fellows, but they have made these contacts and associations more transitory and less stable. A very large part of the populations of great cities, including those who make their homes in tenements and apartment houses, live much as people do in some great hotel, meeting but not knowing one another. The effect of this is to substitute fortuitous and casual relationship for the more intimate and permanent associations of the smaller community.

Under these circumstances the individual's status is determined to a considerable degree by conventional signs—by fashion and "front"—and the art of life is largely reduced to skating on thin surfaces and a scrupulous study of style and manners.

Not only transportation and communication, but the segregation of the urban population tends to facilitate the mobility of the individual man. The processes of segregation establish moral distances which make the city a mosaic of little worlds which touch but do not interpenetrate. This makes it possible for individuals to pass quickly and easily from one moral milieu to another, and encourages the fascinating but dangerous experiment of living at the same time in several different contiguous, but otherwise widely separated, worlds. All this tends to give to city life a superficial and adventitious character; it tends to complicate social relationships and to produce new and divergent individual types. It introduces, at the same time, an element of chance and adventure which adds to the stimulus of city life and gives it, for young and fresh nerves, a peculiar attractiveness. The lure of great cities is perhaps a consequence of stimulations which act directly upon the reflexes. As a type of human behavior it may be explained, like the attraction of the flame for the moth, as a sort of tropism.

The attraction of the metropolis is due in part, however, to the fact that in the long run every individual finds somewhere among the varied manifestations of city life the sort of environment in which he expands and feels at ease; finds, in short, the moral climate in which his peculiar nature obtains the stimulations that bring his innate dispositions to full and free expression. It is, I suspect, motives of this kind which have their basis, not in interest nor even in sentiment, but in something more fundamental and primitive which draw many, if not most, of the young men and young women from the security of their homes in the country into the big, booming confusion and excitement of city life. In a small community it is the normal man, the man without eccentricity or genius, who seems most likely to succeed. The small community often tolerates eccentricity. The city, on the contrary, rewards it. Neither the criminal, the defective, nor the genius has the same opportunity to develop his innate disposition in a small town that he invariably finds in a great city.

Fifty years ago every village had one or two eccentric characters who were treated ordinarily with a benevolent toleration, but who were regarded meanwhile as impracticable and queer. These exceptional individuals lived an isolated existence, cut off by their very eccentricities, whether of genius or of defect, from genuinely intimate intercourse with their fellows. If they had the making of criminals, the restraints and inhibitions of the small community rendered them harmless. If they had the stuff of genius in them, they remained sterile for lack of appreciation or opportunity. Mark Twain's story of *Pudd'n Head Wilson* is a description of one such obscure and unappreciated genius. It is not so true as it was that

> Full many a flower is born to blush unseen
> And waste its fragrance on the desert air.

Gray wrote the "Elegy in a Country Churchyard" before the rise of the modern metropolis.

In the city many of these divergent types now find a milieu in which, for good or for ill, their dispositions and talents parturiate and bear fruit.

In the investigation of those exceptional and temperamental types which the city has produced we should seek to distinguish, as far as possible, between those abstract mental qualities upon which technical excellence is based and those more fundamental native characteristics which find expression in temperament. We may therefore ask:

To what extent are the moral qualities of individuals based on native character? To what extent are they conventionalized habits imposed upon by them or taken over by them from the group?

What are the native qualities and characteristics upon which the moral or immoral character accepted and conventionalized by the group are based?

What connection or what divorce appears to exist between mental and moral qualities in the groups and in the individuals composing them?

Are criminals as a rule of a lower order of intelligence than non-criminals? If so, what types of intelligence are associated with different types of crime? For example, do professional burglars and professional confidence men represent different mental types?

What are the effects upon these different types of isolation and of mobility, of stimulus and of repression?

To what extent can playgrounds and other forms of recreation supply the stimulation which is otherwise sought for in vicious pleasures?

To what extent can vocational guidance assist individuals in finding vocations in which they will be able to obtain a free expression of their temperamental qualities?

The moral region.—It is inevitable that individuals who seek the same forms of excitement, whether that excitement be furnished by a horse race or by grand opera, should find themselves from time to time in the same places. The result of this is that in the organization which city life spontaneously assumes the population tends to segregate itself, not merely in accordance with its interests, but in accordance with its tastes or its temperaments. The resulting distribution of the population is likely to be quite different from that brought about by occupational interests or economic conditions.

Every neighborhood, under the influences which tend to distribute and segregate city populations, may assume the character of a "moral region." Such, for example, are the vice districts, which are found in most cities. A moral region is not necessarily a place of abode. It may be a mere rendezvous, a place of resort.

In order to understand the forces which in every large city tend to develop these detached milieus in which vagrant and suppressed impulses, passions, and ideals emancipate themselves from the dominant moral order, it is necessary to refer to the fact or theory of latent impulses of men.

The fact seems to be that men are brought into the world with all the passions, instincts, and appetites, uncontrolled and undisciplined. Civilization, in the interests of the common welfare, demands the suppression sometimes, and the control always, of these wild, natural dispositions. In the process of imposing its discipline upon the individual, in making over the individual in accordance with the accepted community model, much is suppressed altogether, and much more finds a vicarious expression in forms that are socially valuable, or at least innocuous. It is at this point that sport, play, and art function. They permit the individual to purge himself by means of symbolic expression of these wild and suppressed impulses. This is the catharsis of which Aristotle wrote in his *Poetic*, and which has been given new and more positive significance by the investigations of Sigmund Freud and the psychoanalysts.

No doubt many other social phenomena such as strikes, wars, popular elections, and religious revivals perform a similar function in releasing the subconscious tensions. But within smaller communities, where social relations are more intimate and inhibitions more imperative, there are many exceptional individuals who find within the limits of the communal activity no normal and healthful expression of their individual aptitudes and temperaments.

The causes which give rise to what are here described as "moral regions" are due in part to the restrictions which urban life imposes; in part to the license which these same conditions offer. We have, until very recently, given much consideration to the temptations of city life, but we have not given the same consideration to the effects of inhibitions and suppressions of natural impulses and instincts under the changed conditions of metropolitan life. For one thing, children, which in the country are counted as an asset, become in the city a liability. Aside from this fact it is very much more difficult to rear a family in the city than on the farm. Marriage takes place later in the city, and sometimes it doesn't take place at all. These facts have consequences the significance of which we are as yet wholly unable to estimate.

Investigation of the problems involved might well begin by a study and comparison of the characteristic types of social organization which exist in the regions referred to.

What are the external facts in regard to the life in Bohemia, the half-world, the red-light district, and other "moral regions" less pronounced in character?

What is the nature of the vocations which connect themselves with the ordinary life of these regions? What are the characteristic mental types which are attracted by the freedom which they offer?

How do individuals find their way into these regions? How do they escape from them?

To what extent are the regions referred to the product of the license; to what extent are they due to the restrictions imposed by city life on the natural man?

Temperament and social contagion.—What lends special importance to the segregation of the poor, the vicious, the criminal, and exceptional persons generally, which is so characteristic a feature of city life, is the fact that social contagion tends to stimulate in divergent types the common temperamental differences, and to suppress characters which unite them with the normal types about them. Association with others of their own ilk provides also not merely a stimulus, but a moral support for the traits they have in common which they would not find in a less select society. In the great city the poor, the vicious, and the delinquent, crushed together in an unhealthful and contagious intimacy, breed in and in, soul and body, so that it has often occurred to me that those long genealogies of the Jukes and the tribes of Ishmael would not show such a persistent and distressing uniformity of vice, crime, and poverty unless they were peculiarly fit for the environment in which they are condemned to exist.

We must then accept these "moral regions" and the more or less eccentric and exceptional people who inhabit them, in a sense, at least, as part of the natural, if not the normal, life of a city.

It is not necessary to understand by the expression "moral region" a place or a society that is either necessarily criminal or abnormal. It is intended rather to apply to regions in which a divergent moral code prevails, because it is a region in which the people who inhabit it are dominated, as people are ordinarily not dominated, by a taste or by a passion or by some interest which has its roots directly in the original nature of the individual. It may be an art, like music, or a sport, like horse-racing. Such a region would differ from other social groups by the fact that its interests are more immediate and more fundamental. For this reason its differences are likely to be due to moral, rather than intellectual, isolation.

Because of the opportunity it offers, particularly to the exceptional and abnormal types of man, a great city tends to spread out

[margin handwritten note: association of like with like produces moral support]

and lay bare to the public view in a massive manner all the human characters and traits which are ordinarily obscured and suppressed in smaller communities. The city, in short, shows the good and evil in human nature in excess. It is this fact, perhaps, more than any other, which justifies the view that would make of the city a laboratory or clinic in which human nature and social processes may be conveniently and profitably studied.

ROBERT E. PARK.

CHAPTER II

THE GROWTH OF THE CITY: AN INTRODUCTION TO A RESEARCH PROJECT

The outstanding fact of modern society is the growth of great cities. Nowhere else have the enormous changes which the machine industry has made in our social life registered themselves with such obviousness as in the cities. In the United States the transition from a rural to an urban civilization, though beginning later than in Europe, has taken place, if not more rapidly and completely, at any rate more logically in its most characteristic forms.

All the manifestations of modern life which are peculiarly urban —the skyscraper, the subway, the department store, the daily newspaper, and social work—are characteristically American. The more subtle changes in our social life, which in their cruder manifestations are termed "social problems," problems that alarm and bewilder us, as divorce, delinquency, and social unrest, are to be found in their most acute forms in our largest American cities. The profound and "subversive" forces which have wrought these changes are measured in the physical growth and expansion of cities. That is the significance of the comparative statistics of Weber, Bücher, and other students.

These statistical studies, although dealing mainly with the effects of urban growth, brought out into clear relief certain distinctive characteristics of urban as compared with rural populations. The larger proportion of women to men in the cities than in the open country, the greater percentage of youth and middle-aged, the higher ratio of the foreign-born, the increased heterogeneity of occupation increase with the growth of the city and profoundly alter its social structure. These variations in the composition of population are indicative of all the changes going on in the social organization of the community. In fact, these changes are a part of the growth of the city and suggest the nature of the processes of growth.

The only aspect of growth adequately described by Bücher and Weber was the rather obvious process of the *aggregation* of urban population. Almost as overt a process, that of *expansion*, has been investigated from a different and very practical point of view by groups interested in city planning, zoning, and regional surveys. Even more significant than the increasing density of urban population is its correlative tendency to overflow, and so to extend over wider areas, and to incorporate these areas into a larger communal life. This paper, therefore, will treat first of the expansion of the city, and then of the less-known processes of urban metabolism and mobility which are closely related to expansion.

EXPANSION AS PHYSICAL GROWTH

The expansion of the city from the standpoint of the city plan, zoning, and regional surveys is thought of almost wholly in terms of its physical growth. Traction studies have dealt with the development of transportation in its relation to the distribution of population throughout the city. The surveys made by the Bell Telephone Company and other public utilities have attempted to forecast the direction and the rate of growth of the city in order to anticipate the future demands for the extension of their services. In the city plan the location of parks and boulevards, the widening of traffic streets, the provision for a civic center, are all in the interest of the future control of the physical development of the city.

This expansion in area of our largest cities is now being brought forcibly to our attention by the Plan for the Study of New York and Its Environs, and by the formation of the Chicago Regional Planning Association, which extends the metropolitan district of the city to a radius of 50 miles, embracing 4,000 square miles of

territory. Both are attempting to measure expansion in order to
deal with the changes that accompany city growth. In England,
where more than one-half of the inhabitants live in cities having a
population of 100,000 and over, the lively appreciation of the bearing
of urban expansion on social organization is thus expressed by C. B.
Fawcett:

One of the most important and striking developments in the growth of the
urban populations of the more advanced peoples of the world during the last
few decades has been the appearance of a number of vast urban aggregates,
or conurbations, far larger and more numerous than the great cities of any pre-
ceding age. These have usually been formed by the simultaneous expansion
of a number of neighboring towns, which have grown out toward each other
until they have reached a practical coalescence in one continuous urban area.
Each such conurbation still has within it many nuclei of denser town growth,
most of which represent the central areas of the various towns from which it
has grown, and these nuclear patches are connected by the less densely urban-
ized areas which began as suburbs of these towns. The latter are still usually
rather less continuously occupied by buildings, and often have many open spaces.

These great aggregates of town dwellers are a new feature in the distribution
of man over the earth. At the present day there are from thirty to forty of
them, each containing more than a million people, whereas only a hundred
years ago there were, outside the great centers of population on the waterways
of China, not more than two or three. Such aggregations of people are phenomena of great geographical and social importance; they give rise to new problems in the organization of the life and well-being of their inhabitants and in
their varied activities. Few of them have yet developed a social consciousness
at all proportionate to their magnitude, or fully realized themselves as definite
groupings of people with many common interests, emotions and thoughts.[1]

In Europe and America the tendency of the great city to expand
has been recognized in the term "the metropolitan area of the city,"
which far overruns its political limits, and in the case of New York
and Chicago, even state lines. The metropolitan area may be taken
to include urban territory that is physically contiguous, but it is
coming to be defined by that facility of transportation that enables
a business man to live in a suburb of Chicago and to work in the

[1] "British Conurbations in 1921," *Sociological Review*, XIV (April, 1922), 111-12.

loop, and his wife to shop at Marshall Field's and attend grand opera in the Auditorium.

EXPANSION AS A PROCESS

No study of expansion as a process has yet been made, although the materials for such a study and intimations of different aspects of the process are contained in city planning, zoning, and regional surveys. The typical processes of the expansion of the city can best be illustrated, perhaps, by a series of concentric circles, which may be numbered to designate both the successive zones of urban extension and the types of areas differentiated in the process of expansion.

This chart represents an ideal construction of the tendencies of any town or city to expand radially from its central business district—on the map "The Loop" (I). Encircling the downtown area there is normally an area in transition, which is being invaded by business and light manufacture (II). A third area (III) is inhabited by the workers in industries who have escaped from the area of deterioration (II) but who desire to live within easy access of their work. Beyond this zone is the "residential area" (IV) of high-class apartment buildings or of exclusive "restricted" districts of single family dwellings. Still farther, out beyond the city limits, is the commuters' zone—suburban areas, or satellite cities—within a thirty- to sixty-minute ride of the central business district.

This chart brings out clearly the main fact of expansion, namely, the tendency of each inner zone to extend its area by the invasion of the next outer zone. This aspect of expansion may be called *succession*, a process which has been studied in detail in plant ecology. If this chart is applied to Chicago, all four of these zones were in its early history included in the circumference of the inner zone, the present business district. The present boundaries of the area of deterioration were not many years ago those of the zone now inhabited by independent wage-earners, and within the memories of thousands of Chicagoans contained the residences of the "best families." It hardly needs to be added that neither Chicago

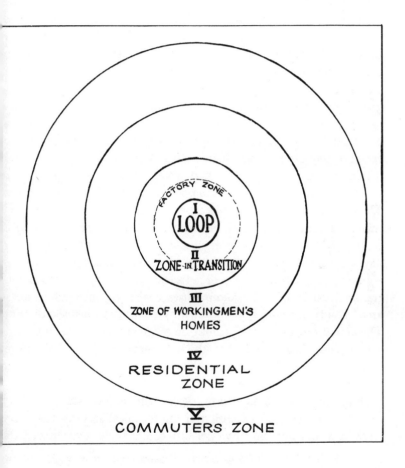

CHART I. The Growth of the City

nor any other city fits perfectly into this ideal scheme. Compli
cations are introduced by the lake front, the Chicago River, railroad
lines, historical factors in the location of industry, the relative degree
of the resistance of communities to invasion, etc.

Besides extension and succession, the general process of expansion in urban growth involves the antagonistic and yet comple
mentary processes of concentration and decentralization. In al
cities there is the natural tendency for local and outside transportation to converge in the central business district. In the down
town section of every large city we expect to find the departmen
stores, the skyscraper office buildings, the railroad stations, the
great hotels, the theaters, the art museum, and the city hall. Quite
naturally, almost inevitably, the economic, cultural, and politica
life centers here. The relation of centralization to the other processes of city life may be roughly gauged by the fact that over hal
a million people daily enter and leave Chicago's "loop." More
recently sub-business centers have grown up in outlying zones
These "satellite loops" do not, it seems, represent the "hoped for'
revival of the neighborhood, but rather a telescoping of several loca
communities into a larger economic unity. The Chicago of yester-
day, an agglomeration of country towns and immigrant colonies
is undergoing a process of reorganization into a centralized decentralized system of local communities coalescing into sub-business
areas visibly or invisibly dominated by the central business district
The actual processes of what may be called centralized decentralization are now being studied in the development of the chain store,
which is only one illustration of the change in the basis of the urban
organization.[1]

Expansion, as we have seen, deals with the physical growth of
the city, and with the extension of the technical services that have
made city life not only livable, but comfortable, even luxurious

[1] See E. H. Shideler, *The Retail Business Organization as an Index of Community
Organization* (in preparation).

Certain of these basic necessities of urban life are possible only through a tremendous development of communal existence. Three millions of people in Chicago are dependent upon one unified water system, one giant gas company, and one huge electric light plant. Yet, like most of the other aspects of our communal urban life, this economic co-operation is an example of co-operation without a shred of what the "spirit of co-operation" is commonly thought to signify. The great public utilities are a part of the mechanization of life in great cities, and have little or no other meaning for social organization.

Yet the processes of expansion, and especially the rate of expansion, may be studied not only in the physical growth and business development, but also in the consequent changes in the social organization and in personality types. How far is the growth of the city, in its physical and technical aspects, matched by a natural but adequate readjustment in the social organization? What, for a city, is a normal rate of expansion, a rate of expansion with which controlled changes in the social organization might successfully keep pace?

SOCIAL ORGANIZATION AND DISORGANIZATION AS PROCESSES OF METABOLISM

These questions may best be answered, perhaps, by thinking of urban growth as a resultant of organization and disorganization analogous to the anabolic and katabolic processes of metabolism in the body. In what way are individuals incorporated into the life of a city? By what process does a person become an organic part of his society? The natural process of acquiring culture is by birth. A person is born into a family already adjusted to a social environment—in this case the modern city. The natural rate of increase of population most favorable for assimilation may then be taken as the excess of the birth-rate over the death-rate, but is this the normal rate of city growth? Certainly, modern cities have increased and are increasing in population at a far higher

rate.   However, the natural rate of growth may be used to measure
the disturbances of metabolism caused by any excessive increase
as those which followed the great influx of southern Negroes into
northern cities since the war.   In a similar way all cities show devia
tions in composition by age and sex from a standard population such
as that of Sweden, unaffected in recent years by any great emigra
tion or immigration.   Here again, marked variations, as any grea
excess of males over females, or of females over males, or in the pro
portion of children, or of grown men or women, are symptomatic
of abnormalities in social metabolism.

Normally the processes of disorganization and organization may
be thought of as in reciprocal relationship to each other, and a
co-operating in a moving equilibrium of social order toward an end
vaguely or definitely regarded as progressive.   So far as disorganiza
tion points to reorganization and makes for more efficient adjust
ment, disorganization must be conceived not as pathological, but as
normal.   Disorganization as preliminary to reorganization of atti
tudes and conduct is almost invariably the lot of the newcomer to
the city, and the discarding of the habitual, and often of what has
been to him the moral, is not infrequently accompanied by sharp
mental conflict and sense of personal loss.   Oftener, perhaps, the
change gives sooner or later a feeling of emancipation and an urge
toward new goals.

In the expansion of the city a process of distribution takes place
which sifts and sorts and relocates individuals and groups by resi
dence and occupation.   The resulting differentiation of the cos
mopolitan American city into areas is typically all from one pattern
with only interesting minor modifications.   Within the central
business district or on an adjoining street is the "main stem" or
"hobohemia," the teeming Rialto of the homeless migratory man of
the Middle West.[1]   In the zone of deterioration encircling the cen
tral business section are always to be found the so-called "slums"

[1] For a study of this cultural area of city life see Nels Anderson, *The Hobo*, Chi
cago, 1923.

and "bad lands," with their submerged regions of poverty, degradation, and disease, and their underworlds of crime and vice. Within

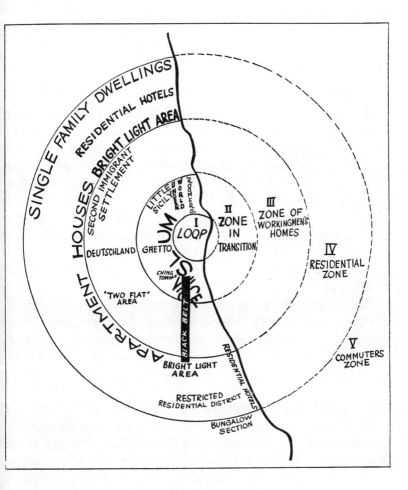

CHART II. Urban Areas

a deteriorating area are rooming-house districts, the purgatory of "lost souls." Near by is the Latin Quarter, where creative and rebellious spirits resort. The slums are also crowded to overflowing with immigrant colonies—the Ghetto, Little Sicily. Greek-town, Chinatown—fascinatingly combining old world heritages and American adaptations. Wedging out from here is the Black Belt, with its free and disorderly life. The area of deterioration, while essentially one of decay, of stationary or declining population, is also one of regeneration, as witness the mission, the settlement, the artists' colony, radical centers—all obsessed with the vision of a new and better world.

The next zone is also inhabited predominatingly by factory and shop workers, but skilled and thrifty. This is an area of second immigrant settlement, generally of the second generation. It is the region of escape from the slum, the *Deutschland* of the aspiring Ghetto family. For *Deutschland* (literally "Germany") is the name given, half in envy, half in derision, to that region beyond the Ghetto where successful neighbors appear to be imitating German Jewish standards of living. But the inhabitant of this area in turn looks to the "Promised Land" beyond, to its residential hotels, its apartment-house region, its "satellite loops," and its "bright light" areas.

This differentiation into natural economic and cultural groupings gives form and character to the city. For segregation offers the group, and thereby the individuals who compose the group, a place and a rôle in the total organization of city life. Segregation limits development in certain directions, but releases it in others. These areas tend to accentuate certain traits, to attract and develop their kind of individuals, and so to become further differentiated.

The division of labor in the city likewise illustrates disorganization, reorganization, and increasing differentiation. The immigrant from rural communities in Europe and America seldom brings with him economic skill of any great value in our industrial, commercial, or professional life. Yet interesting occupational selection has taken place by nationality, explainable more by racial temperament or circumstance than by old-world economic background, as Irish policemen, Greek ice-cream parlors, Chinese laundries, Negro porters, Belgian janitors, etc.

The facts that in Chicago one million (996,589) individuals gainfully employed reported 509 occupations, and that over 1,000 men and women in *Who's Who* gave 116 different vocations, give some notion of how in the city the minute differentiation of occupation "analyzes and sifts the population, separating and classifying the diverse elements."[1] These figures also afford some intimation of the complexity and complication of the modern industrial mechanism and the intricate segregation and isolation of divergent economic groups. Interrelated with this economic division of labor is a corresponding division into social classes and into cultural and recreational groups. From this multiplicity of groups, with their different patterns of life, the person finds his congenial social world and—what is not feasible in the narrow confines of a village— may move and live in widely separated, and perchance conflicting, worlds. Personal disorganization may be but the failure to harmonize the canons of conduct of two divergent groups.

If the phenomena of expansion and metabolism indicate that a moderate degree of disorganization may and does facilitate social organization, they indicate as well that rapid urban expansion is accompanied by excessive increases in disease, crime, disorder, vice, insanity, and suicide, rough indexes of social disorganization. But what are the indexes of the causes, rather than of the effects, of the disordered social metabolism of the city? The excess of the actual over the natural increase of population has already been suggested as a criterion. The significance of this increase consists in the immigration into a metropolitan city like New York and Chicago of tens of thousands of persons annually. Their invasion of the

[1] Weber, *The Growth of Cities*, p. 442.

city has the effect of a tidal wave inundating first the immigrant colonies, the ports of first entry, dislodging thousands of inhabitants who overflow into the next zone, and so on and on until the momentum of the wave has spent its force on the last urban zone. The whole effect is to speed up expansion, to speed up industry, to speed up the "junking" process in the area of deterioration (II). These internal movements of the population become the more significant for study. What movement is going on in the city, and how may this movement be measured? It is easier, of course, to classify movement within the city than to measure it. There is the movement from residence to residence, change of occupation, labor turnover, movement to and from work, movement for recreation and adventure. This leads to the question: What is the significant aspect of movement for the study of the changes in city life? The answer to this question leads directly to the important distinction between movement and mobility.

MOBILITY AS THE PULSE OF THE COMMUNITY

Movement, per se, is not an evidence of change or of growth. In fact, movement may be a fixed and unchanging order of motion, designed to control a constant situation, as in routine movement. Movement that is significant for growth implies a change of movement in response to a new stimulus or situation. Change of movement of this type is called *mobility*. Movement of the nature of routine finds its typical expression in work. Change of movement, or mobility, is characteristically expressed in adventure. The great city, with its "bright lights," its emporiums of novelties and bargains, its palaces of amusement, its underworld of vice and crime, its risks of life and property from accident, robbery, and homicide, has become the region of the most intense degree of adventure and danger, excitement and thrill.

Mobility, it is evident, involves change, new experience, stimulation. Stimulation induces a response of the person to those objects in his environment which afford expression for his wishes. For the person, as for the physical organism, stimulation is essential to growth. Response to stimulation is wholesome so long as it is a correlated *integral* reaction of the entire personality. When the reaction is *segmental*, that is, detached from, and uncontrolled by, the organization of personality, it tends to become disorganizing or pathological. That is why stimulation for the sake of stimulation, as in the restless pursuit of pleasure, partakes of the nature of vice.

The mobility of city life, with its increase in the number and intensity of stimulations, tends inevitably to confuse and to demoralize the person. For an essential element in the mores and in personal morality is consistency, consistency of the type that is natural in the social control of the primary group. Where mobility is the greatest, and where in consequence primary controls break down completely, as in the zone of deterioration in the modern city, there develop areas of demoralization, of promiscuity, and of vice.

In our studies of the city it is found that areas of mobility are also the regions in which are found juvenile delinquency, boys' gangs, crime, poverty, wife desertion, divorce, abandoned infants, vice.

These concrete situations show why mobility is perhaps the best index of the state of metabolism of the city. Mobility may be thought of in more than a fanciful sense, as the "pulse of the community." Like the pulse of the human body, it is a process which reflects and is indicative of all the changes that are taking place in the community, and which is susceptible of analysis into elements which may be stated numerically.

The elements entering into mobility may be classified under two main heads: (1) the state of mutability of the person, and (2) the number and kind of contacts or stimulations in his environment. The mutability of city populations varies with sex and age composition, the degree of detachment of the person from the family and from other groups. All these factors may be expressed numerically. The new stimulations to which a population responds can be measured in terms of change of movement or of increasing contacts. Statistics on the movement of urban population may only measure routine, but an increase at a higher ratio than the increase of population measures mobility. In 1860 the horse-car lines of New York City carried about 50,000,000 passengers; in 1890 the trolley-cars (and a few surviving horse-cars) transported about 500,000,000; in 1921, the elevated, subway, surface, and electric and steam suburban lines carried a total of more than 2,500,000,000 passengers.[1] In Chicago the total annual rides per capita on the surface and elevated lines were 164 in 1890; 215 in 1900; 320 in 1910; and 338 in 1921. In addition, the rides per capita on steam and electric suburban lines almost doubled between 1916 (23) and 1921 (41), and the increasing use of the automobile must not be overlooked.[2] For example, the number of automobiles in Illinois increased from 131,140 in 1915 to 833,920 in 1923.[3]

Mobility may be measured not only by these changes of movement, but also by increase of contacts. While the increase of population of Chicago in 1912–22 was less than 25 per cent (23.6 per cent), the increase of letters delivered to Chicagoans was double that (49.6 per cent)—(from 693,084,196 to 1,038,007,854).[4] In 1912 New York had 8.8 telephones; in 1922, 16.9 per 100 inhabitants. Boston had, in 1912, 10.1 telephones; ten years later, 19.5 telephones per 100 inhabitants. In the same decade the figures for Chicago increased from 12.3 to 21.6 per 100 population.[5] But increase of the use of the telephone is probably more significant than increase

---

[1] Adapted from W. B. Monro, *Municipal Government and Administration*, II, 377.

[2] *Report of the Chicago Subway and Traction Commission*, p. 81, and the *Report on a Physical Plan for a Unified Transportation System*, p. 391.

[3] Data compiled by automobile industries.

[4] Statistics of mailing division, Chicago Post-office.

[5] Determined from *Census Estimates for Intercensual Years*.

in the number of telephones. The number of telephone calls in Chicago increased from 606,131,928 in 1914 to 944,010,586 in 1922,[1] an increase of 55.7 per cent, while the population increased only 13.4 per cent.

Land values, since they reflect movement, afford one of the most sensitive indexes of mobility. The highest land values in Chicago are at the point of greatest mobility in the city, at the corner of State and Madison streets, in the Loop. A traffic count showed that at the rush period 31,000 people an hour, or 210,000 men and women in sixteen and one-half hours, passed the southwest corner. For over ten years land values in the Loop have been stationary, but in the same time they have doubled, quadrupled, and even sextupled in the strategic corners of the "satellite loops,"[2] an accurate index of the changes which have occurred. Our investigations so far seem to indicate that variations in land values, especially where correlated with differences in rents, offer perhaps the best single measure of mobility, and so of all the changes taking place in the expansion and growth of the city.

In general outline, I have attempted to present the point of view and methods of investigation which the department of sociology is employing in its studies in the growth of the city, namely, to describe urban expansion in terms of extension, succession, and concentration; to determine how expansion disturbs metabolism when disorganization is in excess of organization; and, finally, to define mobility and to propose it as a measure both of expansion and metabolism, susceptible to precise quantitative formulation, so that it may be regarded almost literally as the pulse of the community. In a way, this statement might serve as an introduction

[1] From statistics furnished by Mr. R. Johnson, traffic supervisor, Illinois Bell Telephone Company.

[2] From 1912–23, land values per front foot increased in Bridgeport from $600 to $1,250; in Division-Ashland-Milwaukee district, from $2,000 to $4,500; in "Back of the Yards," from $1,000 to $3,000; in Englewood, from $2,500 to $8,000; in Wilson Avenue, from $1,000 to $6,000; but decreased in the Loop from $20,000 to $16,500.

to any one of five or six research projects under way in the department.[1]   The project, however, in which I am directly engaged is
an attempt to apply these methods of investigation to a cross-section
of the city—to put this area, as it were, under the microscope, and
so to study in more detail and with greater control and precision the
processes which have been described here in the large.   For this
purpose the West Side Jewish community has been selected.   This
community includes the so-called "Ghetto," or area of first settlement, and Lawndale, the so-called "Deutschland," or area of second
settlement.   This area has certain obvious advantages for this
study, from the standpoint of expansion, metabolism, and mobility.
It exemplifies the tendency to expansion radially from the business
center of the city.   It is now relatively a homogeneous cultural
group.   Lawndale is itself an area in flux, with the tide of migrants
still flowing in from the Ghetto and a constant egress to more
desirable regions of the residential zone.   In this area, too, it is also
possible to study how the expected outcome of this high rate of
mobility in social and personal disorganization is counteracted in
large measure by the efficient communal organization of the Jewish
community.

ERNEST W. BURGESS

[1] Nels Anderson, *The Slum: An Area of Deterioration in the Growth of the City;*
Ernest R. Mowrer, *Family Disorganization in Chicago;*   Walter C. Reckless, *The
Natural History of Vice Areas in Chicago;*   E. H. Shideler, *The Retail Business Or-
ganization as an Index of Business Organization;*   F. M. Thrasher, *One Thousand
Boys' Gangs in Chicago; a Study of Their Organization and Habitat;*   H. W. Zorbaugh,
The Lower North Side; a Study in Community Organization.

CHAPTER III

THE ECOLOGICAL APPROACH TO THE STUDY OF THE HUMAN COMMUNITY

The young sciences of plant and animal ecology have become fairly well established. Their respective fields are apparently quite well defined, and a set of concepts for analysis is becoming rather generally accepted. The subject of human ecology, however, is still practically an unsurveyed field, that is, so far as a systematic and scientific approach is concerned. To be sure, hosts of studies have been made which touch the field of human ecology in one or another of its varied aspects, but there has developed no science of human ecology which is comparable in precision of observation or in method of analysis with the recent sciences of plant and animal ecology.

I. THE RELATION OF HUMAN ECOLOGY TO PLANT AND ANIMAL ECOLOGY

Ecology has been defined as "that phase of biology that considers plants and animals as they exist in nature, and studies their interdependence, and the relation of each kind and individual to its environment."[1] This definition is not sufficiently comprehensive to include all the elements that logically fall within the range of human ecology. In the absence of any precedent let us tentatively define human ecology as a study of the spatial and temporal[2] relations of human beings as affected by the selective,

[1] *Encyclopedia Americana*, New York (1923), p. 555.

[2] As indicated later on in this paper, ecological formations tend to develop in cyclic fashion. A period of time within which a given ecological formation develops and culminates is the time period for that particular formation. The length of these time periods may be ultimately measured and predicted, hence the inclusion of the temporal element in the definition.

Human ecology concerned with effects of position < Time space upon human institutions & behavior (as spatial relations change social relations are altered; ∴ social & political problems)

distributive, and accommodative forces of the environment. Human ecology is fundamentally interested in the effect of *position*,[1] in both time and space, upon human institutions and human behavior. "Society is made up of individuals spatially separated, territorially distributed, and capable of independent locomotion."[2] These spatial relationships of human beings are the products of competition and selection, and are continuously in process of change as new factors enter to disturb the competitive relations or to facilitate mobility. Human institutions and human nature itself become accommodated to certain spatial relationships of human beings. As these spatial relationships change, the physical basis of social relations is altered, thereby producing social and political problems.

A great deal has been written about the biological, economic, and social aspects of competition and selection, but little attention has been given to the distributive and spatial aspects of these processes. The plant ecologist is aware of the effect of the struggle for space, food, and light upon the nature of a plant formation, but the sociologist has failed to recognize that the same processes of competition and accommodation are at work determining the size and ecological organization of the human community.

The essential difference between the plant and animal organism is that the animal has the power of locomotion which enables it to gather nutriment from a wider environment, but, in addition to the power to move in space, the human animal has the ability to contrive and adapt the environment to his needs. In a word, the human community differs from the plant community in the two dominant characteristics of mobility and purpose, that is, in the power to select a habitat and in the ability to control or

---

[1] The word "position" is used to describe the place relation of a given community to other communities, also the location of the individual or institution within the community itself.

[2] Park and Burgess, *Introduction to the Science of Sociology*, p. 509.

[margin annotation: human communities ≠ purely the product of artifact or design.]

modify the conditions of the habitat. On first consideration this might seem to indicate that human ecology could have nothing in common with plant ecology where the processes of association and adjustment result from natural unmodifiable reactions; but closer examination and investigation make it obvious that human communities are not so much the products of artifact or design *[margin: human community origin]* as many hero-worshipers suppose.[1]

The human community has its inception in the traits of human nature and the needs of human beings. Man is a gregarious animal: *[margin: human natural needs]* he cannot live alone; he is relatively weak and needs not only the company of other human associates but shelter and protection *[margin: house water road]* from the elements as well. Brunhes says there are three essentials to the inception of the human community: the house, the road, *[margin: (shelter food communication]* and water.[2] Food may be transported more easily than shelter or water; the latter two therefore constitute, even under the most nomadic conditions, the essential elements in giving a location and a spatial fixity to human relations.[3] This is exemplified under our present régime of automobile tourist life, where water and *[margin: size & stability of community]* shelter become the determining factors in the location of the camp.

The size and stability of the human community is however a *[margin: function of food supply]* function of the food supply and of the rôle played in the wider ecological process of production and distribution of commodities. When man makes his living from hunting or fishing, the community *[margin: process of production of other commodities]* is small and of but temporary duration; when agriculture becomes the chief source of sustenance, the community is still small but assumes a more permanent character; when trade and commerce develop, larger communities arise at points of break in conveyance,

[1] Although the actions of individuals may be designed and controlled, the total effect of individual action is neither designed nor anticipated.

[2] *Human Geography*, p. 52.

[3] Brunhes points out by a series of maps the very intimate relation between the distribution of human habitations and the water systems of different countries. He also demonstrates the relation of the modern industrial community to the regions of coal deposits.

that is, at the mouths of rivers, junctions of streams, at water-falls, and shallows where streams are forded. As new forms of transportation arise, new points of concentration occur and old points become accentuated or reduced. Again, as goods for trade are made in communities, still other points of concentration come into existence, determined largely by sources of power and raw material.[1]

II. ECOLOGICAL CLASSIFICATION OF COMMUNITIES

From the standpoint of ecology, communities may be divided into four general types: first, the primary service community, such as the agricultural town, the fishing, mining, or lumbering community which serves as the first step in the distributive process of the outgoing basic commodity and as the last stage in the distributive process of the product finished for consumption. The size of such communities depends entirely upon the nature and form of utilization of the extractive industry concerned, together with the extent of the surrounding trade area. The community responds in size to any element that affects the productivity of the economic base or the extent of the area from which it draws its sustenance. But, in any event, so long as such a community does not assume any other function in the larger ecological process, it cannot grow in population beyond a few thousand inhabitants.

The next type of community is the one that fulfils the secondary function in the distributive process of commodities. It collects the basic materials from the surrounding primary communities and distributes them in the wider markets of the world. On the other hand, it redistributes the products coming from other parts of the world to the primary service communities for final consump-

---

[1] The close relation existing between the coal and iron areas and the location of modern industrial communities has frequently been pointed out. L. C. A. Knowles says: "Apart from special and exceptional circumstances industry in Europe and the United States tends to grow up within easy railway access to the great coal areas and on these areas the population is massed in towns" (*The Industrial and Commercial Revolutions in Great Britain during the Nineteenth Century*, p. 24).

tion. This is commonly called the commercial community; it may, however, combine other functions as well. The size of this type of community depends upon the extent of its distributive functions. It may vary from a small wholesale town in the center of an agricultural plain to that of a great port city whose hinterland extends halfway across the continent. Growth depends upon the comparative advantages of the site location.

The third type of community is the industrial town. It serves as the locus for the manufacturing of commodities. In addition it may combine the functions of the primary service and the commercial types. It may have its local trade area and it may also be the distributing center for the surrounding hinterland. The type is characterized merely by the relative dominance of industry over the other forms of service. There is practically no limit to the size to which an industrial community may develop. Growth is dependent upon the scope and market organization of the particular industries which happen to be located within its boundaries. Industrial communities are of two general types: first, those that have diversified and multiple industries organized on a local sale of products, and, second, those that are dominated by one or two highly developed industries organized on a national or world-sale of products.

The fourth type of community is one which is lacking in a specific economic base. It draws its economic sustenance from other parts of the world, and may serve no function in the production or distribution of commodities. Such communities are exemplified in our recreational resorts, political and educational centers, communities of defense, penal or charitable colonies. From the standpoint of growth or decline such communities are not subject to the same laws that govern the development of towns that play a part in the larger productive and distributive processes.[1] They

[1] To be sure, if the interests in question are commercialized, the growth of the community is subject to the same laws of competition as the other types of communities, with the exception that change is likely to be more rapid and fanciful.

In a given state of technology / Communities tend to grow to point of adjustment population (econ. base)

are much more subject to the vicissitudes of human fancies and decrees than are the basic types of human communities. Of course, any community may and usually does have accretions added to its population as a result of such service. It may, for instance, be the seat of a university, of a state prison, or it may be a recreational resort for at least certain seasons of the year.

III. DETERMINING ECOLOGICAL FACTORS IN THE GROWTH OR DECLINE OF COMMUNITY

The human community tends to develop in cyclic fashion. Under a given state of natural resources and in a given condition of the arts the community tends to increase in size and structure until it reaches the point of population adjustment to the economic base. In an agricultural community, under present conditions of production and transportation, the point of maximum population seldom exceeds 5,000.[1] The point of maximum development may be termed the point of culmination or climax, to use the term of the plant ecologist.[2] The community tends to remain in this condition of balance between population and resources until some new element enters to disturb the *status quo*, such as the introduction of a new system of communication, a new type of industry, or a different form of utilization of the existing economic base. Whatever the innovation may be that disturbs the equilibrium of the community, there is a tendency toward a new cycle of adjustment. This may act in either a positive or negative manner. It may serve as a *release* to the community, making for another cycle of growth and differentiation, or it may have a retractive influence, necessitating emigration and readjustment to a more circumscribed base.

Communities tend to remain at that level until something disturbs status quo, then new adjustment

In earlier conditions of life, population was kept down to the community balance by variations in the death-rate, or, as in the

[1] See H. P. Douglass, *The Little Town*, p. 44.

[2] F. E. Clements, *Plant Succession*, p. 3. Carr-Saunders refers to the point of population adjustment to resources as the "optimum."

case of Greek cities, the surplus population emigrated in groups to establish new colonies—offshoots of the mother-city. Under modern conditions of communication and transportation, population adjustment is maintained by a ceaseless process of individual migrations. As a result of the dynamic conditions prevailing throughout the civilized world during the last fifty years, many communities have passed through swift successive cycles of growth or decline, the determining factors being changes in forms and routes of transportation and communication and the rise of new industries.

Some advantage in transportation is the most fundamental and most important of the causes determining the location of a distributing center. It may almost be said to be the only cause for the formation of such centers. For some reason or reasons a particular place is more conveniently and cheaply reached by many people than any surrounding point; and, as a result, they naturally exchange commodities there. The country store is located at the crossing of roads. There also is the village. In a mountain country the market town is at the junction of two, or, still better, of three valleys. Another favorite location is the end of a mountain pass, or a gap that is a thoroughfare between two valleys. If rivers are difficult to cross, settlements will spring up at the safest ferries or fords. In a level plain, a town will be near its center, and a focus of roads or railroads in such a plain, fertile and populous, will almost surely make a city.[1]

It is the railroad and the steamship that determine where a new business shall be developed, quite as often as the government policy. The grant of special rates and privileges to shippers is nowadays the most efficient kind of protection.

It is this quickening and cheapening of transportation that has given such stimulus in the present day to the growth of large cities. It enables them to draw cheap food from a far larger territory and it causes business to locate where the widest business connection is to be had, rather than where the goods or raw materials are most easily produced. And the perfection of the means of communication, the post-office and the telegraph, intensifies the same result.[2]

[1] J. Russell Smith, *Industrial and Commercial Geography* (1913), p. 841.

[2] A. T. Hadley, "Economic Results of Improvement in Means of Transportation," quoted in Marshall, *Business Administration*, p. 35.

The entire net increase of the population of 1870 to 1890 in Illinois, Wisconsin, Iowa, and Minnesota was in cities and towns possessing competitive rates, while those having non-competitive rates decreased in population, and in Iowa it is the general belief that the absence of large cities is due to the earlier policy of the railways giving Chicago discriminating rates.[1]

auto especially has caused dramatic change in rural & small-town institutions

The advent of the trolley line and more recently of the automobile has produced still further disturbing elements in the growth of human communities. Their effect has been chiefly to modify the life of the small town or village, causing the decline of some and the sudden growth of others. The introduction of these two forms of transportation, more particularly of the automobile, has been the most potent force in our recent American history in affecting redistribution of our population and in the disorganization of our rural and small-town institutions which grew up on the basis of a horse-and-vehicle type of mobility.[2]

② new industry

The evolution of new types of industry is another feature that becomes a determining factor in the redistribution of the country's population. As we review our census reports we see the emergence each decade of one or more important industries; first, the textile industry causing concentrations of population in the eastern states, then the development of the iron and steel industry with its center of operations gradually shifting farther and farther west, and more recently the advent of the automobile and oil industries making for enormous concentration of population in certain states of the Union, also the motion-picture industry with its concentrated center in southern California. The emergence of a new industry has a far-reaching effect in disturbing the *status quo* of communal life. Competition soon forces the new industry to concentrate its productive enterprises in one or two communities; these communities then serve as great magnets drawing to themselves the appropriate population elements from communities far and near.

Competition causes industries to concentrate in one or a few cities; then appropriate pop. is attracted to these places

[1] L. C. A. Knowles, *The Industrial and Commercial Revolutions in Great Britain during the Nineteenth Century* (1921), p. 216.

[2] See Gillette, *Rural Sociology* (1922), pp. 472–73.

IV.   THE EFFECT OF ECOLOGICAL CHANGES ON THE SOCIAL ORGANIZATION OF COMMUNITY

Population migrations resulting from such sudden pulls as are the outcomes of unusual forms of release in community growth may cause an expansion in the community's development far beyond the natural culmination point of its cyclic development, resulting in a crisis situation, a sudden relapse, disorganization, or even panic.   So-called "boom towns" are towns that have experienced herd movements of population beyond the natural point of culmination.

On the other hand, a community which has reached the point of culmination and which has experienced no form of release is likely to settle into a condition of stagnation.   Its natural surplus of population is forced to emigrate.   This type of emigration tends to occasion folk-depletion in the parent community.   The younger and more enterprising population elements respond most sensitively to the absence of opportunities in their home town.   This is particularly true when the community has but a single economic base, such as agriculture, lumbering, mining.   Reformers try in vain to induce the young people to remain on the farms or in their native villages, little realizing that they are working in opposition to the general principles of the ecological order.

Again, when a community starts to decline in population due to a weakening of the economic base, disorganization and social unrest follow.[1]   Competition becomes keener within the community, and the weaker elements either are forced into a lower economic level or are compelled to withdraw from the community entirely. There are, of course, periodic and temporary fluctuations in the economic balance, due either to circumstances which affect the entire economic order or to the vicissitudes of the particular industry from which the community draws its sustenance.   These temporary

[1] For a good statistical summary of the decline in village population in the United States from 1900 to 1920 see Gillette, *op. cit.* (1922), p. 465.

Introduction of an innovating element =

fluctuations, however, while important from the standpoint of social well-being, do not comprise the basic determinants of community development.

initial stage of an invasion

The introduction of an innovating element into the adjustment of a community may be designated as the initial stage of an invasion which may make for a complete change in the structure and organization of the community. The introduction of a new mode of transportation, for instance, may transform the economic organization of a community and make for a change in population type.

eg. new railroad link

Thus the Harlem Railroad transformed Quaker Hill from a community of diversified farming, producing, manufacturing, selling, consuming, sufficient unto itself, into a locality of specialized farming. Its market had been Poughkeepsie, twenty-eight miles away, over high hills and indifferent roads. Its metropolis became New York, sixty-two miles away by rail and four to eight miles by wagon-road.

With the railroad's coming, the isolated homogeneous community scattered. The sons of the Quakers emigrated. Laborers from Ireland and other European lands, even negroes from Virginia, took their places. New Yorkers became residents on the Hill, which became the farthest terminus of suburban travel.[1]

eg. new industry

The establishment of a new industry, especially if it displaces the previous economic base, may also make for a more or less complete change of population without greatly modifying the size of the community. This condition is exemplified in many of the small towns of the state of Washington which have changed from lumbering to agriculture or from one type of agriculture to another. In many cases few of the previous inhabitants remained after the invasion of the new economic base.

Larger cities = more able to accommodate selves to invasions

As a community increases in size, however, it becomes better able to accommodate itself to invasions and to sudden changes in number of inhabitants. The city tends to become the reservoir into which the surplus population drains from the smaller communities round about.

[1] Warren H. Wilson, "Quaker Hill," quoted in Sims, *Rural Community*, p. 214.

Community growth
a) simple → complex
b) general → specialized
c) increasing centralization then decentralization

V. ECOLOGICAL PROCESSES DETERMINING THE INTERNAL STRUCTURE OF COMMUNITY

In the process of community growth there is a development from the simple to the complex, from the general to the specialized; first to increasing centralization and later to a decentralization process. In the small town or village the primary universal needs are satisfied by a few general stores and a few simple institutions such as church, school, and home. As the community increases in size specialization takes place both in the type of service provided and in the location of the place of service. The sequence of development may be somewhat as follows: first the grocery store, sometimes carrying a few of the more staple dry goods, then the restaurant, poolroom, barber shop, drug store, dry-goods store, and later bank, haberdashery, millinery, and other specialized lines of service.[1]

skeletal community structure based on routes of travel

The axial or skeletal structure of a community is determined by the course of the first routes of travel and traffic.[2] Houses and shops are constructed near the road, usually parallel with it. The road may be a trail, public highway, railroad, river, or ocean harbor, but, in any case, the community usually starts in parallel relation to the first main highway. With the accumulation of population and utilities the community takes form, first along one side of the highway and later on both sides. The point of junction or crossing of two main highways, as a rule, serves as the initial center of the community.

growth in size — process of differentiation & segregation

As the community grows there is not merely a multiplication of houses and roads but a process of differentiation and segregation takes place as well. Residences and institutions spread out in centrifugal fashion from the central point of the community, while

[1] In actual count of some thirty-odd communities in and around Seattle this was about the sequence of development.

[2] The axial or skeletal structure of civilization, Mediterranean, Atlantic, Pacific, is the ocean around which it grows up. See Ramsay Traquair, "The Commonwealth of the Atlantic," *Atlantic Monthly*, May, 1924.

business concentrates more and more around the spot of highest land values. Each cyclic increase of population is accompanied by greater differentiation in both service and location. There is a struggle among utilities for the vantage-points of position. This makes for increasing value of land and increasing height of buildings at the geographic center of the community. As competition for advantageous sites becomes keener with the growth of population, the first and economically weaker types of utilities are forced out to less accessible and lower-priced areas. By the time the community has reached a population of about ten or twelve thousand, a fairly well-differentiated structure is attained. The central part is a clearly defined business area with the bank, the drugstore, the department store, and the hotel holding the sites of highest land value. Industries and factories usually comprise independent formations within the city, grouping around railroad tracks and routes of water traffic. Residence sections become established, segregated into two or more types, depending upon the economic and racial composition of the population.

The structural growth of community takes place in successional sequence not unlike the successional stages in the development of the plant formation. Certain specialized forms of utilities and uses do not appear in the human community until a certain stage of development has been attained, just as the beech or pine forest is preceded by successional dominance of other plant species. And just as in plant communities successions are the products of invasion, so also in the human community the formations, segregations, and associations that appear constitute the outcome of a series of invasions.[1]

There are many kinds of intra-community invasions, but in general they may be grouped into two main classes: those resulting in change in use of land, and those which introduce merely change in type of occupant. By the former is meant change from one

[1] Compare F. E. Clements, *Plant Succession*, p. 6.

general use to another, such as of a residential area into a business area or of a business into an industrial district. The latter embraces all changes of type within a particular use area, such as the changes which constantly take place in the racial and economic complexion of residence neighborhoods, or of the type of service utility within a business section. Invasions produce successional stages of different qualitative significance, that is, the economic character of the district may rise or fall as the result of certain types of invasion. This qualitative aspect is reflected in the fluctuations of land or rental values.

The conditions which initiate invasions are legion. The following are some of the more important: (1) changes in forms and routes of transportation;[1] (2) obsolescence resulting from physical deterioration or from changes in use or fashion; (3) the erection of important public or private structures, buildings, bridges, institutions, which have either attractive or repellent significance; (4) the introduction of new types of industry, or even a change in the organization of existing industries; (5) changes in the economic base which make for redistribution of income, thus necessitating change of residence; (6) real estate promotion creating sudden demands for special location sites, etc.

Invasions may be classified according to stage of development into (a) initial stage, (b) secondary or developmental stage, (c) climax. The initial stage of an invasion has to do with the point of entry, the resistance or inducement offered the invader by the prior inhabitants of the area, the effect upon land values and rentals. The invasion, of course, may be into an unoccupied territory or into territory with various degrees of occupancy. The resistance to invasion depends upon the type of the invader together with the degree of solidarity of the present occupants. The undesirable

---

[1] For good discussions of the effect of new forms of transportation upon communal structure see McMichael and Bingham, *City Growth and Values* (1923), chap. iv; also Grupp, *Economics of Motor Transportation* (1924), chap. ii.

THE CITY

invader, whether in population type or in use form, usually makes entry (that is, within an area already completely occupied) at the point of greatest mobility. It is a common observation that foreign races and other undesirable invaders, with few exceptions, take up residence near the business center of the community or at other points of high mobility and low resistance. Once established they gradually push their way out along business or transportation thoroughfares to the periphery of the community.

The commencement of an invasion tends to be reflected in changes in land value. If the invasion is one of change in use the value of the land generally advances and the value of the building declines. This condition furnishes the basis for disorganization. The normal improvements and repairs are, as a rule, omitted, and the owner is placed under the economic urge of renting his property to parasitic and transitory services which may be economically strong but socially disreputable and therefore able and obliged to pay higher rentals than the legitimate utilities can afford. It is a well-known fact that the vices under the surveillance of the police usually segregate in such transitional areas.[1]

During the course of development of an invasion into a new area, either of use or type, there takes place a process of displacement and selection determined by the character of the invader and of the area invaded. The early stages are usually marked by keenness of competition which frequently manifests itself in outward clashes. Business failures are common in such areas and the rules of competition are violated. As the process continues, competition forces associational groupings. Utilities making similar or complementary demands of the area tend to group in close proximity to one another, giving rise to subformations with definite service functions. Such associations as amusement areas,

[1] By actual count in the city of Seattle over 80 per cent of the disorderly houses recorded in police records are obsolete buildings located near the downtown business section where land values are high and new uses are in process of establishment.

retail districts, market sections, financial sections, and automobile rows are examples of this tendency.

The climax stage is reached in the invasion process, once the dominant type of ecological organization emerges which is able to withstand the intrusions of other forms of invasion. For example, in the development of a residential district, when it is not controlled in advance by building restrictions, the early stages of growth are usually marked by wide variations in the type and value of buildings constructed. But, in the process of development, a uniform cost type of structure tends to dominate, gradually eliminating all other types that vary widely from the norm, so that it is customary to find a considerable degree of economic homogeneity in all established residential districts. The same process operates in areas devoted to business uses, competition segregates utilities of similar economic strength into areas of corre-sponding land values, and at the same time forces into close prox-imity those particular forms of service which profit from mutual association such as financial establishments or automobile display-rooms. Once a dominant use becomes established within an area, competition becomes less ruthless among the associational units, rules of control emerge, and invasion of a different use is for a time obstructed.

The general effect of the continuous processes of invasions and accommodations is to give to the developed community well-defined areas, each having its own peculiar selective and cultural character-istics. Such units of communal life may be termed "natural areas,"[1] or formations, to use the term of the plant ecologist. In any case, these areas of selection and function may comprise many subfor-mations or associations which become part of the organic structure of the district or of the community as a whole. It has been sug-gested that these natural areas or formations may be defined in

---

[1] A term used by members of the Department of Sociology in the University of Chicago.

terms of land values,[1] the point of highest land value representing the center or head of the formation (not necessarily the geographic center but the economic or cultural center), while the points of lowest land value represent the periphery of the formation or boundary line between two adjacent formations.

Each formation serves to attract similars to it.

Each formation or ecological organization within a community serves as a selective or magnetic force attracting to itself appropriate population elements and repelling incongruous units, thus making for biological and cultural subdivisions of a city's population. Everyone knows how racial and linguistic colonies develop in all of our large cities, but the age and sex segregations which take place are not quite so obvious to common perception. In the city of Seattle, which has in general a sex composition of 113 males to 100 females, the downtown district, comprising an area inscribed by a radius of half a mile or so, has from 300 to 500 males to every 100 females. But in the outlying districts of the city, except in one or two industrial sections, these ratios are reversed. Females predominate in numbers over males in all the residential neighborhoods and in the suburbs of the city. This same condition is true with regard to the age distribution of population. The school census shows an absolute decline in the number of children of school age in the central districts of the city although the total population for this area has shown an increase for each decade. It is obvious, then, that the settler type of population, the married couples with children, withdraw from the center of the city while the more mobile and less responsible adults herd together in the hotel and apartment regions near the heart of the community.

This process of population-sifting produces not only increasing mobility with approach from the periphery to the center of the formation, but also different cultural areas representing different mores, attitudes, and degrees of civic interest. The neighborhoods in which the settler type of population resides, with their preponder-

[1] This has also been suggested by the Chicago group.

ance of women and children, serve as the custodians of the stabilizing and repressive mores.   It is in the Seattle neighborhoods, especially those on the hill-tops, that the conservative, law-abiding, civic-minded population elements dwell.   The downtown section and the valleys, which are usually industrial sites, are populated by a class of people who are not only more mobile but whose mores and attitudes, as tested by voting habits, are more vagrant and radical.

R. D. McKenzie

CHAPTER IV

THE NATURAL HISTORY OF THE NEWSPAPER

I. THE STRUGGLE FOR EXISTENCE

The newspaper has a history; but it has, likewise, a natural history. The press, as it exists, is not, as our moralists sometimes seem to assume, the wilful product of any little group of living men. On the contrary, it is the outcome of a historic process in which many individuals participated without foreseeing what the ultimate product of their labors was to be.

The newspaper, like the modern city, is not wholly a rational product. No one sought to make it just what it is. In spite of all the efforts of individual men and generations of men to control it and to make it something after their own heart, it has continued to grow and change in its own incalculable ways.

The type of newspaper that exists is the type that has survived under the conditions of modern life. The men who may be said to have made the modern newspaper—James Gordon Bennett, Charles A. Dana, Joseph Pulitzer, and William Randolph Hearst— are the men who discovered the kind of paper that men and women would read and had the courage to publish it.

The natural history of the press is the history of this surviving species. It is an account of the conditions under which the existing newspaper has grown up and taken form.

A newspaper is not merely printed. It is circulated and read. Otherwise it is not a newspaper. The struggle for existence, in the case of the newspaper, has been a struggle for circulation. The newspaper that is not read ceases to be an influence in the community. The power of the press may be roughly measured by the number of people who read it.

The growth of great cities has enormously increased the size of the reading public.   Reading, which was a luxury in the country, has become a necessity in the city.   In the urban environment literacy is almost as much a necessity as speech itself.   That is one reason there are so many foreign-language newspapers.

Mark Villchur, editor of the *Russkoye Slovo*, New York City, asked his readers how many of them had read newspapers in the old country.   He found that out of 312 correspondents only 16 had regularly read newspapers in Russia; 10 others from time to time read newspapers in the Volast, the village administration center, and 12 were subscribers to weekly magazines.   In America all of them were subscribers or readers of Russian newspapers.

This is interesting because the immigrant has had, first and last, a profound influence on the character of our native newspapers. How to bring the immigrant and his descendants into the circle of newspaper readers has been one of the problems of modern journalism.

The immigrant who has, perhaps, acquired the newspaper habit from reading a foreign-language newspaper is eventually attracted to the native American newspapers.   They are for him a window looking out into the larger world outside the narrow circle of the immigrant community in which he has been compelled to live.   The newspapers have discovered that even men who can perhaps read no more than the headlines in the daily press will buy a Sunday paper to look at the pictures.

It is said that the most successful of the Hearst papers, the *New York Evening Journal*, gains a new body of subscribers every six years.   Apparently it gets its readers mainly from immigrants. They graduate into Mr. Hearst's papers from the foreign-language press, and when the sensationalism of these papers begins to pall, they acquire a taste for some of the soberer journals.   At any rate, Mr. Hearst has been a great Americanizer.

In their efforts to make the newspaper readable to the least-instructed reader, to find in the daily news material that would thrill the crudest intelligence, publishers have made one important discovery. They have found that the difference between the high-brow and the low-brow, which once seemed so profound, is largely a difference in vocabularies. In short, if the press can make itself intelligible to the common man, it will have even less difficulty in being understood by the intellectual. The character of present-day newspapers has been profoundly influenced by this fact.

II. THE FIRST NEWSPAPERS

What is a newspaper? Many answers have been given. It is the tribune of the people; it is the fourth estate; the Palladium of our civil liberties, etc.

On the other hand, this same newspaper has been characterized as the great sophist. What the popular teachers did for Athens in the period of Socrates and Plato the press has done in modern times for the common man.

The modern newspaper has been accused of being a business enterprise. "Yes," say the newspaper men "and the commodity it sells is news." It is the truth shop. (The editor is the philosopher turned merchant.) By making information about our common life accessible to every individual at less than the price of a telephone call we are to regain, it is urged—even in the complicated life of what Graham Wallas calls the "Great Society"—some sort of working democracy.

The advertising manager's notion is again something different. For him the newspaper is a medium for creating advertising values. The business of the editor is to provide the envelope which incloses the space which the advertising man sells. Eventually the newspaper may be conceived as a sort of common carrier, like the railway or the post office.

The newspaper, according to the author of the *Brass Check*, is a crime. The brass check is a symbol of prostitution. "The brass check is found in your pay envelope every week—you who write and print and distribute our newspapers and magazines. The brass check is the price of your shame—you who take the fair body of truth and sell it in the market place, who betray the virgin hopes of mankind into the loathsome brothel of big business."

This is the conception of a moralist and a socialist—Upton Sinclair.

Evidently the newspaper is an institution that is not yet fully understood. What it is, or seems to be, for any one of us at any time is determined by our differing points of view. As a matter of fact, we do not know much about the newspaper. It has never been studied.

One reason we know so little about the newspaper is that as it exists today it is a very recent manifestation. Besides, in the course of its relatively brief history, it has gone through a remarkable series of transfigurations. The press today is, however, all that it was and something more. To understand it we must see in its historic perspective.

The first newspapers were written or printed letters; news-letters they were called. In the seventeenth century English country gentlemen used to employ correspondents to write them once a week from London the gossip of the court and of the town.

The first newspaper in America, at least the first newspaper that lasted beyond its first issue, was the *Boston News-Letter*. It was published by the postmaster. The village post-office has always been a public forum, where all the affairs of the nation and the community were discussed. It was to be expected that there, in close proximity to the sources of intelligence, if anywhere, a newspaper would spring up. For a long time the position of post-master and the vocation of editor were regarded as inseparable.

The first newspapers were simply devices for organizing gossip, and that, to a greater or less extent, they have remained. Horace

Greeley's advice to a friend who was about to start a country paper is as good today as it was then.

Begin with a clear conception that the subject of deepest interest to an average human being is himself; next to that, he is most concerned about his neighbors. Asia and the Tongo Islands stand a long way after these in his regard. It does seem to me that most country journals are oblivious as to these vital truths. If you will, so soon as may be, secure a wide awake, judicious correspondent in each village and township of your county, some young lawyer, doctor, clerk in a store, or assistant in a post office who will promptly send you whatever of moment occurs in his vicinity, and will make up at least half your journal of local matter thus collected, nobody in the county can long do without it. Do not let a new church be organized, or new members be added to one already existing, a farm be sold, a new house be raised, a mill be set in motion, a store be opened, nor anything of interest to a dozen families occur, without having the fact duly though briefly chronicled in your columns. If a farmer cuts a big tree, or grows a mammoth beet, or harvests a bounteous yield of wheat or corn, set forth the fact as concisely and unexceptionally as possible.

What Greeley advises friend Fletcher to do with his country paper the city editor of every newspaper, as far as it humanly is possible, is still trying to do. It is not practicable, in a city of 3,000,000 and more, to mention everybody's name. For that reason attention is focused upon a few prominent figures. In a city where everything happens every day, it is not possible to record every petty incident, every variation from the routine of the city life. It is possible, however, to select certain particularly picturesque or romantic incidents and treat them symbolically, for their human interest rather than their individual and personal significance. In this way news ceases to be wholly personal and assumes the form of art. It ceases to be the record of the doings of individual men and women and becomes an impersonal account of manners and life.

The motive, conscious or unconsious, of the writers and of the press in all this is to reproduce, as far as possible, in the city the conditions of life in the village. In the village everyone knew everyone else. Everyone called everyone by his first name. The village was democratic.   We are a nation of villagers.   Our institutions are fundamentally village institutions.   In the village, gossip and public opinion were the main sources of social control.

"I would rather live," said Thomas Jefferson, "in a country with newspapers and without a government than in a country with a government and without newspapers."

If public opinion is to continue to govern in the future as it has in the past, if we propose to maintain a democracy as Jefferson conceived it, the newspaper must continue to tell us about ourselves. We must somehow learn to know our community and its affairs in the same intimate way in which we knew them in the country villages.   The newspaper must continue to be the printed diary of the home community.   Marriages and divorce, crime and politics, must continue to make up the main body of our news. Local news is the very stuff that democracy is made of.

But that, according to Walter Lippmann, is just the difficulty. "As social truth is organized today, so he says, "the press is not constituted to furnish from one edition to the next the amount of knowledge which the democratic theory of public opinion demands . . . . When we expect it to supply such a body of truth, we employ a misleading standard of judgment.   We misunderstand the limited nature of news, the illimitable complexity of society; we overestimate our own endurance, public spirit, and all-round competence. We suppose an appetite for uninteresting truths which is not discovered by any honest analysis of our own tastes. . . . . Unconsciously the theory sets up the single reader as theoretically incompetent, and puts upon the press the burden of accomplishing whatever representative government, industrial organization, and diplomacy have failed to accomplish.   Acting upon everybody for thirty minutes in twenty-four hours, the press is asked to create a mystical force called 'public opinion' that will take up the slack in public institutions."[1]

[1] Walter Lippmann, *Public Opinion*, pp. 361–62.

It is evident that a newspaper cannot do for a community of 1,000,000 inhabitants what the village did spontaneously for itself through the medium of gossip and personal contact. Nevertheless the efforts of the newspaper to achieve this impossible result are an interesting chapter in the history of politics as well as of the press.

III. THE PARTY PAPERS

The first newspapers, the news-letters, were not party papers. Political journals began to supersede the news-letters at the beginning of the eighteenth century. The news with which the reading public was most concerned at that time was the reports of the debates in Parliament.

Even before the rise of the party press certain prying and curious individuals had made a business of visiting the Strangers' Gallery during the sessions of the House of Commons in order to write up from memory, or from notes taken down surreptitiously, accounts of the speeches and discussions during an important debate. At this time all the deliberations of Parliament were secret, and it was not until 100 years later that the right of reporters to attend the sessions of the House of Commons and record its proceedings was officially recognized. In the meantime reporters were compelled to resort to all sorts of subterfuges and indirect methods in order to get information. It is upon this information, gathered in this way, that much of our present history of English politics is based.

One of the most distinguished of these parliamentary reporters was Samuel Johnson. One evening in 1770, it is reported, Johnson, with a number of other celebrities, was taking dinner in London. Conversation turned upon parliamentary oratory. Someone spoke of a famous speech delivered in the House of Commons by the elder Pitt in 1741. Someone else, amid the applause of the company, quoted a passage from this speech as an illustration of an orator who had surpassed in feeling and beauty of language the finest efforts of the orators of antiquity. Then Johnson, who up to that point had taken no part in the discussion, spoke up. "I wrote that speech," he said, "in a garret in Exeter Street."

The guests were struck with amazement. He was asked, "How could it have been written by you, sir?"

"Sir," said Johnson, "I wrote it in Exeter Street. I never was in the gallery of the House of Commons but once. Cave had interest with the doorkeepers; he and the persons employed under him got admittance; they brought away the subjects of discussion, the names of the speakers, the side they took, and the order in which they rose, together with notes of the various arguments adduced in the course of the debate. The whole was afterward communicated to me, and I composed the speeches in the form they now have in the "Parliamentary Debates," for the speeches of that period are all printed from Cave's magazine."[1]

Someone undertook to praise Johnson's impartiality, saying that in his reports he seems to have dealt out reason and eloquence with an equal hand to both political parties. "That is not quite true," was Johnson's reply. "I saved appearances tolerably well; but I took care that the Whig dogs should not have the best of it."

This speech of William Pitt, composed by Johnson in Exeter Street, has long held a place in school books and collections of oratory. It is the famous speech in which Pitt answered the accusation of the "atrocious crime of being a young man."

Perhaps Pitt thought he delivered that speech. At any rate there is no evidence that he repudiated it. I might add that Pitt, if he was the first, was not the last statesman who is indebted to the reporters for his reputation as an orator.

The significant thing about this incident is that it illustrates the manner in which, under the influence of the parliamentary reporters, something like a constitutional change was effected in the character of parliamentary government. As soon as the

[1] Michael MacDonagh, *The Reporters' Gallery*. Pp. 139-40.

parliamentary orators discovered that they were addressing not only their fellow-members but, indirectly, through the medium of the press, the people of England, the whole character of parliamentary proceedings changed. Through the newspapers the whole country was enabled to participate in the discussions by which issues were framed and legislation was enacted.

Meanwhile, the newspapers themselves, under the influence of the very discussions which they themselves instigated, had become party organs. Whereupon the party press ceased to be a mere chronicle of small gossip and came to be what we know as a "journal of opinion." The editor, meanwhile, no longer a mere newsmonger and humble recorder of events, found himself the mouthpiece of a political party, playing a rôle in politics.

During the long struggle for freedom of thought and speech in the seventeenth century, popular discontent had found literary expression in the pamphlet and broadside. The most notable of these pamphleteers was John Milton, and the most famous of these pamphlets was Milton's *Areopagitica: A Defence of the Liberty of Unlicensed Printing*, published in 1646; "the noblest piece of English prose" it has been called by Henry Morley.

When the newspaper became, in the early part of the eighteenth century, a journal of opinion, it took over the function of the political pamphlet. The opinion that had formerly found expression in a broadside was now expressed in the form of editorial leading articles. The editorial writer, who had inherited the mantle of the pamphleteer, now assumed the rôle of a tribune of the people.

It was in this rôle, as the protagonist of the popular cause, that the newspaper captured the imagination of our intelligentsia.

When we read in the political literature of a generation ago references to "the power of the press," it is the editor and the editorial, rather than the reporter and the news, of which these writers are thinking. Even now when we speak of the liberty of the press it is the liberty to express an opinion, rather than the liberty to investigate and publish the facts, which is meant.   The activities of the reporter, upon which any opinion that is relevant to existing conditions is likely to be based, are more often regarded as an infringement of our personal rights than an exercise of our political liberties.

The liberty of the press for which Milton wrote the *Areopagitica* was the liberty to express an opinion.   "Give me the liberty," he said, "to know, to alter, and to argue freely according to conscience, above all liberties."

Carlyle was thinking of the editorial writer and not of the reporter when he wrote: "Great is journalism!   Is not every able editor a ruler of the world, being a persuader of it?"

The United States inherited its parliamentary government, its party system, and its newspapers from England.   The rôle which the political journals played in English politics was re-enacted in America.   The American newspapers were a power with which the British government had to reckon in the struggle of the colonies for independence.   After the British took possession of New York City, Ambrose Serle, who had undertaken to publish the *New York Gazette* in the interest of the invaders, wrote as follows to Lord Dartmouth in regard to the patriot-party press.

> Among other engines which have raised the present commotion, next to the indecent harangues of the preachers, none has had a more extensive or stronger influence than the newspapers of the respective colonies.   One is astonished to see with what avidity they are sought after, and how implicitly they are believed by the great bulk of the people.[1]

It was nearly a century later, in the person of Horace Greeley, editor of the *New York Tribune* during the anti-slavery struggle, that the journal of opinion reached its highest expression in America. America has had better newspaper men than Horace Greeley, although none, perhaps, whose opinions exercised so wide an influence.   "The *New York Tribune*," says Charles Francis Adams,

[1] George Henry Payne, *History of Journalism in the United States*, p. 120.

"during those years was the greatest educational factor, economically and morally, this country has ever known."

IV. THE INDEPENDENT PRESS

The power of the press, as represented by the older type of newspaper, rested in the final analysis upon the ability of its editors to create a party and lead it. The journal of opinion is, by its very nature, predestined to become the organ of a party, or at any rate the mouthpiece of a school.

So long as political activities were organized on the basis of village life, the party system worked. In the village community, where life was and still is relatively fixed and settled, custom and tradition provided for most of the exigencies of daily life. In such a community, where every deviation from the ordinary routine of life was a matter of observation and comment and all the facts were known, the political process was, at any rate, a comparatively simple matter. Under these circumstances the work of the newspaper, as a gatherer and interpreter of the news, was but an extension of the function which was otherwise performed spontaneously by the community itself through the medium of personal contact and gossip.

But as our cities expanded and life grew more complicated, it turned out that political parties, in order to survive, must have a permanent organization. Eventually party morale became a greater value than the issues for the determination of which the parties are supposed to exist. The effect upon the party press was to reduce it to the position of a sort of house organ of the party organization. It no longer knew from day to day just what its opinions were. The editor was no longer a free agent. It was of this subjugated *Tribune* that Walt Whitman was thinking when he coined the phrase, "the kept editor."

When, finally, the exigencies of party politics, under conditions of life in great cities, developed the political machine, some of the more independent newspapers revolted. This was the origin of the independent press. It was one of the independent papers, the *New York Times* of that day, that first assailed and eventually overthrew, with the aid of a cartoonist, Thomas Nast, the Tweed Ring, the first and most outrageous of the political machines that party politics in this country has so far produced. Presently there was a general breaking away, particularly by the metropolitan, as distinguished from the country, papers, from the domination of the parties. Party loyalty ceased to be a virtue.

Meanwhile a new political power had arisen and found expression in the press. This power was embodied, not in the editorial and the editorial writer, however, but in the news and the reporter. In spite of the fact that the prestige of the press, up to this time, had rested on its rôle of champion of popular causes, the older newspapers were not read by the masses of the people.

The ordinary man is more interested in news than he is in political doctrines or abstract ideas. H. L. Mencken has called attention to the fact that the average man does not understand more than two-thirds of what "comes from the lips of the average political orator or clergyman."

The ordinary man, as the *Saturday Evening Post* has discovered, thinks in concrete images, anecdotes, pictures, and parables. He finds it difficult and tiresome to read a long article unless it is dramatized and takes the form of what newspapers call a "story." "News story" and "fiction story" are two forms of modern literature that are now so like one another that it is sometimes difficult to distinguish them.

The *Saturday Evening Post*, for example, writes the news in the form of fiction, while the daily press frequently writes fiction in the form of news. When it is not possible to present ideas in the concrete, dramatic form of a story, the ordinary reader likes them stated in a short paragraph.

It is said that James E. Scripps, founder of the *Detroit News*, which specializes in afternoon papers in secondary cities, built up his whole string of papers upon the basis of the very simple psychological principle that the ordinary man will read newspaper items in the inverse ratio to their length. His method of measuring the efficiency of his newspapers, therefore, was to count the number of items they contained. The paper that had the largest number of items was the best paper. This is just the reverse of Mr. Hearst's methods; his papers have fewer items than other papers.

The old-time journalist was inclined to have a contempt for news. News was for him simply material upon which to base an editorial. If God let things happen that were not in accordance with his conception of the fitness of things, he simply suppressed them. He refused to take the responsibility of letting his readers learn about things that he knew ought not to have happened.

Manton Marble, who was editor of the *New York World* before Joseph Pulitzer took it and made it yellow, used to say there were not 18,000 people in New York City to whom a well-conducted newspaper could offer to address itself. If the circulation of the paper went above that figure he thought there must be something wrong with the paper. Before Mr. Pulitzer took it over, the circulation had actually sunk to 10,000. The old *New York World* preserved the type of the old conservative high-brow paper down to the eighties. By that time in the larger cities the political independent newspapers had become the accepted type of journal.

Long before the rise of what was later to be called the independent press, there had appeared in New York two journals that were the forerunners of the present-day newspapers. In 1883 Benjamin Day, with a few associates, started a paper for "mechanics and the masses generally." The price of this paper was one cent, but the publishers expected to make up by larger circulation and by advertising the loss sustained by the lower price. At that time most of the other New York papers were selling for six cents.

It was, however, the enterprise of James Gordon Bennett,

the founder of the *New York Herald*, who set the pace in the new form of journalism. In fact, as Will Irwin says in the only adequate account that has ever been written of the American newspaper, "James Gordon Bennett invented news as we know it." Bennett, like some others who have contributed most to modern journalism, was a disillusioned man, and for that very reason, perhaps, a ruthless and cynical one. "I renounce all so-called principles," he said in his announcement of the new enterprise. By principles he meant, perhaps, editorial policies. His salutatory was at the same time a valedictory. In announcing the purposes of the new journalism he bade adieu to the aims and aspirations of the old. Henceforth the editors were to be news gatherers and the newspaper staked its future on its ability to gather, print, and circulate news.

What is news? There have been many answers. I think it was Charles A. Dana who said, "News is anything that will make people talk." This definition suggests at any rate the aims of the new journalism. Its purpose was to print anything that would make people talk and think, for most people do not think until they begin to talk. Thought is after all a sort of internal conversation.

A later version of the same definition is this: "News is anything that makes the reader say, 'Gee Whiz!'" This is the definition of Arthur McEwen, one of the men who helped make the Hearst papers. It is at the same time the definition of the latest and most successful type of journal, the yellow press. Not all successful journals are, to be sure, yellow. The *New York Times*, for example, is not. But the *New York Times* is not yet a type.

V. THE YELLOW PRESS

There seem to be, as Walter Lippmann has observed, two types of newspaper readers. "Those who find their own lives interesting" and "those who find their own lives dull, and wish to live a more thrilling existence." There are, correspondingly, two types of newspapers: papers edited on the principle that readers are mainly interested in reading about themselves, and papers edited upon the principle that their readers, seeking some escape from the dull routine of their own lives, are interested in anything which offers them what the psychoanalyists call "a flight from reality."

The provincial newspaper with its record of weddings, funerals, lodge meetings, oyster suppers, and all the small patter of the small town represents the first type. The metropolitan press, with its persistent search in the drab episodes of city life for the romantic and the picturesque, its dramatic accounts of vice and crime, and its unflagging interest in the movements of personages of a more or less mythical high society represents the latter type.

Up to the last quarter of the nineteenth century, that is to say, up to about 1880, most newspapers, even in our large cities, were conducted on the theory that the best news a paper can print is a death notice or marriage announcement.

Up to that time the newspapers had not yet begun to break into the tenements, and most people who supported a newspaper lived in homes rather than in apartments. The telephone had not yet come into popular use; the automobile was unheard of; the city was still a mosaic of little neighborhoods, like our foreign-language communities of the present day, in which the city dweller still maintained something of the provincialism of the small town.

Great changes, however, were impending. The independent press was already driving some of the old-time newspapers to the wall. There were more newspapers than either the public or the advertisers were willing to support. It was at this time and under these circumstances that newspaper men discovered that circulation could be greatly increased by making literature out of the news. Charles A. Dana had already done this in the *Sun*, but there still was a large section of the population for whom the clever writing of Mr. Dana's young men was caviar.

The yellow press grew up in an attempt to capture for the newspaper a public whose only literature was the family story paper or the cheap novel. The problem was to write the news in such a way that it would appeal to the fundamental passions. The formula was: love and romance for the women; sport and politics for the men.

The effect of the application of this formula was enormously to increase the circulation of the newspapers, not only in the great cities, but all over the country. These changes were brought about mainly under the leadership of two men, Joseph Pulitzer and William Randolph Hearst.

Pulitzer had discovered, while he was editor of the *St. Louis Post Dispatch,* that the way to fight popular causes was not to advocate them on the editorial page but to advertise them—write them up—in the news columns. It was Pulitzer who invented muckraking. It was this kind of journalism which enabled Pulitzer, within a period of six years, to convert the old *New York World,* which was dying of inanition when he took it, into the most talked about, if not the most widely circulated, paper in New York City.

Meanwhile, out in San Francisco Mr. Hearst had succeeded in galvanizing the old moribund *Examiner* into new life, making it the most widely read newspaper on the Pacific Coast.

It was under Mr. Hearst that the "sob sister" came into vogue. This is her story, as Will Irwin told it in *Collier's,* February 18, 1911:

Chamberlain (managing editor of the *Examiner*) conceived the idea that the city hospital was badly managed. He picked a little slip of a girl from among his cub reporters and assigned her to the investigation. She invented her own method; she "fainted" on the street, and was carried to the hospital for treatment. She turned out a story "with a sob for the unfortunate in every line." That was the professional beginning of "Annie Laurie" or Winifred Black, and of a departure in newspaper writing. For she came to have many imitators, but none other could ever so well stir up the primitive emotions of sympathy and pity; she was a "sob squad" all by herself. Indeed, in the discovery of this symphathetic "woman writing," Hearst broke through the crust into the thing he was after.

With the experience that he had gained on the *Examiner* in San Francisco and with a large fortune that he had inherited from his father, Hearst invaded New York in 1896. It was not until he reached New York and started out to make the *New York Journal* the most widely read paper in the United States that yellow journalism reached the limit.

Pulitzer's principal contribution to yellow journalism was muckraking, Hearst's was mainly "jazz." The newspaper had been conducted up to this time upon the theory that its business was to instruct. Hearst rejected that conception. His appeal was frankly not to the intellect but to the heart. The newspaper was for him first and last a form of entertainment.

It was about the time the yellow press was engaged in extending the newspaper habit to the masses of people, including women and immigrants—who up to this time did not read newspapers—that the department store was beginning to attract attention.

The department store is, in a sense, a creation of the Sunday newspaper. At any rate, without the advertising that the Sunday newspaper was able to give it, the department store would hardly have gained the vogue it has today. It is important in this connection that women read the Sunday paper before they did the dailies. The women are buyers.

It was in the Sunday newspaper that the methods of yellow journalism were first completely worked out. The men who are chiefly responsible for them are Morrill Goddard and Arthur Brisbane. It was Goddard's ambition to make a paper that a man would buy even if he could not read it. He went in for pictures, first in black and white and then in colors. It was in the *Sunday World* that the first seven-column cut was printed. Then followed the comic section and all the other devices with which we are familiar for compelling a dull-minded and reluctant public to read.

After these methods had been worked out in the Sunday paper, they were introduced into the daily. The final triumph of the yellow journal was Brisbane's "Heart-to-Heart Editorials"—a column of predigested platitudes and moralizing, with half-page diagrams and illustrations to re-enforce the text. Nowhere has Herbert Spencer's maxim that the art of writing is economy of attention been so completely realized.

Walter Lippmann, in his recent study of public opinion, calls attention to the fact that no sociologist has ever written a book on news gathering. It strikes him as very strange that an institution like the press, from which we expect so much and get so little of what we expect, should not have been the subject of a more disinterested study.

It is true that we have not studied the newspaper as the biologists have studied, for example, the potato bug. But the same may be said of every political institution, and the newspaper is a political institution quite as much as Tammany Hall or the board of aldermen are political institutions. We have grumbled about our political *institutions*, sometimes we have sought by certain magical legislative devices to exercise and expel the evil spirits that possessed them. On the whole we have been inclined to regard them as sacred and to treat any fundamental criticism of them as a sort of blasphemy. If things went wrong, it was not the institutions, but the persons we elected to conduct them, and an incorrigible human nature, who were at fault.

What then is the remedy for the existing condition of the newspapers? There is no remedy. Humanly speaking, the present newspapers are about as good as they can be. If the newspapers are to be improved, it will come through the education of the people and the organization of political information and intelligence. As Mr. Lippmann well says, "the number of social phenomena which are now recorded is small, the instruments of analysis are very crude, and the concepts often vague and uncriticized." We must improve our records and that is a serious task. But first of all we must learn to look at political and social life objectively and cease to think of it wholly in moral terms! In that case we shall have less news, but better newspapers.

The real reason that the ordinary newspaper accounts of the incidents of ordinary life are so sensational is because we know so little of human life that we are not able to interpret the events of life when we read them. It is safe to say that when anything shocks us, we do not understand it.

ROBERT E. PARK

CHAPTER V

COMMUNITY ORGANIZATION AND JUVENILE DELINQUENCY

I. THE "NATURAL DEPRAVITY" OF MANKIND

In view of the fact that man is so manifestly—as Aristotle described him—a political animal, predestined to live in association with, and dependence upon, his fellows, it is strange and interesting to discover, as we are compelled to do, now and again, how utterly unfitted by nature man is for life in society.

It is true, no doubt, that man is the most gregarious of animals, but it is nevertheless true that the thing of which he still knows the least is the business of carrying on an associated existence. Here, as elsewhere, it is those who have given the subject the closest study—the educator, the criminologist, and the social worker—who are most aware of the incalculable elements in every social situation and feel most keenly their inability to control human behavior.

In his recent study, *The Unadjusted Girl*, Dr. W. I. Thomas, referring to this matter, calls attention to the fact that "The whole criminal procedure is based on punishment, and yet we do not even know that punishment deters from crime. Or, rather, we know that it sometimes deters, and sometimes stimulates to further crime, but we do not know the conditions under which it acts in one way or another."[1]

So ill-adapted is the natural, undomesticated man to the social order into which he is born, so out of harmony are all the native impulses of the ordinary healthy human with the demands which society imposes, that it is hardly an exaggeration to say that if his

[1] William I. Thomas, *The Unadjusted Girl—with Cases and Standpoint for Behavior Analysis, Criminal Science*, Monograph No. 4, Boston, 1923.

childhood is spent mainly in learning what he must not do, his youth will be devoted mainly to rebellion. As to the remainder of his life—his recreations will very likely turn out to be some sort of vacation and escape from this same social order to which he has finally learned to accommodate, but not wholly reconcile, himself.

So far is this description true that our ancestors, living under a sterner discipline and in a moral order less flexible and accommodating than our own, were so impressed with the innate cantankerousness of ordinary mankind that they were driven to the assumption that there was something fundamentally diabolical in human nature, a view which found expression in the well-known doctrine of the "natural depravity of man."

One reason why human beings, in contrast with the lower animals, seem to be so ill-adapted to the world in which they are born is that the environment in which human beings live is so largely made up of the experience and memories and the acquired habits of the people who have preceded them.

This experience and these memories—crystallized and embodied in tradition, in custom, and in folk-ways—constitute the social, as distinguished from the biological, environment; for man is not merely an individual with certain native and inherited biological traits, but he is at the same time a person with manners, sentiments, attitudes, and ambitions.

It is the social environment to which the person, as distinguished from the individual, responds; and it is these responses of the person to his environment that eventually define his personality and give to the individual a character which can be described in moral terms.

II. SOCIETY AND THE SOCIAL MILIEU

This social environment in which mankind has acquired nearly if not all the traits that we regard as characteristically human is what we call society, society in the large; what Comte called "humanity."

When, however, we attempt to consider a little more in detail this society which ideally includes all mankind, we discover that it is composed of a number of smaller groups, little societies, each of which represents some single aspect or division of this all-enveloping social milieu in which we live and of which we are at the same time a part.

The first and most intimate portion of man's social environment, strange as the statement may at first seem, is his own body. After that, his clothing, tools, and property, which are in some sense a part of his personality, may, under certain circumstances, be regarded as a part of his environment. They become part of his social environment as soon as he becomes conscious of them; as soon as he becomes self-conscious.

Most of us have known, at some time in our lives, that "sickening sense of inferiority" that comes over one when in competition with his fellows, he realizes for the first time, perhaps, the inadequacy of his personal resources—physical, mental, and moral—to achieve his personal ambitions. But we who are presumably normal have very little understanding of the struggles of the physically or mentally handicapped to accommodate themselves to a world to which they are constitutionally not adapted.

So important to the development of personality is this interest which, with the advent of self-consciousness, the individual discovers in himself, that it has been made the basis of one of the numerous schools of psychiatry in Europe. Dr. Alfred Adler's theory of "psychic compensation" is based on the observation that an individual who is conscious of his inferiority inevitably seeks to compensate himself for this lowered self-esteem by greater concentration and effort. Eventually he may, in this way, succeed in overcoming his constitutional handicap; or he may find compensation for failure in one field by success in another and different one. Adler points out that there are numerous instances in which individuals have made striking successes in fields in which they were least fitted,

constitutionally, to succeed. The classic illustration is that of De-
mosthenes, who, according to the anecdote that has come down to
us, was a stutterer, but, by putting pebbles in his mouth and talk-
ing to the waves on the seashore, overcame his handicap and became
the greatest of Athenian orators.

When this sense of inferiority is acute because of some physical
deformity, or in consequence of any other constitutional inferiority,
so that the person is peculiarly sensitive about himself, the result is
frequently what Adler describes as "psychic overcompensation,"
which manifests itself in certain definite neurotic and socially
pathological tendencies, usually described as "egocentrism."

In such cases, according to Adler, "the neurotic shows a series
of sharply emphasized traits of character which exceed the normal
standard. The marked sensitiveness, the irritable debility, the suggestibility, the egotism, the penchant for the fantastic, the estrange-
ment from reality, but also more special traits such as tyranny, ma-
levolence, a self-sacrificing virtue, coquetry, anxiety, and absent-
mindedness are met with in the majority of case histories."

As soon as we become conscious of ourselves, self-control—
which is not fundamentally different from the control we exercise
over external volume—tends to become one of our most difficult and
absorbing problems. Man has many advantages over the lower
animals. On the other hand, the lower animals are not subject to
what Frazer describes as "the perils of the soul"; they do not have
the problem of managing themselves. This was evidently what Walt
Whitman meant when he wrote:

> I think I could turn and live with animals, they are so placid and
>   self-contained, ...
> They do not sweat and whine about their condition,
> They do not lie awake in the dark and weep for their sins,
> They do not make me sick discussing their duty to God,
> No one is dissatisfied—not one is demented with the mania of owning
>   things,

Not one kneels to another, nor to his kind that lived thousands of years ago,

Not one is respectable or industrious over the whole earth.

III. THE FAMILY AS A CORPORATE PERSON

After the individual's own person, the most intimate environment to which the person responds is the family. The family is, or was, under earlier and simpler conditions of life, a sort of larger corporate person. Among the Polish peasants, for example, where the family completely dominates the individual, "husband and wife," we are told, "are not individuals more or less closely connected according to their personal sentiments, but group members, controlled by both the united families."[1] It is on this basis that we can understand completely the letters written by immigrant boys to their parents asking them to send them wives:

DEAREST PARENTS:

Please do not be angry with me for what I shall write. I write you that it is hard to live alone, so please find some girl for me, but an orderly [honest] one, for in America there is not even one single orderly [Polish] girl. . . . . [December 21, 1902.] I thank you kindly for your letter, for it was happy. As to the girl, although I don't know her, my companion, who knows her, says that she is stately and pretty, and I believe him, as well as you, my parents. . . . . Please inform me which one (of the sisters) is to come, the older or the younger one, whether Aledsandra or Stanislawa.[2]

Of such a family it may almost be said that the unrebellious and completely accommodated individuals who compose it have ceased to exist as persons. They have no independent social status and no personal responsibilities except as members of the family group.

The family, as it exists under modern conditions, has fallen from the high estimation in which it was held by an earlier generation.

[1] Thomas and Znaniecki, *The Polish Peasant*, I, 87–97, quoted in Park and Miller, *Old-World Traits Transplanted*, p. 34.

[2] *Ibid.*, II, 259, quoted in Park and Miller, *Old-World Traits Transplanted*, pp. 39–40.

I once heard a distinguished psychologist say that he had been forced to the conclusion, after much patient study, that the family was probably the worst possible place in which to bring up a child. In general, I should say the psychiatrists seem to have a very poor opinion of the modern family as an environment for children. This opinion, if it is not justified, is at least supported by studies of juvenile delinquency made some years ago, in which it appeared that 50 per cent of the delinquencies studied were from broken homes.

The "one-child family" is now generally recognized as one of the characteristic social situations in which egocentric behavior is likely to manifest itself. It is certain that parents, just because of their solicitude for the welfare of their offspring, are not always safe companions for them. However that may be today, it is certain that in the past it was within the limits of the family group that most of the traits which we may describe as human were originally developed.

Outside the circle of the family and the neighborhood, within which intimate and the so-called "primary relations" are maintained, there is the larger circle of influences we call the community; the local community, and then the larger, organized community, represented by the city and the nation. And out beyond the limits of these there are beginning to emerge the vast and vague outlines of that larger world-community which Graham Wallas has described under the title, *The Great Society*.

The community, then, is the name that we give to this larger and most inclusive social milieu, outside of ourselves, our family, and our immediate neighborhood, in which the individual maintains not merely his existence as an individual, but his life as a person.

The community, including the family, with its wider interests, its larger purposes, and its more deliberate aims, surrounds us, incloses us, and compels us to conform; not by mere pressure from without, not by the fear of censure merely, but by the sense of our interest in, and responsibility to, certain interests not our own.

The sources of our actions are, no doubt, in the organic impulses of the individual man; but actual conduct is determined more or less by public opinion, by custom, and by a code which exists outside of us in the family, in the neighborhood, and in the community. This community, however, with its less immediate purposes and its more deliberate aims, is always more or less outside of, and alien to, us; much more so than the family, for example, or any other congenial group. This is to such an extent true that certain sociological writers have conceived society as having an existence quite independent of the individuals who compose it at any given time. Under these circumstances the natural condition of the individual in society is one of conflict; conflict with other individuals, to be sure, but particularly conflict with the conventions and regulations of the social group of which he is a member. Personal freedom—self-expression, as we have learned to call it in recent years—is, therefore, if not a fruitless, still a never ending, quest.

Only gradually, as he succeeds in accommodating himself to the life of the larger group, incorporating into the specific purposes and ambitions of his own life the larger and calmer purposes of the society in which he lives, does the individual man find himself quite at home in the community of which he is a part.

If this is true of mankind as a whole, it is still more true of the younger person. The natural impulses of the child are inevitably so far from conforming to the social situation in which he finds himself that his relations to the community seem to be almost completely defined in a series of "don'ts." Under these circumstances juvenile delinquency is, within certain age-limits at least, not merely something to be expected; it may almost be said to be normal.

It is in the community, rather than in the family, that our moral codes first get explicit and formal definition and assume the external and coercive character of municipal law.

IV. SOCIAL CHANGE AND SOCIAL DISORGANIZATION

In the family and in the neighborhood such organization as exists is based upon custom and tradition, and is fixed in what Sumner calls the folk-ways and the mores. At this stage, society is a purely natural product; a product of the spontaneous and unreflective responses of individuals living together in intimate, personal, and face-to-face relations. Under such circumstances conscious efforts to discipline the individual and enforce the social code are directed merely by intuition and common sense.

In the larger social unit, the community, where social relations are more formal and less intimate, the situation is different. It is in the community, rather than in the family or the neighborhood, that formal organizations like the church, the school, and the courts come into existence and get their separate functions defined. With the advent of these institutions, and through their mediation, the community is able to supplement, and to some extent supplant, the family and the neighborhood as a means for the discipline and control of the individual. However, neither the orphan asylum nor any other agency has thus far succeeded in providing a wholly satisfactory substitute for the home. The evidence of this is that they have no alumni association. They create no memories and traditions that those who graduate from them are disposed to cherish and keep alive.

It is in this community with its various organizations and its rational, rather than traditional, schemes of control, and not elsewhere, that we have delinquency. Delinquency is, in fact, in some sense the measure of the failure of our community organizations to function.

Historically, the background of American life has been the village community. Until a few years ago the typical American was, and perhaps still is, an inhabitant of a middle western village; such a village, perhaps, as Sinclair Lewis describes in *Main Street*. And still, today, the most characteristic trait of Homo Americanus is an inveterate individualism which may, to be sure, have been temperamental, but in that case temperament has certainly been considerably reinforced by the conditions of life on the frontier.

But with the growth of great cities, with the vast division of labor which has come in with machine industry, and with movement and change that have come about with the multiplication of the means of transportation and communication, the old forms of social control represented by the family, the neighborhood, and the local community have been undermined and their influence greatly diminished.

This process by which the authority and influence of an earlier culture and system of social control is undermined and eventually destroyed is described by Thomas—looking at it from the side of the individual—as a process of "individualization." But looking at it from the point of view of society and the community it is social disorganization.

We are living in such a period of individualization and social disorganization. Everything is in a state of agitation—everything seems to be undergoing a change. Society is, apparently, not much more than a congeries and constellation of social atoms. Habits can be formed only in a relatively stable environment, even if that stability consists merely—as, in fact, it invariably does, since there is nothing in the universe that is absolutely static—in a relatively constant form of change. Any form of change that brings any measurable alteration in the routine of social life tends to break up habits; and in breaking up the habits upon which the existing social organization rests, destroys that organization itself. Every new device that affects social life and the social routine is to that extent a disorganizing influence. Every new discovery, every new invention, every new idea, is disturbing. Even news has become at times so dangerous that governments have felt it wise to suppress its publication.

It is probable that the most deadly and the most demoralizing single instrumentality of present-day civilization is the automobile. The automobile bandit, operating in our great cities, is much more successful and more dangerous than the romantic stage robber of fifty years ago. The connection of the automobile with vice is notorious. "The automobile is connected with more seductions than happen otherwise in cities altogether."[1]

The newspaper and the motion picture show, while not so deadly, are almost as demoralizing. If I were to attempt to enumerate all the social forces that have contributed to the disorganization of modern society I should probably be compelled to make a catalogue of everything that has introduced any new and striking change into the otherwise dull routine of our daily life. Apparently anything that makes life interesting is dangerous to the existing order.

The mere movement of the population from one part of the country to another—the present migration of the Negroes northward, for example—is a disturbing influence. Such a movement may assume, from the point of view of the migrants themselves, the character of an emancipation, opening to them new economic and cultural opportunities, but it is none the less disorganizing to the communities they have left behind and to the communities into which they are now moving. It is at the same time demoralizing to the migrating people themselves, and particularly, I might add, to the younger generation.

The enormous amount of delinquency, juvenile and adult, that exists today in the Negro communities in northern cities is due in part, though not entirely, to the fact that migrants are not able to accommodate themselves at once to a new and relatively strange environment. The same thing may be said of the immigrants from Europe, or of the younger generation of women who are just now entering in such large numbers into the newer occupations and the freer life which the great cities offer them.

"Progress," as I once heard William James remark, "is a terrible thing." It is a terrible thing in so far as it breaks up the routine upon which an existing social order rests, and thus destroys the cultural and the economic values, i.e., the habits of thrift, of skill, of industry, as well as the personal hopes, ambitions, and life-programs which are the content of that social order.

[1] W. I. Thomas, *The Unadjusted Girl*, p. 71.

Our great cities, as those who have studied them have learned, are full of junk, much of it human, i.e., men and women who, for some reason or other, have fallen out of line in the march of industrial progress and have been scrapped by the industrial organization of which they were once a part.

A recent study by Nels Anderson of what he calls "Hobohemia," an area in Chicago just outside the "Loop," that is to say, the downtown business area, which is almost wholly inhabited by homeless men, is a study of such a human junk heap. In fact, the slum areas that invariably grow up just on the edge of the business areas of great cities, areas of deteriorated houses, of poverty, vice, and crime, are areas of social junk.

I might add, because of its immediate connection with the problems and interests of this association, that recent studies made in Chicago of boys' gangs seem to show that there are no playgrounds in the city in which a boy can find so much adventure, no place where he can find so much that may be called "real sport," as in these areas of general deterioration which we call the slums.

In order to meet and deal with the problems that have been created by the rapid changes of modern life, new organizations and agencies have sprung into existence. The older social agencies, the church, the school, and the courts, have not always been able to meet the problems which new conditions of life have created. The school, the church, and the courts have come down to us with their aims and methods defined under the influence of an older tradition. New agencies have been necessary to meet the new conditions. Among these new agancies are the juvenile courts, juvenile protective associations, parent-teachers' associations, Boy Scouts, Young Men's Christian Associations settlements, boys' clubs of various sorts, and I presume, playgrounds and playground associations. These agencies have taken over to some extent the work which neither the home, the neighborhood, nor the other older communal institutions were able to carry on adequately.

These new institutions, perhaps because they are not to the same extent hampered by our earlier traditions, are frankly experimental and are trying to work out a rational technique for dealing with social problems, based not on sentiment and tradition, but on science.

Largely on the basis of the experiments which these new agencies are making, a new social science is coming into existence. Under the impetus which the social agencies have given to social investigation and social research, sociology is ceasing to be a mere philosophy and is assuming more and more the character of an empirical, if not an exact, science.

As to the present condition of our science and of the devices that we have invented for controlling conduct and social life, I can only repeat what I said at the very outset of our paper: "The thing of which we still know least is the business of carrying on an associated existence."

V. THE GANG AND THE LOCAL COMMUNITY

I have sought, in what has been said, to indicate what seems to me to be the relation of the work of the playground association and other social agencies to the more general problem of community organization and juvenile delinquency. But I have a feeling that this paper lacks a moral, and I know that every paper on a social topic should have a moral. If I were asked to state in a few words what seems to me to be suggested by our discussion so far I should say:

1. That the problem of juvenile delinquency seems to have its sources in conditions over which, with our present knowledge, we have very little control; that the whole matter needs, therefore, a more searching investigation than we have yet been able to give it.

2. That the encouraging factor in the situation is: (1) that our social agencies are definitely experimenting with the problem; (2) that there is growing up in the universities and elsewhere a body of knowledge about human nature and society which will presently enable us to interpret these experiments, redefine the problem, and

eventually gain a deeper insight into the social conditions and the social processes under which not merely juvenile delinquency but other forms of personal and social disorganization occur.

3. That what we already know about the intimate relations between the individual and the community makes it clear that delinquency is not primarily a problem of the individual, but of the group. Any effort to re-educate and reform the delinquent individual will consist very largely in finding for him an environment, a group in which he can live, and live not merely in the physical or biological sense of the word, but live in the social and in the sociological sense. That means finding a place where he can have not only free expression of his energies and native impulses, but a place where he can find a vocation and be free to formulate a plan of life which will enable him to realize in some adequate way all the fundamental wishes that, in some form or other, every individual seeks to realize, and must realize, in order to have a wholesome and reasonably happy existence.

4. This suggests to me that the playground should be something more than a place for working off steam and keeping children out of mischief. It should be a place where children form permanent associations. The play group is certainly one of the most important factors in the defining of the wishes and the forming of the character of the average individual. Under conditions of urban life, where the home tends to become little more than a sleeping-place, a dormitory, the play group is assuming an increasing importance. Mr. Frederic M. Thrasher has recently been studying the boys' gangs in Chicago. He has located one thousand gangs, and it is interesting to notice where these gangs are located. They are for the most part in the slums. The gangs he has located and studied are by no means all the gangs in Chicago. They are, rather, the gangs that have attracted attention because they have been troublesome, because they are connected directly or indirectly with juvenile delinquency and adolescent crime.

If I ventured to state my opinion in regard to the matter, I should say that these gangs have exercised a considerably greater influence in forming the character of the boys who compose them than has the church, the school, or any other communal agency outside of the families and the homes in which the members of the gangs are reared. And it is quite possible that the influence of these homes have not been always and altogether wholesome.

5. Finally, playgrounds should, as far as possible, be associated with character-forming agencies like the school, the church, and other local institutions. For however much the older generation may have been detached by migration and movement from their local associations, the younger generation, who live closer to the ground than we do, are irresistibly attached to the localities in which they live. Their associates are the persons who live next to them. In a great city, children are the real neighbors; their habitat is the local community; and when they are allowed to prowl and explore they learn to know the neighborhood as no older person who was not himself born and reared in the neighborhood is ever likely to know it.

This is one thing that makes the gang, a little later on, when perhaps it has become an athletic club, important politically. Our political system is based upon the theory that the people who live in the same locality know one another and have the same political and social interests. The gang is not infrequently a vocational school for ward politicians.

ROBERT E. PARK

CHAPTER VI

COMMUNITY ORGANIZATION AND THE ROMANTIC TEMPER

I. THE PROBLEM STATED

Recent local studies in Chicago seem to show that the number of competent persons in the community is frequently no real measure of the competency—if one may use that expression in this connection—of the community itself. A high communal intelligence quotient does not always, it seems, insure communal efficiency.

The explanation that at once suggests itself is that competent persons presumably are specialists deeply concerned in the little area of human experience in which they have chosen to operate, but profoundly indifferent to the interests of the particular geographical area in which they may happen to reside.

It is the incompetent persons, apparently, who still maintain an interest that could in any sense be called lively in the local communities of our great cities. Women, particularly women without professional training, and immigrants who are locally segregated and immured within the invisible walls of an alien language are bound to have some sort of interest in their neighbors. Children in great cities, who necessarily live close to the ground, however, are the real neighbors. Boys' gangs are neighborhood institutions. Politicians are professional neighbors. When the boys' gangs are graduated, as they frequently are, into local politics, the local political boss assumes toward them the rôle of patron, and they assume toward him the rôle of clients.

The competent people—that is to say, the professional people— are, on the other hand, either physically or in imagination, abroad most of the time. They live in the city—in their offices and in their clubs. They go home to sleep. Most of our residential suburbs tend to assume, as far as the professional classes are concerned, the character of dormitories. It is seldom that anyone who is sufficiently eminent or sufficiently competent to find a place in *Who's Who* has time for anything more than a benevolent interest in his local community.

On the other hand, the competent people are keenly alive to the interests of their professions, and if we could organize our politics, as the Russians have sought to organize theirs, on the basis of occupations, that is, in soviets, it might be possible to awaken in our intelligenzia a more than dilettante and sporting interest in local politics and the problems of the local community. But the actual stituation is different.

Our political system is founded on the presumption that the local community is the local political unit. If the local community is organized, knows its own local interests, and has a mind of its own, democracy prospers. It is said that 50 per cent of the qualified voters in this country do not exercise the franchise. So far as this is an index of their indifference to local community interests, it is at the same time a measure of the efficiency or inefficiency of the local community.

The National Community Center Association represents one of many efforts in recent years to alter the situation of which non-voting is perhaps one evidence. Community organizations aim, for one thing, to discover, to organize, and to make available for the local community the local community's resources, particularly its human resources. The extent to which it succeeds is the measure of its efficiency. How to assess these resources, how to use them: these are problems.

II. THE COMMUNITY DEFINED

But what is a community and what is community organization? Before assessing the communal efficiency one should at least be able to describe a community. The simplest possible description of a community is this: a collection of people occupying a more or less clearly defined area. But a community is more than that. A community is not only a collection of people, but it is a collection of institutions. Not people, but institutions, are final and decisive in distinguishing the community from other social constellations.

Among the institutions of the community there will always be homes and something more: churches, schools, playgrounds, a communal hall, a local theater, perhaps, and, of course, business and industrial enterprises of some sort. Communities might well be classified by the number and variety of the institutions—cultural, political, and occupational—which they possess. This would indicate the extent to which they were autonomous or, conversely, the extent to which their communal functions were mediatized, so to speak, and incorporated into the larger community.

There is always a larger community. Every single community is always a part of some larger and more inclusive one. There are no longer any communities wholly detached and isolated; all are interdependent economically and politically upon one another. The ultimate community is the wide world.

a) *The ecological organization.*—Within the limits of any community the communal institutions—economic, political, and cultural—will tend to assume a more or less clearly defined and characteristic distribution. For example, the community will always have a center and a circumference, defining the position of each single community to every other. Within the area so defined the local populations and the local institutions will tend to group themselves in some characteristic pattern, dependent upon geography, lines of communication, and land values. This distribution of population and institutions we may call the ecological organization of the community.

Town-planning is an attempt to direct and control the ecological organization. Town-planning is probably not so simple as it seems.

Cities, even those like the city of Washington, D.C., that have been most elaborately planned, are always getting out of hand. The actual plan of a city is never a mere artifact, it is always quite as much a product of nature as of design. But a plan is one factor in communal efficiency.

b) The economic organization.—Within the limits of the ecological organization, so far as a free exchange of goods and services exists, there inevitably grows up another type of community organization based on the division of labor. This is what we may call the occupational organization of the community.

The occupational organization, like the ecological, is a product of competition. Eventually every individual member of the community is driven, as a result of competition with every other, to do the thing he *can do* rather than the thing he *would like to do*. Our secret ambitions are seldom realized in our actual occupations. The struggle to live determines finally not only where we shall live within the limits of the community, but what we shall do.

The number and variety of professions and occupations carried on within the limits of a community would seem to be one measure of its competency, since in the wider division of labor and the greater specialization—in the diversities of interests and tasks—and in the vast unconscious co-operation of city life, the individual man has not only the opportunity, but the necessity, to choose his vocation and develop his individual talents.

Nevertheless, in the struggle to find his place in a changing world there are enormous wastes. Vocational training is one attempt to meet the situation; the proposed national organization of employment is another. But until a more rational organization of industry has somehow been achieved, little progress may be expected or hoped for.

c) The cultural and political organization.—Competition is never unlimited in human society. Always there is custom and law which sets some bounds and imposes some restraints upon the wild and wilful impulses of the individual man. The cultural and political organization of the community rests upon the occupational organization, just as the latter, in turn, grows up in, and rests upon, the ecological organization.

It is this final division or segment of the communal organization with which community-center associations are mainly concerned. Politics, religion, and community welfare, like golf, bridge, and other forms of recreation, are leisure-time activities, and it is the leisure time of the community that we are seeking to organize.

Aristotle, who described man as a political animal, lived a long time ago, and his description was more true of man then than it is today. Aristotle lived in a world in which art, religion, and politics were the main concerns of life, and public life was the natural vocation of every citizen.

Under modern conditions of life, where the division of labor has gone so far that—to cite a notorious instance—it takes 150 separate operations to make a suit of clothes, the situation is totally different. Most of us now, during the major portion of our waking hours, are so busy on some minute detail of the common task that we frequently lose sight altogether of the community in which we live.

On the other hand, our leisure is now mainly a restless search for excitement. It is the romantic impulse, the desire to escape the dull routine of life at home and in the local community, that drives us abroad in search of adventure. This romantic quest, which finds its most outrageous expression in the dance halls and jazz parlors, is characteristic of almost every other expression of modern life. Political revolution and social reform are themselves often merely expressions of this same romantic impulse. Millennialism in religion, the missionary enterprises, particularly those that are limited to "regions beyond," are manifestations of this same wish to escape reality.

We are everywhere hunting the bluebird of romance, and we are hunting it with automobiles and flying machines. The new devices of locomotion have permitted millions of people to realize, in actual life, flights of which they had only dreamed previously. But this physical mobility is but the reflection of a corresponding mental instability.

This restlessness and thirst for adventure is, for the most part, barren and illusory, because it is uncreative. We are seeking to escape from a dull world instead of turning back upon it to transform it.

Art, religion, and politics are still the means through which we participate in the common life, but they have ceased to be our chief concern. As leisure-time activities they must now compete for attention with livelier forms of recreation. It is in the improvident use of our leisure, I suspect, that the greatest wastes in American life occur.

III.   THE MEASUREMENT OF COMMUNAL EFFICIENCY

This, then, is our community. How are we to measure its efficiency? Here, I am bound to confess, we have still much to learn.

The simplest and most elementary way of estimating the competency and efficiency of a community, as something different from the competency and efficiency of the individual men and women who compose it, is by a comparative study of that community's social statistics. Poverty, disease, and delinquency have frequently been called social diseases. They may be said to measure the extent to which the community has been able to provide an environment in which the individuals which compose it are able to live, or, to state it from the opposite point of view, they measure the extent to which the individuals who compose the community have been able to adapt themselves to the environment which the community provided.

The immigrant community manifestly exists to enable the immigrant to live. By life, however, we mean something more than mere physical existence. Man is a creature such that when he lives at all he lives in society, lives in his hopes, in his dreams, and in the minds of other men. In some way or another, man is bound to realize all his fundamental wishes, and these wishes, according to Dr. W. I. Thomas, are four:

He must have (1) security, that is, a home; some place to go out from and return to.

He must have (2) new experience, recreation, adventure, new sensations.

He must have (3) recognition, i.e., he must belong to some society in which he has status, some group in which he is somebody; somewhere or other, in short, he must be a person, rather than a mere cog in the economic or social machine.

Finally (4) he must have affection, intimate association with someone or something, even though it be merely a cat or a dog, for which he feels affection and knows that affection is returned. All special human wishes reduce finally to these four categories, and no human creature is likely to be wholesome and happy unless, in some form or manner, all four of these wishes are more or less adequately realized.[1]

While I was on the Pacific Coast a few months ago, studying what we have called "race relations," I was impressed by the marked differences, as between immigrant groups, with respect to their ability to accommodate themselves to the American environment and, within the limitations imposed upon them by our customs and our laws, to provide for all the interests of life.

Immigrant communities are likely to include within the circle of their interests and their organizations all the interests of life. Every immigrant community will have a religious organization— a synagogue, a temple, or a church—with its related, often dependent, mutual aid and welfare organizations. It will have also its own business enterprises, its clubs, lodges, coffee houses, restaurants and gathering places, and a press. Every immigrant community is likely to have its press in America even if it did not have one in the home country. The immigrant colony is frequently nothing more than a transplanted village, for America actually has been colonized not by races or by nationalities, but by villages.

[1] Robert E. Park, "The Significance of Social Research in Social Service," *Journal of Applied Sociology* (May-June, 1924), pp. 264-65.

As to the competence of these immigrant communities to provide
an environment in which immigrants can live, Raymond Pearl's
paper, "The Racial Origin of Almshouse Paupers in the United
States," published in *Science* (October 31, 1924), throws some light.

One paragraph in that paper states the situation as between the
nation and the foreign-born. It says:

> While on January 1, 1923, there were in almshouses 59.8 native-born white
> persons per 100,000 of the same class in the population, the corresponding
> figure for the foreign-born was 173.6. This is by some regarded as a fact of dread
> significance. Perhaps it is. To me it seems possibly only an interesting expres-
> sion of the difficulties which the human organism finds in adapting itself to a
> new environment.

If these figures may be regarded, as Dr. Pearl suggests that they
should, as an index of the difficulties which the human organism
finds in adapting itself to a new environment, the more detailed
study of the various racial groups exhibits some surprising results.

They show, in the first place, wide divergencies in the capacity
of different immigrant groups to adapt themselves to American life;
they show, in the second place, that the races and nationalities that
have lived here longest are the least able to meet the demands of
the new environment. Dr. Pearl states it in this way:

> With a few trifling exceptions, all the countries from which the present
> law *encourages* immigration contributed to almshouse pauperism in 1923 in
> *excess* of their representation in the population in 1920. On the other hand,
> again with a few trifling exceptions, those countries from which the present
> immigration law was especially framed to *discourage* immigration appear in the
> lower part of the diagram, because they contribute a *smaller* proportion to
> almshouse pauperism in 1923 than their representation in the general popula-
> tion in 1920.

Two things strike me as significant in this connection: (1) It is
the recent immigrants who contribute least to the almshouse population; (2) among these recent immigrants it is, apparently, those who
for one reason or another are least willing or able to participate in
American life who contribute the least to our almshouse population.

Why is this true? My own inference is that the decisive factors are not biological, but sociological. The explanation of the almshouse statistics, in other words, is less a matter of racial temperament than of social tradition. It is the immigrants who have maintained in this country their simple village religions and mutual aid organizations who have been most able to withstand the shock of the new environment.

The whole subject needs to be investigated further. What would a comparative study of different racial and language groups with reference to disease, delinquency, and family disorganization show? What would a comparison of the Japanese, Chinese, and Mexicans show with reference to crime? I mention these three groups because they are living and working side by side on the Pacific Coast.

The census of 1910 showed the Mexicans to have the highest crime rate of any immigrant group in the United States. My conviction is that when we obtain the facts we shall find that the Japanese have the lowest crime rate, at least the lowest of any immigrant group on the Coast.

The explanation is that the Japanese—and the same is true of the Chinese—have organized what we may call "control organizations" to deal at once with disputes arising among themselves and with the larger community outside.

The Japanese Association, like the Chinese Six Companies, is organized to keep their nationals out of the courts. But the Japanese Association is more than a court of arbitration and conciliation. Its function is not merely to settle disputes, but to maintain the morale of the local Japanese community and to promote in every practical way, mainly by education, the efforts of the Japanese people to make their way in the communities in which they live. With the possible exception of the Jews, the Japanese are better informed than any other group about the condition of their own people in America.

One thing that has sensibly raised the morale of the Japanese, as it has, indeed of the Jews, is its struggle to maintain its racial status in the United States. Nothing, as Sumner observed, so easily establishes solidarity within the group as an attack from without Nothing so contributes to the discipline of a racial or national minority as the opposition of the racial or national majority.

The peoples who are making, or have made in recent years, the most progress in America today are, I suspect, the Jews, the Negroes and the Japanese. There is, of course, no comparison to be made between the Jew, the Japanese, and the Negro as to their racial competence. Of all the immigrant peoples in the United States, the Jews are the most able and the most progressive; the Negro, on the other hand, is just emerging, and is still a little afraid of the consequences of his newly acquired race-consciousness.

What is alike in the case of the Jew, the Negro, and the Japanese is that their conflict with America has been grave enough to create in each a new sense of racial identity, and to give the sort of solidarity that grows out of a common cause. It is the existence in a people of the sense of a cause which finally determines their group efficiency.

In some sense these communities in which our immigrants live their smaller lives may be regarded as models for our own. We are seeking to do, through the medium of our local community organizations, such things as will get attention and interest for the little world of the locality. We are encouraging a new parochialism, seeking to initiate a movement that will run counter to the current romanticism with its eye always on the horizon, one which will recognize limits and work within them.

Our problem is to encourage men to seek God in their own village and to see the social problem in their own neighborhood. These immigrant communities deserve further study.

ROBERT E. PARK

CHAPTER VII

MAGIC, MENTALITY, AND CITY LIFE

I. MAGIC AND PRIMITIVE MENTALITY

Few words of African origin have survived and found a permanent place in the popular speech of the English West Indies. One of these is "obeah." Of this word, J. Graham Cruickshank, in a little pamphlet entitled *Black Talk* says:

> *Obeah*—which is Negro witchcraft, and whose worst aspect was the poisonous *idea* put into the mind of the subject—has gone under to a great extent. Extraordinary cases of it crop up now and again in the newspapers. It is the most difficult of all anthropological data on which to "draw" the old Negro. Burton gives an Old Calabar proverb: "Ubio nkpo ono onya" (They plant Obeah for him) and adds this note: "'Ubio' means any medicine or charm put in the ground to cause sickness or death. It is manifestly the origin of the West Indian 'obeah.' We shall be the less surprised to hear that the word has traveled so far when told by Clarkson, in his *History of the Slave Trade*, that when the traffic was a legitimate branch of commerce as many slaves were annually exported from Bonny and the Old Calabar River as from all the rest of the West African Coast."[1]

Obeah is Negro magic. The paper which follows was suggested by observation on Negro magic during a recent visit to the English Islands in the Carribean.

During the past year two very important books have been published, in English, dealing with the subject of magic. The first is a translation of Lévy-Bruhl's *La Mentalité Primitive*, and the other is Lynn Thorndyke's *A History of Magic and Experimental Science during the First Thirteen Centuries of the Christian Era*.

In venturing to include two volumes so different in content and point of view in the same general category, I have justified myself

[1] J. Graham Cruickshank, *Black Talk*, p. 8.

by adopting Thorndyke's broad definition, which includes unde: "magic" "all occult arts and sciences, superstition and folklore."

Lévy-Bruhl's book is an attempt, from a wide survey of anthro pological literature, to define a mode of thought characteristic o primitive peoples.

Thorndyke, on the other hand, is interested mainly, as the title of his volume indicates, in the beginnings of empirical science The points of view are different, but the subject-matter is the same namely, magical beliefs and practices, particularly in so far as they reflect and embody a specific type of thought.

Lévy-Bruhl has collected, mainly from the writings of mission- aries and travelers, an imposing number of widely scattered obser- vations. These have been classified and interpreted in a way that is intended to demonstrate that the mental life and habits of thought of primitive peoples differ fundamentally from those of civilized man.

Thorndyke, on the other hand, has described the circumstances under which, during the first thirteen centuries of our era, the fore- runners of modern science were gradually discarding magical practices in favor of scientific experiment.

There is, of course, no historical connection between the culture of Europe in the thirteenth century and that of present-day savages, although the magical beliefs and practices of both are surprisingly similar and in many cases identical, a fact which is intelligible enough when we reflect that magic is a very ancient, widespread, characteristically human phenomenon, and that science is a very recent, exceptional, and possibly fortuitious manifestation of social life.

Lévy-Bruhl described the intelligence and habits of thought characteristic of savage peoples as a type of mentality. The civilized man has another and a different mentality. "Mentality," used in this way, is an expression the precise significance of which is not at once clear. We use the expression "psychology" in a similar but somewhat different way when we say, for example, that the rural and urban populations "have a different 'psychology,'" or that such and such a one has the "psychology" of his class—meaning that a given individual or the group will interpret an event or respond to a situation in a characteristic manner. But "mentality," as ordinarily used, seems to refer to the form, rather than to the content, of thought. We frequently speak of the type or grade of mentality of an individual, or of a group. We would not, however, qualify the word "psychology" in any such way. We would not, for example, speak of the grade or degree of the bourgeoise, or the proletarian "psychology." The things are incommensurable and "psychology," in this sense, is a character but not a quantity.

The term "mentality," however, as Lévy-Bruhl uses it, seems to include both meanings. On the whole, however, "primitive mentality" is used here to indicate the form in which primitive peoples are predisposed to frame their thoughts. The ground pattern of primitive thought is, as Lévy-Bruhl expresses it, "pre-logical."

As distinguished from Europeans and from some other peoples somewhat less sophisticated than ourselves, the primitive mind "manifests," he says, "a decided distaste for reasoning and for what logicians call the discursive operations of thought. This distaste for rational thought does not arise out of any radical incapacity or any inherent defect in their understanding," but is simply a method—one might almost say a tradition—prevalent among savage and simple-minded people of interpreting as wilful acts the incidents, accidents, and unsuspected changes of the world about them.

What is this pre-logical form of thought which characterizes the mentality of primitive people? Lévy-Bruhl describes it as "participation." The primitive mind does not know things as we do, in a detached objective way. The uncivilized man enters, so to speak, into the world about him and interprets plants, animals, the changing seasons, and the weather in terms of his own impulses and conscious purposes. It is not that he is lacking in observation, but he has no mental patterns in which to think and describe the shifts and changes of the external world, except those offered by the mutations of his own inner life. His blunders of interpretation are due to what has been described as the "pathetic fallacy," the mistake of attributing to other persons, in this case, to physical nature and to things alive and dead, the sentiments and the motives which they inspire in him. As his response to anything sudden and strange is more likely to be one of fear than of any other emotion, he interprets the strange and unfamiliar as menacing and malicious. To the civilized observer it seems as if the savage lived in a world peopled with devils.

One difference between the savage and the civilized man is that the savage is mainly concerned with incidents and accidents, the historical, rather than scientific, aspects of life. He is so actively engaged in warding off present evil and meeting his immediate needs that he has neither time nor inclination to observe routine. It is the discovery and explanation of this routine that enables natural science to predict future consequences of present action and so enable us to prepare today for the needs of tomorrow. It is the discovery and explanation, in terms of cause and effect, of this routine that constitutes, in the sense in which Lévy-Bruhl uses the term, rational thought.

What the author of primitive mentality means by "participation" is familiar enough, though the expression itself is unusual as description of a form of thought. Human beings may be said to know one another immediately and intuitively by "participation." Knowledge of this kind is dependent, however, upon the ability of human beings to enter imaginatively into one another's minds and to interpret overt acts in terms of intentions and purposes. What Lévy-Bruhl's statement amounts to, then, is that savage people think, as poets have always done, in terms of wills rather than forces. The universe is a society of wilful personalities, not an irrefragable chain of cause and effect.   For the savage, there are events, but neither hypotheses nor facts, since facts, in the strict sense of the word, are results of criticism and reflection and presuppose an amount of detachment that primitive man does not seem to possess.   Because he thinks of his world as will rather than force, primitive man seeks to deal with it in terms of magic rather than of mechanism.

II.   MAGIC AS A FORM OF THOUGHT

Thorndyke's *History of Magic* is an account of the manner and circumstances under which, within the period it covers, not all at once, but gradually, first in one field of knowledge and practice, and then in another—haltingly, painfully, and step by step—the transition from magic to science was made.

Anthropologists have not always agreed as to the precise relation between magic and science.   Is magic to be regarded as an earlier and more primitive form of science, or is it not?   It is at least true that science, as means of control of the external world, has always found some form of magic in existence, and has always displaced it. But magic is probably never *merely* a tool or a technique which men use to control and fashion the world after their desire.   It is primarily a form of emotional expression, a gesture, or dramatic performance.   It has something, also, of the character of a prayer or solemn formulation of a wish, but always with the hope that in some—not quite intelligible—way the formulation of the wish will bring its own fulfilment.   Magic ceases to interest us where the relation of the means to ends assumes the definiteness and certainty of a scientific demonstration.

Farmers in some parts of the country still pray for rain—at least they did so up to a few years ago.   They will quit doing so, however, as soon as someone invents a sure-fire device for making it.[1]

[1] Archbishop E. J. Hanna, head of the Catholic diocese of California, recently, during the drouth on the Pacific Coast, issued formal instructions to the pastors of all Catholic churches to offer the following prayer immediately after mass: "O God, in

We still believe in magic in medicine and in politics—partly, I suspect, because in those fields science has not been able to give us the positive knowledge it has in other regions of our experience, and partly because in the field of medicine and of politics our solemn formulations of our wishes so frequently bring the results desired. In many cases the method of social reformers in dealing with social evils is not unlike the technique of Christian Science in dealing with bodily and spiritual ailments; it consists mainly in solemnly and ceremonially asserting that a given evil no longer exists. Society formulates its wish, consecrates it—through the solemn referendum of a popular election, perhaps—and writes it on the statute books. As far as the public is concerned, the thing is then finished. Fortunately, this form of magic often works—but unfortunately, it does not work so often as it used to.[1]

What has been said indicates that magic may be regarded as a form of thought characteristic of, but not confined to, primitive— or what Professor Ellsworth Faris has called preliterate—man. It suggests, also, that primitive thought and primitive mentality are ordinarily associated with a definite organization of life and experience, perhaps even a definite economic organization of society. We all are disposed to think in magical terms in those regions of our experience that have not been rationalized, and where our control is

---

whom we live and move and are, grant us seasonal rain that we, enjoying a sufficiency of support in this life, may with more confidence strive after things eternal."—From *Los Angeles Evening Herald*, January 17, 1924.

[1] Thomas and Znaniecki, *The Polish Peasant in Europe and America* (Boston, 1918), I, 3: "The oldest but most persistent form of social technique is that of 'ordering-and-forbidding'—that is, meeting a crisis by an arbitrary act of will decreeing the disappearance of the undesirable or the appearance of the desirable phenomena, and the using arbitrary physical action to enforce the decree. This method corresponds exactly to the magical phase of natural technique. In both, the essential means of bringing a determined effect is more or less consciously thought to reside in the act of will itself by which the effect is decreed as desirable, and of which the action is merely an indispensable vehicle or instrument; in both, the process by which the cause (act of will and physical action) is supposed to bring its effect to realization remains out of reach of investigation."

uncertain and incomplete. The stock exchange and the golf course, where success is uncertain and fortuitous, all tend to breed their own superstition.

"Magic," as Thorndyke says, "implies a mental state, and so may be viewed from the standpoint of the history of thought." But magic, if it is a form of thought, is not science; neither is it art. The arts may be said to begin with the lower animals. But in the art with which the beaver constructs a dam and the bird builds a nest there is neither magic nor science.

We can best understand magic and its relation to science if we recall that thought is itself an interrupted act, "a delayed response" to use the language of the behaviorists. There is the impulse to act, which is interrupted by reflection, but eventually the impulse completes itself in action. Magic has the character of thought in so far as it is an impulse that is interrupted and so becomes conscious. But it is not rational thought because it does not foresee and seek to define the relation between the end it seeks and the means necessary to achieve that end. Between ends and means there is always a hiatus in which there is feeling but not clear intuition of how that end is to be achieved.

All human activities tend to assume the character of magic in so far as they become purely traditional and conventional, defined in some sacred formula piously transmitted. It is peculiarly characteristic of modern life, however, that all our inherited forms of behavior tend to become rationalized. It is characteristic of modern life that nothing is accepted merely on authority, every tradition is subject to criticism.

It is only in very recent years that we have achieved scientific agriculture and scientific cooking. On the other hand we have already scientific advertising and scientific "cheering." "Yelling" at ball games, once so spontaneous, has now become an art, if not a duty.[1]

[1] The following telegram was recently in the *San Francisco Bulletin:* "Stanford University, Jan. 24, 1924—Stanford has established what is termed a unique course in

III. MENTALITY AND CITY LIFE

The reason the modern man is a more rational animal than his more primitive ancestor is possibly because he lives in a city, where most of the interests and values of life have been rationalized, reduced to measurable units, and even made objects of barter and sale. In the city—and particularly in great cities—the external conditions of existence are so evidently contrived to meet man's clearly recognized needs that the least intellectual of peoples are inevitably led to think in deterministic and mechanistic terms.

The embodiment of rational thought is the tool, the machine, in which all the parts are manifestly designed to achieve a perfectly intelligible end. The primitive man lives in a vastly different world, where all the forces about him are mysterious and uncontrollable, and where nature seems as wild, as romantic, and as unpredictable as his own changing moods. The primitive man has almost no machinery, and relatively few tools.

The mentality of the modern man, on the other hand, is based upon the machine and upon the application of science to all the interests of life—to education, to advertising, and, presently, perhaps, to politics. The culture of the modern man is characteristically urban, as distinguished from the folk culture, which rests on personal relations and direct participation in the common life of the family, the tribe, and the village community.

In fact, if we define them strictly, as Lévy-Bruhl seems to do, we may say that reason and reflective thinking were born in the city. They came, if not into existence, at least into vogue, in Athens, in the time of Socrates and the Sophists. The Sophists were, in fact, a distinctly urban phenomenon, and we owe to Socrates— who was one of them—the first clear recognition of conceptional,

---

the curriculum of western universities. It teaches scientific yell-leading, according to the rally committee, which sponsors the course. The course is open to sophomores only. Practices will be held in Encina gymnasium."

as distinguished from perceptional, knowledge. We owe to Plato, Socrates' disciple, the definition of the most fundamental tool of modern scientific thought, namely, the concept, i.e., the Platonic idea.

Magic may be regarded, therefore, as an index, in a rough way, not merely of the mentality, but of the general cultural level of races, peoples, and classes. It is even possible that a more thorough-going analysis of the mental processes involved in magic and rational thought will permit us to measure the mentalities of social groups with as much precision, at least, as we now measure and grade—with the aid of the Binet-Simon tests—the intelligence of individuals. At least we should know in this case what we were measuring, namely, the extent and degree to which a given group or class had acquired the ability and the habit of thinking in rational rather than magical terms.

With a more precise conception of the nature of magic and of the mechanisms of prelogical thinking, we shall, no doubt, be able not merely to compare and perhaps measure with a certain degree of accuracy and objectivity the mentality and cultural levels of different cultural groups, but we shall be able also to describe the process by which races and peoples make the transition from one cultural level to another. This transition, which Thorndyke has described in his history of magic, is everywhere in progress. These changes in a contemporary and living society are open and accessible to investigation, now that history has enabled us to see them, as they can never see them later, when they have become history.

In a recent paper in the *American Journal of Sociology*, Professor U. G. Weatherly has called attention to the advantages of the West Indies as a sociological laboratory.

Islands are peculiarly interesting sociologically, provided, of course, that they are inhabited. For one thing, they are physically defined. The island community is, for this reason, invariably isolated, geographically and socially, and because the means of communication are known, the extent of isolation can be reduced to relatively measurable terms.

This isolation tends to give to each separate island community an individuality that one rarely finds elsewhere. Because islands are geographically limited and isolated, the influence of climate and physiographic characteristics, as well as of economic organization, in defining cultural traits, can be estimated and assessed with greater accuracy than elsewhere. Until one has visited some of the Lesser Antilles, he is not likely to understand or appreciate Frederick A. Ober's rather drastic summary of their history—"Discovered by the Spaniards, appropriated by the Dutch, Danish, or English, and finally abandoned to the semi-barbarous blacks from Africa, this has been the usual succession in the islands."[1]

The rather bitter note of this statement probably reflects the tone of the white planters, whose position in the islands has gradually declined since the emancipation of the slaves.

It directs attention, however, to what is, from the point of view of the student of human nature and of society, the most interesting and unique feature of the islands, namely, the racial situation. As Professor Weatherly has said, "Perhaps nowhere else is there a better opportunity for securing definite evidence bearing on the opposing theories of race and contact as factors in cultural growth." Every island, in fact, is a separate racial melting-pot in which the mingled cultures and races of Europe, Africa, and Asia seem to be gradually, very gradually, simmering down to a single cultural, and eventually, also, to a single racial, blend.

IV. OBEAH: THE MAGIC OF THE BLACK MAN

Outside the Spanish Islands, Negroes are the dominant race in the West Indies. In regions where they have not been replaced by Hindus, as they have been in Trinidad and Demerara, British

[1] Frederick A. Ober, *A Guide to the West Indies Bermudas*, New York, 1908, p. 351.

Guiana, they constitute 90 per cent of the population. They are, in fact, the only people who regard themselves as natives. The Asiatics and the Europeans are, for the most part, mere sojourners.

So far as the islands now have a native culture it is the culture of the Negro folk. It is, at the same time, the most characteristic manifestation of the mentality of the West Indian black man, so far as he has preserved what Lévy-Bruhl describes as the mentality of primitive man.

What is more interesting about obeah is that while as a practice and a belief it is universal among the uneducated classes of the black population in the islands, it is everywhere different, and everywhere in process of change. Practices that were originally imported from Africa tend to assimilate and fuse with related practices and traits of the European and Hindu cultures wherever the Africans have come into contact with them.

This is evident, in the first place, from the fact that the obeah man is not always a Negro; he may be, and not infrequently is, a Hindu. In the second place, the ritual of obeah may include anything from patent medicine to Guinea pepper. Among the instruments of obeah in the possession of the police of Trinidad recently were a stone image, evidently of Hindu origin, and a book of magic ritual published in Chicago, which pretended to be, and no doubt had been, translated originally from the writings of Albertus Magnus, the great medieval writer on magic. A book called *Le Petit Albert* is said to be extremely popular among obeah men in the French Islands.

The favorite decoctions in use among witch doctors consist of bones, ashes, "grave dirt," human nail parings—mixed, perhaps, with asafetida or any other substance having a pungent odor. But in addition to these, obeah men in the West Indies use the candles, the little shrines, or "chapels," as they call them, and various other portions of the ritual of the Catholic church.

In January, 1917, a woman known as Valentine Sims, a native of

St. Lucia, was convicted, in Port-of-Spain, Trinidad, of obtaining money by the assumption of supernatural powers. The testimony in the case showed that, among other things, she attended the Roman Catholic church, and, on pretense of receiving holy communion, took the altar bread distributed to the worshipers during the communion, and used it in practicing obeah.

All this suggests that obeah, as one finds it in the West Indies, is not so much a tradition and a cultural inheritance as it is an innate predisposition, like a sense of humor, or "the will to believe," as James describes it. Behind these practices, and supporting them, are all sorts of fears and a general sense of insecurity in regard to the physical and spiritual environment that more cultivated persons either do not feel, or they find escape from in quite different practices.

This is clearly indicated in the letters found among the papers of obeah adepts which have been confiscated from time to time by the police. From these letters one gains an insight into the nature and extent· of the terrors, anxieties, and perils of the soul which trouble the dreams and imaginations of the black man, whom we ordinarily think of as roaming, cheerful, care-free, and unconcerned in a worried and troubled world.

The black man in the West Indies is greatly troubled about a great many things. He has more than the usual number of obscure pains and aches, which he worries about a great deal, and for which he, like most of us, is in search of some sovereign remedy. He is disturbed about his relations with his employer. Not that, like the workingman we know, he talks or thinks about his rights and the rights of labor. He is not class-conscious. Quite the contrary, he is constantly worried because he is not in favor with his employer. If he is scolded or scowled at, he is troubled. His first assumption, in such circumstances, is that some fellow-employee in some dark way is influencing his employer against him, and he seeks the obeah charm which will discover and circumvent his enemy and win back his employer's good will.

If he gets into a quarrel with the family next door, if his sweetheart looks coldly upon him, if his wife deserts him, he inevitably assumes that there are personal and magical influences at work, seeking to undermine otherwise sweet and happy relations. Frequently he is right. At any rate the obeah man exploits these suspicions, and that is the reason strenuous efforts are being made in the British Islands to stamp the superstition out.

Visiting the police courts in the English islands, one is profoundly impressed by the patient efforts of most of the judges to discover and apply the rules of law to the petty personal and neighborhood difficulties that the natives are so fond of airing in the courts. One gets the impression that the most difficult thing for the primitive mind to conceive and administer for himself is justice. On the other hand, the Negro, at least, knows and appreciates justice when he meets it. That is probably one reason why he likes to take his troubles to court.

V.   FASHIONS IN OBEAH

One gets the impression that there are fashions in obeah. Dominica, for example, is noted for its use of love-philters; in Montserrat, obeah is mainly a protection against evil spirits and a means of communication with the dead; in Antigua, obeah is most generally a form of medicine. Amulets, "guards," as they are popularly called, intended to ward off evil spirits or protect one against the ill-will of an evil-minded neighbor are also popular. Nevis has a reputation for "black magic."

The older generation of obeah men were supposed to have a knowledge of vegetable poisons the effects of which cannot be detected on postmortem. In Nevis the older tradition has apparently lingered longer than elsewhere. At any rate, magical practices seem to have assumed a more malignant form in Nevis than in some of the other islands.

In 1916 an old woman, Rose Eudelle, deaf and bedridden, was convicted of practicing obeah. She seems to have been one of the few witch doctors who believed sincerely in the efficacy of their own practices. She had a great reputation, and boasted that she had killed one man and sent another to the asylum. Curiously enough, she practiced obeah mainly through correspondence, and when she was finally arrested, some fifty letters from clients in various islands, one of them in New York City, were discovered. There was great excitement in Nevis when she was arrested. As she had solemnly threatened the colored police sergeant who arrested her, the whole black population was confidently expecting that some dramatic misfortune would overtake him. Here there seemed to be something more nearly approaching primitive and African magic than in any of the other thirty-eight cases of which I obtained some sort of record.

Not only is the fashion in obeah different in the different islands, but interest in magic, which is said to be declining everywhere, is less modified in some islands than in others. In Barbados, though the practices still persist, prosecutions for obeah have almost entirely ceased. In the police station at Castries, St. Lucia, on the other hand, there are still preserved the heart and hand of a Negro boy who was killed some years ago to furnish an obeah man with the instruments of magic to enable him to open the vaults of the local bank and rob it of the treasure which was supposed to be amassed there.

The fact is, then, that the mentality of the black population of the West Indies, as that of Africa, is changing under the influence of contact with the white man's culture, and particularly under the influence of the very energetic prosecutions which not only have made the profession less profitable, but by undermining faith in his supernatural powers, have robbed the obeah man of the terror which he at one time inspired.

Aside from the superficial changes in the original superstition and the gradual decline of interest and belief in magic, it seems as if certain more fundamental changes, reflected in these practices, were taking place. First, the obeah man tends to become, on the one hand, a sort of unlicensed physician, as in the case of Percival Duval, an obeah man who maintained regular office hours, wrote prescriptions, and prescribed medicines. Actually, Duval seems to have used a little less medicine and a little more hocus pocus than the average medical practitioner in our own country did a few years ago. But he was convicted, and upon appeal to the higher court his conviction was confirmed. Another obeah man in St. John's, Antigua, was found to be dealing, along with the other instruments of obeah, very largely in patent medicines and homely household remedies. Among the instruments of obeah taken from his office when it was raided were the following: (1) Exhibit labeled "ground bones and ashes." The sample consisted of a mixture of a calcium compound and probably lime, wood-ashes, and incense. The incense content was 26.3 per cent. (2) Exhibit labeled "ground glass and smith coal." This sample consisted of a coarse commercial oxygen mixture. (3) Yellow powder. This consisted of a cheap, scented starch powder. (4) Supposed dog's tongue. This consisted entirely of vegetable matter composed principally of starch cells. (5) Exhibit labeled "ashes and incense." The sample consisted of incense, wood-ashes, and charcoal, earth, and small pebbles, with a small proportion of oxygen mixture. It contained 17.3 per cent of incense in lump and powdered form. (6) Exhibit "vial with yellow liquid." The sample consisted of ordinary commercial oil of anise. (7) Vial with brownish liquid. The sample consisted of a solution of iodine in potassium iodine of approximately 15 per cent strength.

The fact is, the obeah man in the West Indies is in a way to become a quack doctor. This represents one direction in which change is taking place.

On the other hand, there is a disposition of the obeah man to become a sort of confessor and privy counselor in all the intimate and personal affairs of the common people. The black people—

and not only black, but occasionally Portuguese, who are the traders in the smaller islands—go to him with affairs of business and of the heart. They write him long personal letters, and he sends them a magical prayer or incantation to cure them of bodily ailments, to protect them from dangers of travel, and to insure general good fortune. In an affair of the heart, the witch doctor frequently prescribed a magic powder, sweetly scented, to accompany and lend a delicate and stimulating fragrance to a love letter. In principle, this aspect of the obeah man's practice is like Mr. Coué's—"Every day, in every way, I am better and better"—only that the uses of obeah are more specific. In any case, there is here a very evident tendency of the practice to assume a form in which the ritual of obeah is merely a device, like the prayers of primitive folk, for magically re-enforcing the expression of a wish. So closely are the magical practices of the obeah man connected—in the mind of the ordinary black man—with religion that in one case, at any rate, he pretended to cure a boy of insanity by making believe that he was operating as the agent or proxy of the priest.

This, then, represents a second tendency to change in the practices of magic by the black man.   If obeah in some instances seems to be taking the form of popular medicine, in others it tends to assume the form of a pagan religious ceremony, adapting itself to the forms and the ritual of the local church.

VI.   THE PROBLEM STATED

In a recent volume, *Studies in Human Nature*, Mr. J. B. Baillie has suggested that the disposition and the ability to think abstractly, disinterestedly, and scientifically is not only a relatively recent acquisition of the human race, but at the same time is a local phenomenon.

This geographical limitation of science is indeed a remarkable fact, the importance of which our familiarity with the scientific mood and our insularity of mind constantly tend to obscure. . . . . We should not forget that millions of human beings have no interest in the scientific mood at all, and seem by constitution to have no capacity for it. . . . . Some individuals among these non-scientific peoples may, and do, assimilate the science of the West. But experience seems to show that such acquisition is at best a mere accomplishment, and leaves the racial structure and composition of their minds unaffected. . . . . The non-scientific peoples take up science as they put on Western clothes. One may change one's clothes, but there is no changing the skin. The fact is that the scientific mood arises from a peculiar attitude of the mind to the world found amongst certain peoples of the globe; and without this attitude science will always appear a curiosity or an irrelevance.[1]

The author assumes that the disposition to think rationally and to cultivate abstract and scientific thought is a racial attribute. Perhaps a more accurate statement of the matter would take account of the fact that even within the comparatively limited area where science is in vogue, there are large numbers of people who still—even while using the language of science—think in the more elementary forms of folk-thought. This seems to be true wherever large masses of the population are still illiterate, or where, for any reason, even when able to read, they habitually think in terms of the spoken language, rather than in the language of the printed page. Literacy itself is very largely a product of modern city life. Books and reading which used to be, and to a certain extent are yet, a luxury in the country, become a necessity in the city.

The Negroes migrating in such large numbers from the West Indies to the United States are bringing with them habits of thought which have largely disappeared among the Negro population native to this country. The obeah men of the West Indies have many clients in the United States, and a recent issue of the *New York Age* announced that the Negro quarter around 135th Street, New York, was overrun with fortune tellers and witch doctors, many or most of them from the West Indies.

Within a few years, however, most of these superstitions will have disappeared, or at any rate will have assumed those more

[1] J. B. Baillie, *Studies in Human Nature,* p. 242.

conventional forms with which we are familiar and have learned to tolerate.   This is certainly true of the city population.

Great changes are taking place, with the introduction of modern methods of education, in our own insular possessions.   Mr. Axel Holst, of the National Bank of the Danish West Indies, who has been a close and assiduous student of Negro folklore in the Virgin Islands, says that the effect of the American system of education will within a few years totally change the mental habits of the natives of St. Thomas.   Since the younger generation have begun to read books, they are not so interested as they were in the Nansi stories, which correspond to the Bre'r Rabbit stories of the States. Since the introduction of American rule, newspapers have come into vogue, and the young men have taken to political discussion.

The changes in the "mentality" of the Negro population are, Mr. Holst says, going on visibly, and at a surprising rate.   These changes, if they are actually taking place, should be made the subject of further investigation.   Such study should enable us to determine, among other things, more precisely than we have been able to determine hitherto, the rôle which cultural contacts, social heritages, and racial temperament play in the whole cultural process.

It is evident that we are not to assume, as otherwise we might, that there is no area of the experience in which primitive or pre-literate people think realistically and rationally.   On the other hand, in contrasting primitive mentality with that of civilized man, we need not assume—except for the sake of the contrast— that the thinking of civilized man is always and everywhere either rational or scientific.   As a matter of fact, there are still wide areas of our experience that have not as yet been fully rationalized, nota-bly the fields of medicine and religion.   In medicine, at least—if we are to believe a recent medical critic of what, in imitation of Lévy-Bruhl, we might call "medical mentality"—the majority of practitioners still think of diseases as morbid entities instead of convenient labels for groups of symptoms.

The following paragraph from a recent writer states the matter from the point of view of a critic of "medical mentality."

It is not to be thought that any educated medical man indeed believes "a disease" to be a material thing, although the phraseology in current use lends colour to such supposition. Nevertheless, in hospital jargon, "diseases" are "morbid entities," and medical students fondly believe that these "entities" somehow exist in *rebus Naturae* and were discovered by their teachers, much as was America by Columbus. . . . . In fact, for these gentlemen "diseases" are Platonic realities; universals *ante rem*. This unavowed belief, which might be condoned were it frankly admitted, is an inheritance from Galen, and carries with it the corollary that our notions concerning this, that, or the other "diseases" are either absolutely right or absolutely wrong, and are not merely matters of mental convenience.

But if the practitioners think of diseases in pre-logical terms what can we expect of the layman, whose medical education has been largely confined to the reading of patent medical advertisements? What has been said suggests a problem which may be perhaps stated in this way: How far is the existence of magic and magical mode of thought a measure of the mentality of a racial or cultural group in which it is found to persist? How far is what Ballie calls "the scientific mood" an effect of the urban environment?

ROBERT E. PARK

CHAPTER VIII

CAN NEIGHBORHOOD WORK HAVE
A SCIENTIFIC BASIS?

Neighborhood work at present and as now practiced cannot, for two reasons, be said to be based upon science. First, the social sciences—and I refer to sociology in particular—have at present little to offer as a scientific basis for social work; secondly, what knowledge the social sciences have accumulated has been used little, or not at all, by neighborhood workers.

The trend of neighborhood work to a scientific basis.—But if neighborhood work has not had a scientific basis, it has had, from its inception, as one of its conscious or unconscious motives, the search after knowledge as the basis of human relations. Settlement work, especially, represents not only the most devoted and the most idealistic, but also the most intelligent, phase of social work of the past generation. The settlement in its origin was an extension of the university. It carried over into a new environment the love of truth and, it may be added, the spirit of science. The residents of the settlement were brought at once into touch with social reality; that is, with the concrete facts of human life.

This early venture into intimate contact with social reality may accordingly be called the first stage in the trend of neighborhood work toward a scientific basis. But settlement workers soon found that sympathetic understanding and intimate contacts failed to solve many of the actual problems of neighborhood work. The recalcitrancy of the boys' gang, the opposition and manipulations of the ward boss, the competition of commercialized recreation, the unsolvable cultural conflict between immigrant parents and Americanized children are only a few of the many perplexing conditions of neighborhood life in immigrant areas which resisted the spirit of good will of settlement workers. They therefore began to study their communities in the attempt to state the factors at work by an analysis of the elements in the situation. *Hull House Maps and Papers*, *The City Wilderness*, and *Americans in Process* are illustrations of the careful study and keen observation of these very early efforts to determine and to take account of the many and different conditions affecting neighborhood work. This interest in the discovery of factors in the social situation may therefore be called the second stage in the trend of neighborhood work toward a scientific basis.

Science, however, is concerned not with factors, but with forces. The distinction is not always clearly drawn between a factor and a force. "Factors are the elements that co-operate to make a given situation. Forces are type-factors operative in typical situations."[1] A factor is thought of as a concrete cause for an individual event; a force is conceived to be an abstract cause for events in general so far as they are similar. A particular gang of boys, the Torpedo gang, of which Tony is the leader—and which is made up of eight street Arabs—is a factor in the situation which a certain settlement in an Italian colony in Chicago faces. But as soon as the attention shifts from this one gang and this particular settlement to settlements in general and to gangs in general the transition is made from a factor to a force. A gang is a factor to a given settlement; the gang is a force from the standpoint of all settlements.

The study of social forces in the community.—If neighborhood work can have a scientific basis, it is because there are social forces in community life—forces like geographical conditions, human wishes, community consciousness—that can be studied, described, analyzed, and ultimately measured. In a series of research projects now in progress in the Department of Sociology in the University of Chicago, studies are being made of the social forces of community life. While the city of Chicago is used as the laboratory for this

[1] A distinction made by Professor Robert E. Park.

investigation, it is assumed that the processes of urban life in one community are in certain ways typical of city life throughout the United States.

The term "community" is widely used by sociologists, neighborhood workers, and others, but often with widely divergent meanings. In research in any field it is necessary to define our concepts and to make relevant distinctions. In the literature of the subject there is a growing disposition to emphasize as one of the fundamental aspects of the community its geographical setting. Whatever else the community may be, it signifies individuals, families, groups, or institutions located upon an area and some or all of the relationships which grow out of this common location. "'Community' is the term which is applied to societies and social groups where they are considered from the point of view of the geographical distribution of the individuals and institutions of which they are composed."[1]

Upon reflection it is evident that markedly different social relationships may have their roots in the conditions of a common territorial location. Indeed, it is just these outstanding differences in communal activities, viewed in relation to their geographic background, which have caused much of the confusion in the use of the term "community." For community life, as conditioned by the distribution of individuals and institutions over an area, has at least three quite different aspects.

First of all, there is the community viewed almost exclusively in terms of location and movement. How far has the area itself, by its very topography and by all its other external and physical characteristics, as railroads, parks, types of housing, conditioned community formation and exerted a determining influence upon the distribution of its inhabitants and upon their movements and life? To what extent has it had a selective effect in sifting and sorting families over the area by occupation, nationality, and economic or social class? To what extent is the work of neighborhood or community

[1] Park and Burgess, *Introduction to the Science of Sociology*, p. 163.

institutions promoted or impeded by favorable or unfavorable location? How far do geographical distances within or without the community symbolize social distances? This apparently "natural"
organization of the human community, so similar in the formation
of plant and animal communities, may be called the "ecological
community."

No comprehensive study of the human community from this
standpoint has yet been made. A prospectus for such a study is out-
lined in an earlier chapter by Professor R. D. McKenzie, in this
volume, under the title, "The Ecological Approach to the Study of
the Human Community."[1] Yet there are several systematic treatises
and a rapidly growing literature of scientific research in the two
analogous fields of plant ecology and animal ecology. The processes
of competition, invasion, succession, and segregation described in
elaborate detail for plant and animal communities seem to be
strikingly similar to the operation of these same processes in the
human community. The assertion might even be defended that the
student of community life or the community organization worker
might secure at present a more adequate understanding of the basic
factors in the natural organization of the community from Warm-
ing's *Oecology of Plants* or from Adams's *Guide to the Study of Animal
Ecology* than from any other source.

In the second place, the community may be conceived in terms
of the effects of communal life in a given area upon the formation or
the maintenance of a local culture. Local culture includes those
sentiments, forms of conduct, attachments, and ceremonies which
are characteristic of a locality, which have either originated in the
area or have become identified with it. This aspect of local life may
be called "the cultural community." This relationship of cultural
patterns to territorial areas has not yet been adequately studied
unless in the phenomena of language. What, for example, are
studies in dialect but one illustration of how local areas with their

[1] P. 163.

entailed isolation differentially affect customs of speech? Concrete materials for a wider study of culture in relation to location are increasing, notably upon preliterate peoples and upon retarded groups geographically isolated, as the southern mountaineers or the remote inhabitants of Pitcairn Island.

The immigrant colony in an American city possesses a culture unmistakably not indigenous but transplanted from the Old World. The telling fact, however, is not that the immigrant colony maintains its old-world cultural organization, but that in its new environment it mediates a cultural adjustment to its new situation. How basically culture is dependent upon place is suggested by the following expressions, "New England conscience," "southern hospitality," "Scottish thrift," "Kansas is not a geographical location so much as a state of mind." Neighborhood institutions like the church, the school, and the settlement are essentially cultural institutions, and recognition of this fact has far-reaching implications for the policies and programs of these local centers.

There remains a third standpoint from which the relation of a local area to group life may be stated. In what ways and to what extent does the fact of common residence in a locality compel or invite its inhabitants to act together? Is there, or may there be developed upon a geographical basis, a community consciousness? Does contiguity by residence insure or predispose to co-operation in at least those conditions of life inherent in geographic location, as transportation, water supply, playgrounds, etc.? Finally, what degree of social and political action can be secured on the basis of local areas? This is the community of the community organization worker and of the politician, and may be described as "the political community." It is upon this concept of the community as a local area that American political organization has been founded.

These three definitions of the community are not perhaps altogether mutually exclusive. They do, however, represent three distinctly different aspects of community life that will have to be recognized in any basic study of the community and of community organization. A given local area, like Hyde Park in Chicago, may at the same time constitute an ecological, cultural, and political community, while another area like the lower North Side in the same city, which forms a distinct ecological unit, falls apart into several cultural communities and cannot, at any rate from the standpoint of a common and effective public opinion, be said to constitute a going political community. The Black Belt in Chicago comprises one cultural community but overflows several ecological areas and has no means of common political action except through ward lines arbitrarily drawn.

It follows that the boundaries of local areas determined ecologically, culturally, and politically seldom, if ever, exactly coincide. In fact, for American cities it is generally true that political boundaries are drawn most arbitrarily, without regard either to ecological or cultural lines, as is notoriously the case in the familiar instance of the gerrymander. Therefore it is fair to raise the question: How far are the deficiencies in political action through our governmental bodies and welfare action through our social agencies the result of the failure to base administrative districts upon ecological or cultural communities?[1]

This analysis of the community into its threefold aspects suggests that the study of social forces in a local area should assume that the neighborhood or the community is the resultant of three main types of determining influences: first, ecological forces; second, cultural forces; and third, political forces.

Ecological forces.—The ecological forces are those which have to do with the process of competition and the consequent distribution and segregation by residence and occupation. Through competition

---

[1] One of the committees of the Chicago Council of Social Agencies has a subcommittee which is studying this problem in connection with the subject of uniform districts for social agencies. Several departments of the city government are interested in considering the possibilities of uniform administrative districts.

and the factors which affect it, as trade centers, etc., every neighborhood in the city becomes a component and integral part of the larger community, with a destiny bound up by its relation to it. In the study of the growth of the city it is found that the life of any neighborhood is determined, in the long run, not altogether by the forces within itself, but even more by the total course of city life. To think of the neighborhood or the community in isolation from the city is to disregard the biggest fact about the neighborhood.

Studies of urban growth reveal that the city grows outward from its central business district (1) in a series of expanding zones.[1] There is a "zone of transition" (2) encircling the downtown area. This is the area of deterioration, the so-called "slum", created in large part by the invasion of business and light manufacture. A third area (3) is inhabited by workers in industry who have escaped from the area of deterioration (2) and who desire to live within easy access of their work. Beyond this zone is the "residential area" (4) of high-class apartment buildings or of exclusive "restricted" districts of single family dwellings. Still farther, out beyond the city limits, is the "commuters' zone" (5) of suburban areas or satellite cities within a sixty-minute ride of the central business district.

Within these zones of urban growth are to be found local districts or communities, and these in turn subdivide into smaller areas called neighborhoods. In the long run, geographical factors and the process of competition fix the boundaries and the centers of these areas. It is important that neighborhood work be in accordance with, rather than in opposition to, these silent but continuous influences. A map of local communities was prepared to show the way in which rivers, railroads, large industrial establishments, parks, and boulevards divide the city into its constituent local communities—residential and industrial.

The centers of local communities are to be found at the point of

[1] See chapter "The Growth of the City" for a more elaborate analysis of urban pexansion (pp. 47–62).

highest land value in the intersection of two business streets. These local community centers are also characterized by the concentration of retail business, of banks, of restaurants, and of the large and magnificent palaces of amusement, like motion picture houses and public dance halls. If high land values indicate the center of the community, the lowest land values generally define its periphera.

CHART I

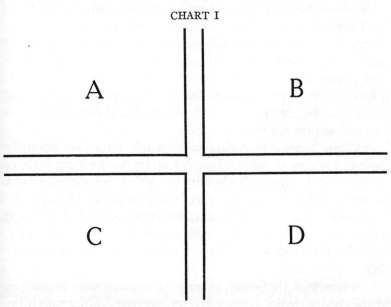

SCHEMATIC REPRESENTATION OF THE DIVISION OF A COMMUNITY INTO NEIGHBORHOODS BY THE INTERSECTION OF TWO BUSINESS STREETS.

But if the intersection of two business streets determines the trade center, these same streets divide it into neighborhoods. In Chart I on this page is offered a schematic representation of a Chicago local community, Woodlawn, with its economic center at the intersection of the two main business streets of Sixty-Third Street and Cottage Grove Avenue. At this intersection land values are five thousand dollars a front foot. Woodlawn falls into four neighbor-

hoods, A, B, C, and D, divided from each other by these same inter-
secting business streets. It is interesting that each of these neighborhoods has its own public school. Even more significant is the fact
that an attempt to unite two struggling churches of the same
denomination in two of these neighborhoods into one strong church
failed because neither would surrender its location.

It seems almost axiomatic to state that community and neighborhood work must take into account the operation of these silent but
continuous ecological forces and work with them rather than against
them. Yet how often are social centers located on the edge, rather
than at the center, of a neighborhood. In the location of a neighborhood center the consequences which flow from the play of ecological
forces must be heeded, because they condition the development of
its work and the radius of its influence.

Cultural forces.—Ecological or economic forces are naturally
basic to the play of cultural forces. Culture, as the social heritage
of the group, implies both a locality to which it is indigenous and a
constant, rather than a changing, social situation. Chicago, like
other large cities, has its cultural communities, each of which has, if
not a local area, at least a local center. Hobohemia, Bohemia,
Philistia, the Ghetto, and the Gold Coast are cultural communities.

Movement in the person, as from one social location to another,
or any sudden change as caused by an invention, carries with it the
possibility or the probability of cultural decadence. The cultural
controls over conduct disintegrate; impulses and wishes take random
and wild expression. The result is immorality and delinquency; in
short, personal and social disorganization. An illustration of cultural decadence as a result of movement is the excessively high rate
of juvenile delinquency among the children of immigrant parents.
To what extent have neighborhood workers gauged the effect of the
daily newspaper, the motion picture, the automobile, and the radio,
in releasing the child, the youth, and the adult from the confines of

the neighborhood and of bringing them into contact with the city-wide, nation-wide, and world-wide life of our time?

These changes taking place in community life may be observed in a dramatic form in commercialized recreation. The day of the neighborhood public dance hall and the neighborhood motion picture show has passed, or at least is passing. Young people are deserting the neighborhood recreation centers and are thronging to centers outside the local community, to the high-class, magnificent dance gardens and palaces, and to the so-called "wonder" theaters of the "bright light" areas.

A realignment of the leisure-time movements of urban young people is taking place, which every agency engaged in neighborhood work must take into account. Is the neighborhood as a factor in the lives of youth soon to become a situation of the past? Can settlements and social centers expect to hold back the tide of the forces of city life?

A map of the residences of dance hall patrons which shows both the disappearance of the small public dance hall from the neighborhood and the concentration of large dance halls in "bright light" areas is all the more significant because it portrays the phenomenon of promiscuity. By promiscuity is meant primary and intimate behavior upon the basis of secondary contacts. In the village type of neighborhood, where everyone knows everyone else, the social relationships of the young people were safeguarded by the primary controls of group opinion. But in the public dance hall, where young people are drawn from all parts of the city, this old primary control breaks down. Is not this the basic reason why social workers find the dance hall so recurring a factor in personal disorganization and delinquency? As yet, however, we have no satisfactory study of the dance hall as a social world of youth. Two new social types—the "sheik" and the "flapper"—have been created by the dance hall and the motion picture, but they are regarded as subjects for jest rather than for serious study.

A study by Miss Evelyn Buchan of girl delinquency shows the effect of the increasing mobility and promiscuity of city life upon the behavior of youth, and suggests an interesting method of study.

FORM I.—The Neighborhood Triangle.

To bring into clearer relief the rôle of mobility and promiscuity asfactors in behavior, a device called "the delinquency triangle" was employed. The three points of the triangle were located by spotting the home of the girl, the home of her male companion, and the place of delinquency. Three typical forms of the triangle soon appeared.

Form I represents the traditional form of sex delinquency, where all three points of the triangle are within the community. This may be called the "neighborhood triangle." In this case the intimacy of the boy and girl might be little more than the continuance in this country of old-world folkways, but without the protection for the girl in subsequent marriage which the European peasant mores afford.

Form 2, which is "the mobility triangle," stands for delinquency of the type related to increased freedom of movement, where two points of the triangle or its base, formed by the homes of the girl and the boy, lie within the same community, but where its apex, or the place of delinquency, is situated outside. In this case the bright-light area becomes a place of freedom from the narrower, distant controls of the home and the neighborhood.

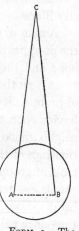

FORM 2.—The Mobility Triangle.

In form 3, delinquency is of the type of promiscuity, because here all the points of the triangle lie in different communities. The intimacy developing from the casual acquaintance of the metal worker from the steel mills with the girl from the West Side whom he "picked up" at an amusement park may be so transient that neither knows the family name or the address of the other.

The total effect of forces of city life, like mobility and promiscuity, upon the neighborhood and upon our traditional culture seems to be subversive and disorganizing. Particularly is this true of deteriorating areas, where neighborhood work originated, and where it is still, in any completely developed state, for the most part confined. A series of maps has been prepared which shows graphically what, of course, is known to social students—that the zone of deterioration and the areas of the greatest mobility in the city have the greatest concentration of poverty, vice, crime, juvenile delinquency, divorce, desertion, abandoned infants, murder, and suicide.

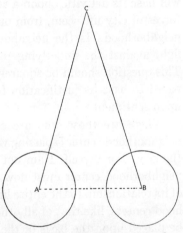

FORM 3.—The Promiscuity Triangle

Political forces.—The political forces have to do with the more formal control of public opinion and law. Neighborhood work is concerned with political forces whenever social action is desired. Our whole scheme of social work may be regarded, from this standpoint at least, as social politics. But has the social worker, who is the social politician, the same intimate knowledge of his neighborhood that the professional politician possesses? A minimum of information which he needs is a card catalogue of, plus some direct contact with, all the local dynamic personalities, including gang leaders, pool hall proprietors, leaders of all the neighborhood organizations, and of all professional persons, like representatives of social agencies, physicians, lawyers, clergymen, at work in his locality. More than that, he needs to know the basic interests, the driving wishes, and the vital problems of the men and women, the youth and the children, living in the community.

The knowledge of these forces in neighborhood life will suggest feasible projects and programs. Too often, however, attempts at social control rise from ignorant good will rather than from the facts of the situation. This is particularly true of the many futile efforts to impose neighborly relationships upon areas which are no longer neighborhoods.

What, then, is our answer to the question, Can neighborhood work have a scientific basis? It can have a scientific foundation if it will base its activities upon a study of social forces. But the social forces of city life seem, from our studies, to be destroying the city neighborhood. Is the neighborhood center to engage in a losing fight against the underlying tendencies of modern urban society? This question should be squarely faced: Is neighborhood work prepared to base its justification for existence upon facts rather than upon sentiment?

There are those who are convinced that the function of the neighborhood center is passing with the decay of the neighborhood in the city. For myself, I am not so certain. Surely the work of the neighborhood center must now be conceived and planned in terms of its relationship to the entire life of the city. The work of neighborhood centers, like that of all other social agencies, must increasingly be placed upon the basis of the scientific study of the social forces with which they have to deal. Especially are studies desired of the actual effect and rôle of intimate contacts in personal development and social control.

A feasible way for neighborhood centers to place their work upon a scientific basis would be to stress the impulse to research that has always been associated with the settlement movement. Thirty years ago Mr. Robert A. Woods read a paper on "University Settlements as Laboratories in Social Science." The argument for research in its relations to neighborhood work is contained in that article. He conceived the advantage of research both to social science and to the settlement. The growing fluidity and complexity of urban life has but increased the force of his argument.

Neighborhood work, by the logic of the situation, if it is to evolve a successful technique, will be compelled more and more to depend upon research into the social forces of modern life.

ERNEST W. BURGESS

CHAPTER IX

THE MIND OF THE HOBO: REFLECTIONS UPON THE RELATION BETWEEN MENTALITY AND LOCOMOTION

In the evolutionary hierarchy, as Herbert Spencer has sketched it for us, the animal series occupied a higher position than that of the plants. But in spite of all the progress represented in the long march from the amoeba to man, it is still strue that the human creature is a good deal of a vegetable. This is evident in the invincible attachment of mankind to localities and places; in man's, and particularly woman's, inveterate and irrational ambition to have a home—some cave or hut or tenement—in which to live and vegetate; some secure hole or corner from which to come forth in the morning and return to at night.

As long as man is thus attached to the earth and to places on the earth, as long as nostalgia and plain homesickness hold him and draw him inevitably back to the haunts and places he knows best, he will never fully realize that other characteristic ambition of mankind, namely, to move freely and untrammeled over the surface of mundane things, and to live, like pure spirit, in his mind and in his imagination alone.

I mention these things merely to emphasize a single point, namely, mind is an incident of locomotion. The first and most convincing indication of mind is not motion merely, but, as I have said, locomotion. The plants don't locomote, don't move through space; they respond more or less to stimulation, even though they have no nerves, but they do not move through space, certainly not of their own motion. And when they do move, they have no goal, no destination, and that is because they have no imagination.

Now it is characteristic of animals that they can and do change their spots. The ability to do this implies that they are able not merely to wag a tail or move a limb, but that they are able to co-ordinate and mobilize the whole organism in the execution of a single act. Mind, as we ordinarily understand it, is an organ of control. It does not so much initiate new movements as co-ordinate impulses, and so mobilize the organism for action; for mind, in its substantive aspect, is just our disposition to act; our instincts and attitudes, in other words.

Mental activity begins on the periphery, with stimuli which are antecedent to, but ultimately discharged in, actions. But mind in the transitive, verbal aspect is a process by which, as we say, we "make up our minds" or change them; that is to say, it is a process by which we define the direction in which we are going to move, and locate in imagination the goal that we intend to seek.

Plants carry on, apparently, all the processes of metabolism which are characteristic of animals—these are, in fact, what we mean by the vegetative processes—but they do not go anywhere. If the plants have minds, as some people assume they do, they must be of that brooding, vegetative sort characteristic of those mystics who, quite forgetful of the active world, are absorbed in the contemplation of their own inner processes. But the characteristic of the animal, and of the higher types of animal—everything above the oyster, in fact—is that they are made for locomotion and for action. Furthermore, it is in the processes of locomotion—involving, as they do, change of scene and change of location—that mankind is enabled to develop just those mental aptitudes most characteristic of man, namely, the aptitude and habit of abstract thought.

It is in locomotion, also, that the peculiar type of organization that we call "social" develops. The characteristic of a social organism—if we may call it an organism—is the fact that it is made up of individuals capable of independent locomotion. If society were, as some individuals have sought to conceive it, an organism in the biological sense—if it were made up of little cells all neatly and safely inclosed in an outer integument, or skin, in which all cells were so controlled and protected that no single cell could by any chance have any adventures or new experience of its own—there would be no need for men in society to have minds, for it is not because men are alike that they are social, but because they are different. They are moved to act by individual purposes, but in doing so they realize a common end. Their impulses are private, but actions are public.

In view of all this we may well ask ourselves what, if anything, is the matter with the hobo's mind. Why is it that with all the variety of his experiences he still has so many dull days? Why, with so much leisure, has he so little philosophy? Why, with so wide an acquaintance with regions, with men, and with cities, with life in the open road and in the slums, has he been able to contribute so little to our actual knowledge of life?

We need not even pause for a reply. The trouble with the hobo mind is not lack of experience, but lack of a vocation. The hobo is, to be sure, always on the move, but he has no destination, and naturally he never arrives. Wanderlust, which is the most elementary expression of the romantic temperament and the romantic interest in life, has assumed for him, as for so many others, the character of a vice. He has gained his freedom, but he has lost his direction. Locomotion and change of scene have had for him no ulterior significance. It is locomotion for its own sake. Restlessness and the impulse to escape from the routine of ordinary life, which in the case of others frequently marks the beginning of some new enterprise, spends itself for him in movements that are expressive merely. The hobo seeks change solely for the sake of change; it is a habit, and, like the drug habit, moves in a vicious circle. The more he wanders, the more he must. It is merely putting the matter in an another way to say that the trouble with the hobo, as Nels Anderson has pointed out in his recent volume, *The Hobo*, is that he is an individualist. He has sacrificed the human need of association and organization to a romantic passion for individual freedom. Society is, to be sure, made up of independent, locomoting individuals. It is this fact of locomotion, as I have said, that defines the very nature of society. But in order that there may be permanence and progress in society the individuals who compose it must be located; they must be located, for one thing, in order to maintain communication, for it is only through communication that the moving equilibrium which we call society can be maintained.

All forms of association among human beings rest finally upon locality and local association. The extraordinary means of communication that characterize modern society—the newspaper, the radio, and the telephone—are merely devices for preserving this permanence of location and of function in the social group, in connection with the greatest possible mobility and freedom of its members.

The hobo, who begins his career by breaking the local ties that bound him to his family and his neighborhood, has ended by breaking all other associations. He is not only a "homeless man," but a man without a cause and without a country; and this emphasizes the significance, however, futile of the efforts of men like James Eads How to establish hobo colleges in different parts of the country, places where hobos can meet to exchange experiences, to discuss their problems, and all of the problems of society; places, also, where they can maintain some sort of corporate existence and meet and exchange views with the rest of the world on a basis of something like equality and with some hope of understanding.

The same thing may be said of the Industrial Workers of the World, the only labor organization that has persistently sought and to some extent succeeded in organizing the unorganizable element among laboring men, namely, the seasonal and casual laborers. The tendency of their efforts to organize the hobo in his own interest has been, so far as they have been successful, to give him what he needed most, namely, a group-consciousness, a cause, and a recognized position in society.

If they have failed, it is due in part to the fact that so large a part of modern industry is organized in a way which tends inevitably to the casualization of labor. It is due, in part, to the fact that the hobo, in so far as he is a congenital type, finds in casual and seasonal labor a kind of occupation congenial to his temperament, for the hobo is the bohemian in the ranks of common labor. He has the artistic temperament. Aside from the indispensable labor of his hands, the only important contribution which he has made to the permanent common fund of our experience which we call our culture has been his poetry. It is an interesting fact, however, that some of the best of this poetry has been produced in jail. During these periods of enforced quietude, when he could no longer move, the hobo has vented his habitual restlessness in songs, songs of protest, the hymns of the rebellious I.W.W., tragic little ballads describing some of the hardships and tragedies of life on the long, gray road.

There have been many hobo poets. The most eminent of them, Walt Whitman, reflected the restlessness and rebelliousness and individualism of the hobo mind not only in the content but in the very formlessness of his verse.

What do you suppose will satisfy the soul, except to walk free and own no superior?

Nothing could better express the spirit of the old frontier which, more than any other feature in American life, has served to characterize American institutions and American mores. The hobo is, in fact, merely a belated frontiersman, a frontiersman at a time and in a place when the frontier is passing or no longer exists.

ROBERT E. PARK

CHAPTER X

A BIBLIOGRAPHY OF THE URBAN COMMUNITY

The task of compiling a bibliography on the city which is to be of use to the sociologist involves many difficulties. The materials are scattered over many fields of investigation ranging all the way from the various branches of the natural and social sciences to the practical arts and crafts. Much of the material is highly technical and abstract, while the rest is popular and full of human interest. If one attempts to survey the whole field he is likely to be led into tempting bypaths which lead far afield and in the end arrive nowhere. Moreover, the bibliographer has neither chart nor compass to guide him in his search, for the sociologist himself is not yet certain of the meaning of the concept "city" and of the relationship of his science to the phenomenon.

Specialization has gone so far that no one can hope to become an expert in more than one field in a lifetime. The sanitary engineer, interested in urban sanitation, is mainly concerned with drainage systems, pumps, sewer pipes, and incinerators; but the accountant, the political scientist, and the sociologist are not primarily interested in these matters. At first glance the sociologist might be tempted to pass over such material as lying outside his province, while he would be less likely to pass over materials relating to parks, playgrounds, schools, infant mortality, city-planning, and non-voting, because these institutions and processes have traditionally held the sociologist's interest. And yet it is within the realm of possibility that such a question as that of the type of sewer pipe that is to be employed in a city drainage system may become one with which the sociologist is as legitimately concerned as the question of city-planning or juvenile delinquency.

The problem of deciding what is pertinent and what is extraneous is, then, obviously an important one. While the sociologist may be intensely interested in a subject matter pertaining to another science or craft, he has his own distinctive point of view, methodology, and objective, and since he cannot be an expert engineer, city manager, and sociologist all at the same time, he must accept the data of these other specialists when they happen to form the subject matter of his investigation. The sociologist is no more a housing specialist or a zoning specialist or a social case worker in a metropolitan social agency than he is an urban engineer or health officer, but he may have an important contribution to make to all of these activities, and may in turn acquire from these technicians a body of materials which shed light on his own problems and yield to sociological analysis. What is to be included or excluded from a sociological bibliography of the city depends upon the sociological definition of the city.

Although the literature on the city extends as far back as the city itself, the subject is now being studied with renewed interest and with a new point of view. If we were compiling a complete bibliography we would most likely begin with the classical discussion of Socrates in the second book of Plato's *Republic* and follow the increasingly complex and scattered writings up to the present day, when we can scarcely find a science that does not have something to contribute to the subject. But this is not the aim of this bibliography. The attempt is here made to note just that part of the literature which has something to offer to the sociologist in the way of source material, point of view, method, and interpretation. A great deal, no doubt, has been included which is of little value. At the same time much has been necessarily omitted which is important. Some effort was made to avoid excessive duplication, but this attempt has not been wholly successful. The list of books and articles includes many works which were inaccessible at the time the bibliography was compiled, and whose contents could therefore not be

examined. They are included because either the titles were suggestive or else the reputation of the authors merited attention.

The contribution which a bibliography is able to make to the
study of any subject lies probably as much in the viewpoint it
incorporates and the method of presentation it uses as in the references it presents. The scheme of classification here employed may
lay claim to offering a rather new approach to the study of the city.
It will probably have to be modified as new material is discovered
and as the sociologists themselves continue to make their own
distinctive contributions. It ought to offer an index to the aspects
of the city that promise most in the way of results from research.
At the same time it may be of assistance in organizing and funding
the rapidly increasing body of knowledge concerning the sociology
of the city.

A TENTATIVE SCHEME FOR THE CLASSIFICATION OF THE LITERATURE OF THE SOCIOLOGY OF THE CITY[1]

I. The City Defined
 1. Geographically: by site, situation, topography, density
 2. Historically: by political status, title, law
 3. Statistically: by census
 4. As an economic unit
 5. Sociologically

II. The Natural History of the City
 1. Ancient cities: Asia, Egypt, Greece, Rome
 2. The medieval city
 3. The modern city

III. Types of Cities
 1. Historical types
 2. Location types: sea coast, inland, river, lake
 3. Site types: plain, valley, mountain, hill, harbor, island
 4. Functional types: capital, railroad, port, commercial, industrial, resort, cultural
 5. The town, the city, and the metropolis
 6. Structural types: the natural city and the planned city

[1] Numbers in parentheses after titles indicate that the work cited contains material bearing on the topics in the outline corresponding to these numbers.

IV. The City and Its Hinterland
1. The trade area
2. The commuting area: the metropolitan area
3. The administrative city
4. The city and its satellites
5. The city and its cultural periphery
6. The city and world economy

V. The Ecological Organization of the City
1. Natural areas
2. The neighborhood
3. The local community
4. Zones and zoning
5. The city plan

VI. The City as a Physical Mechanism
1. Public utilities: water, gas, electricity
2. Means of communication: telephone, mails, telegraph, street-car, busses, automobile
3. Streets and sewers
4. Public safety and welfare: fire, police, health departments, social agencies
5. Schools, theaters, museums, parks, churches, settlements
6. Recreation
7. City government: the city manager, the boss
8. Food supply, stores (department and chain stores)
9. Steel construction: the skyscraper
10. Housing and land values

VII. The Growth of the City
1. Expansion
2. Allocation and distribution of population: "city building"
3. Population statistics: natural growth and migration
4. Mobility and metabolism in city life
5. Social organization and disorganization and city growth

VIII. Eugenics of the City
1. Birth, death, and marriage rates: the span of life
2. Sex and age groups
3. Fecundity

IX. Human Nature and City Life
1. The division of labor: professions and specialization of occupations
2. The mentality of city life

I. THE CITY DEFINED

Differences in standpoint and method in the various sciences show graphically in the definitions that each formulates of the same object. This is strikingly illustrated by a comparison of the definitions held by various scientific groups of the phenomenon of the city.

1. The city has been regarded by geographers as an integral part of the landscape. From this standpoint the city is an elevation, rising from the ground like a mountain. Such observations as changes in wind velocity and atmospheric conditions produced by the city regarded as an obstruction of the landscape have been noted. Human geography has lately come to regard the city as the most significant human transformation of the natural environment, and as part of the general product arising out of man's relation with the natural environment. Urban geography has recently been gaining ground as a phase of regional geography. The location, physical structure, size, density, and economic function of cities are the chief factors emphasized. A substantial literature has grown up which has a direct bearing on the sociological study of the city.

Aurousseau, M. "Recent Contributions to Urban Geography," *Geog. Rev.*, XIV (July, 1924), 444–55.
   A concise statement of the geographical approach to the city, with a bibliography of the most authoritative and recent literature. Points out the recency of the study of urban geography and the difficulties involved in the methods. (II, 3; III.)

Barrows, Harlan H. "Geography as Human Ecology," *Annals of the Association of American Geographers*, Vol. XIII (March, 1923), No. 1.
While not specifically concerned with the city, defines the viewpoint and method of the geographer.

Blanchard, Raoul. "Une méthode de géographie urbaine," *La Vie Urbaine*, IV (1922) 301–19.
An exposition of the principles and methods of urban geography by one of the leading authorities. (III, 2, 3, 4, 6.)

Chisholm, G. G. "Generalizations in Geography, Especially in Human Geography," *Scott. Geog. Mag.*, XXXII (1916), 507–19. (III, 2, 3, 4.)
Hassert, Kurt. *Die Städte geographisch betrachtet* (Leipzig, 1907).
One of the early outlines of urban geography. (III, 2, 3, 4, 6.)

————. Über Aufgaben der Städtekunde," *Petermann's Mitteilungen*, LVI (Part II, 1910), 289–94. (III.)
Jefferson, M. "Anthropography of Some Great Cities: A Study in Distribution of Population." *Bull. Amer. Geog. Soc.*, XLI (1909), 537–66.
Argues the need for a geographical definition of the city and suggests one based on density of population. (I, 3, 4; III, VII, 2.)

Schrader, F. "The Growth of the Industrial City," *Scott. Geog. Mag.*, XXXIII (1917), 348–52.
An extensive review of an article by Professor Schrader printed in *Annales de Géographie*, January, 1917. A statement of the forces responsible for the emergence of the geographical entity "the city," especially of the industrial city. (I, 4; III, 2, 3, 4; IV, 1, 6; V, 5; VII, 1.)

Smith, J. Russell. "The Elements of Geography and the Geographic Unit," *School and Society*, Vol. XVII, No. 441. (III, 2, 3, 4.)

2. The rise of the city introduced an entirely novel element into the historical process. As a result we find the historians among the first to study this phenomenon of human aggregation which culminated in the city. The historian is mainly interested in tracing the development of this new form of social life from the standpoint of structure and formal organization. The origin of the city has been traced, the ancient cities have been described, the Greek city-state, Rome, the rise of the medieval city, and its transformation into the modern city have found an important place in historical literature. The earlier studies are mainly political in nature. Only recently have

historians devoted themselves to describing the new modes of life to which the city gave rise, and the interrelations between city and country. The city has been regarded chiefly as a political unit. The name "city" was given to a settlement because it had achieved a certain degree of political autonomy from the central government, or as an honorary title conferred for service rendered to a superior political entity, or, finally, as a result of incorporation or legal enactment.

Bücher, Karl. "Die Grossstädte in Gegenwart und Vergangenheit," in the volume, *Die Grossstadt*, edited by Th. Petermann, Dresden, 1903. (I, 4; II; III; IV.)

Cunningham, William. *Western Civilization* (Cambridge, 1898–1900).
Has many references to the changing historical conceptions of the city. (I, 4; II, 2, 3.)

The Encyclopedia Americana, 1918 edition, Vol. VI, article, "City." (II; IV, 3.)

The Encyclopedia Brittanica, 1911 edition, article, "City." (II; IV, 3.)

Schäfer, D. "Die politische und militärische Bedeutung der Grossstädte," in the volume *Die Grossstadt*, edited by Th. Petermann, Dresden, 1903.
A summary of the city as a political unit, together with its function from the military standpoint. (II; III, 1, 2, 3, 4; IV, 5.)

3. The statisticians have at various times been forced to define a city because census-taking and interpreting presupposes the existence of definite statistical units. The principal statistical methods of defining the city are: (1) by extent of the area of settlement, and (2) by number of inhabitants. In the history of the United States Census the city has been variously defined as an incorporated community of 8,000 inhabitants or more, then of 4,000, and at the present time of 2,500 inhabitants.

Blankenburg, R. "What Is a City?" *Independent*, XXCV (January 17, 1916), 84–85.

Meuriot, P. M. G. "Du criterium adopté pour la définition de la population urbaine," *Soc. de Statist. de Paris*, LV (October, 1914), 418–30.

Reuter, E. B. *Population Problems* (Philadelphia and London, 1924).
Shows the changing statistical definitions of the city adopted at various times by the United States Census. Contains a great deal of other material relating to urban population. (VII, 2, 3; VIII, 1, 2.)

4. The economists have been interested in tracing the development of the city as an economic unit. The city, from this standpoint, may be regarded as typical of a certain stage in economic development. The rise of the city is intimately associated with the transition from handicraft to machine industry, the division of labor, the market, and exchange. Besides the great number of economic histories which trace the general movement toward urban economy there are many monographs of special cities whose economic history has been studied, and some instances of present-day developments in metropolitan economy.

Below, George von. "Die Entstehung des modernen Kapitalismus und die Hauptstädte," *Schmollers Jahrbuch*, XLIII (1919), 811–28. (III, 4; IV, 1, 4, 6.)

Cheney, Edward Potts. *Industrial and Social History of England* (New York, 1910). (II, 2, 3; IV, 6.)

Day, Clive. *History of Commerce* (New York, 1926). (II; III, 4; IV, 6.)

Dillen, Johannes Gerard van. *Het Economisch karakter der Middeleeuwsche Stad*. I. *De Theorie der gesloten Stad-Huishanding* (Amsterdam, 1914). (II, 2; III, 4, 5; IV, 6.)

Gras, Norman S. B. *An Introduction to Economic History* (New York, 1922). Considerable material on the rise of the city as an economic unit. (II, 2, 3; III, 4, 5; IV, 1, 2, 6; X, 1.)

Sombart, Werner. *The Quintessence of Capitalism: A Study of the History and Psychology of the Modern Business Man*. Translated by M. Epstein (New York, 1915). (II, 3; IV, 6; IX, X; 3.)

Waentig, H. "Die wirtschaftliche Bedeutung der Grossstädte," in the volume, *Die Grossstadt*, edited by Th. Petermann, Dresden, 1903. A thorough study of the increasing significance of the city as an economic unit. (III, 4; IV, 6.)

5. A sociological definition of the city must recognize that such a complex phenomenon cannot be adequately characterized in terms of any one single distinguishing mark or any set of formal and arbitrary characteristics. The city is, to be sure, a human group

occupying a definite area, with a set of technical devices, institutions, administrative machinery, and organization which distinguish it from other groupings. But in this conglomeration of buildings, streets, and people the sociologist discovers a psychophysical mechanism. For him the city is a set of practices, of common habits, sentiments and traditions which have grown up through several generations of life and are characteristic of a typical cultural unit. Within this larger entity which is called the city he sees many other groupings of people and areas which are the result of growth and of a continuous process of sifting and allocation, each one of which areas has a character of its own and produces its special type of inhabitant. He sees a number of occupational and cultural groups whose interests and characteristics mark them off one from the other, but who, nevertheless, are conscious of their membership in some common larger group known as the city, and who participate in its life.

From another point of view the city is an institution which has arisen and maintains itself to some extent independently of the population because it satisfies certain fundamental wants, not only of the local inhabitants, but also of a larger area which has become dependent upon what the city has to give.

The city, finally, may be regarded as the product of three fundamental processes: the ecological, the economic, and the cultural, which operate in the urban area to produce groupings and behavior which distinguish that area from its rural periphery.

Izoulet, Jean. *La Cité moderne et la métaphysique de la sociologie* (Paris, 1894).

Maunier, René. "The Definition of the City." Translated by L. L. Bernard, *Amer. Jour. Sociol.*, XV, 536–48.
    A critical examination of the existing definitions of the city in the light of sociological theory. (I, 1, 2, 3, 4.)

Almost every textbook in the field of sociology has some sort of a working definition of the city. In addition there are available the various conceptions of the city underlying the social surveys.

II. THE NATURAL HISTORY OF THE CITY

The history of the city is almost synonymous with the history of civilization. The sociologist is interested in the natural history of the city as a phase of social evolution. Unlike the historian, he is not aiming to get the concrete facts of the rise and the decay of any particular city, but rather seeks to find in the study of the history of various cities the genesis of the typical city as a basis for the classification of types of cities and of social processes, irrespective of time and place.

1. Most of our ideas as to the origin of the city we owe to the findings of the archeologists. Exactly when cities began to appear in the story of mankind is still a doubtful question. We hear of cave cities in the paleolithic age. When we come down to historic times we find numerous cities whose main purpose was defense. The ancient cities of Memphis, Thebes, Babylon, and several others were already imposing aggregations of human beings and were centers of administration and of culture. Such a vast literature exists on the Greek city-state and on Rome, that is available in almost any library, that only a few references need be cited here.

Clerget, Pierre. "Urbanism: A Historic, Geographic, and Economic Study," *Smithsonian Institution Annual Report, 1912* (Washington, D.C., 1913), pp. 653–67. (II, 2, 3; III; V, 1, 2, 3; VI, VII, VIII.)

Coulanges, Fustel de. *The Ancient City: A Study of the Religion, Laws, and Institutions of Greece and Rome* (Boston, 1894). Translated by Willard Small.

Davis, W. S. *A Day in Old Athens: A Picture of Athenian Life* (New York, 1914).

Fowler, W. W. *The City-State of the Greeks and Romans* (London and New York, 1895). (I, 2.)

Friedländer, L. *Roman Life and Manners under the Early Empire.* Authorized translation by L. A. Magnus from the 7th rev. ed. of the *Sittengeschichte Roms* (London, 1908–13), 4 vols. (III, 4.)

Rostovtzeff, Michael. "Cities in the Ancient World," in volume *Urban Land Economics*, edited by R. T. Ely, Institute for Research in Land Economics, Ann Arbor, 1922.

Zimmern, Alfred E. *The Greek Commonwealth: Politics and Economics in Fifth-Century Athens* (2d rev. edition; Oxford, 1915).

2. Historians are still doubtful whether the medieval city was the product of a continuous growth starting with Rome or whether, around the year 1000, the city was born anew after some centuries of reversion to a simpler form of social life. There is little doubt, however, that the medieval city not only had a different structure but also played a decidedly different rôle than the Greek or the Roman city. The typical medieval city was fortified and had achieved a certain degree of political autonomy from the central government. It played its leading rôle, however, as the center of trade and commerce and the home of the guilds. With the sixteenth century there came an important change over the urban life of Europe. New inventions, such as that of gunpowder, made the city wall obsolete. The beginnings of industry spelled the doom of the narrow guild system. In the light of this new order of things the medieval city of a former day—which was really a town—either had to adapt itself to the new forces that had become operative and join the ranks of growing cities or else become sterile and sink into decay.

Bax, E. B. *German Culture, Past and Present* (London, 1915).
  Traces the development of the medieval German city. (II, 3).

Benson, E. *Life in a Medieval City, Illustrated by York in the Fifteenth Century* (London, 1920).

Consentius, Ernst. *Alt-Berlin, Anno 1740* (2d ed.; Berlin, 1911).
  One of a great number of special studies in the early history of German towns and cities. (III, 6.)

Coulton, George Gordon. *Social Life in Britain from the Conquest to the Reformation* (Cambridge, 1918).

Green, Alice S. A. (Mrs. J. R.) *Town Life in the Fifteenth Century* (2 vols., New York, 1894). (III, 5.)

Pirenne, Henry. *Medieval Cities: Their Origins and the Revival of Trade.* (Princeton, N.J., 1925).
Traces the growth of cities and their institutions in relation to the revival of trade. (I, 4; III, 4; IV, 4; VII, 1.)

Preuss, Hugo. *Die Entwicklung des Deutschen Städtewesens* (Leipzig, 1906).
A standard history of the development of the German city. (I, 2; II, 3; IV, 3; VI, 7; VII, 1.)

Stow, John. *The Survey of London* (1598) (London and New York, 1908).

3. The modern city marks the advent of a new epoch in civilization. Its rise has been accompanied by, and, in turn, is the result of a profound revolution in economic, political, intellectual, and social life. The modern man is to so great an extent a product of the modern city that in order to grasp the full significance of the transformation the city has wrought we must get a view of its origins and development. The city, as we find it today, is by no means a finished product. Its growth is so rapid and its energy so great that it changes its complexion almost daily, and with it the character of mankind itself.

Baily, W. L. "Twentieth Century City," *Amer. City*, XXXI (August, 1924), 142–43.

Beard, C. A. "Awakening of Japanese Cities," *Review of Reviews*, LXIX (May, 1924), 523–27.

Bücher, Karl. *Industrial Evolution.* Translated by S. M. Wickett (London and New York, 1901).
The modern city from the standpoint of industrial society. (II, 1, 2; III, 4, 5; IV, 6; VII, 1; IX, 1.)

Die Stadt Danzig: ihre geschichtliche Entwickelung und ihre öffentlichen Einrichtungen (Danzig, 1904).
Shows the development of a modern city and its characteristic institutions. (III, 1, 2, 3; VI.)

Ebeling, Martin. "Grossstadtsozialismus." Vol. XLIV of *Grossstadtdokumente*, edited by Hans Ostwald (Berlin, 1905).
A cross-section of the modern city from the standpoint of the workingman. (IV, 3, 6; V, 2, 3; VI; VII, 2, 5; VIII, 1.)

Ende, A. von. *New York* (Berlin, 1909).
Typical of a great number of descriptions of cities by travelers and writers of tourists' guidebooks. The best known are those of Baedeker, of Leipzig, covering every important European city.

George, M. Dorothy. *London life in the XVIIIth Century* (New York, 1925).
Contains an excellent selected bibliography on the city of London. A cross-section of London life on the threshold of the modern era. (III; VII, 1, 2.)

Hare, Augustus J. C. *Paris* (London, 1900).
One of a series of books of various European cities, being intended as a guide for tourists.

Hessel, J. F. *The Destiny of the American City*. Champaign, Illinois, 1922.
The trend of American city growth and its problems.

Howe, Frederic C. *The Modern City and Its Problems* (New York, 1915).
A short outline of the development of the modern city, a statement of the implications of city civilization, a discussion of the city as a physical mechanism, and suggestions for an extension of the principle of municipal ownership and management, city-planning, and co-operation. (III, 5; IV, 2, 3; V, 4, 5; VI; VII, 1, 2; IX, 3.)

Irwin, Will. *The City That Was: A Requiem of Old San Francisco* (New York, 1906).

Johnson, Clarence Richard (editor). *Constantinople Today, or, the Pathfinder Survey of Constantinople: A Study in Oriental Social Life* (New York and London, 1923). (III, 2; V; VI; VII; VIII; IX, 1, 3.)

Kirk, William (editor). *A Modern City: Providence, Rhode Island, and Its Activities* (Chicago, 1909). (III, 4; VI; VII.)

"London: A Geographical Synthesis," *Geog. Rev.*, XIV (1924), 310–12.
A summary of the co-ordinated geographical study of a modern city. (III; IV; V; VI, 3.)

Pollock, H. M., and Morgan, W. S. *Modern Cities* (New York, 1913).
A general study of American cities and their problems. (III, 6; V, 5, VI.)

Strong, Josiah. *The Twentieth Century City* (New York, 1898).

Zueblin, Charles. *American Municipal Progress* (new and revised edition; New York, 1916).
Attempts to formulate a science of "municipal sociology." (VI; VII; VIII, 1.)

Almost every modern city has several histories of its recent development, and the current magazines contain a great deal of general information about particular cities. The list of typical works on the modern city might be extended indefinitely, but the numerous bibliographies already available make this task unnecessary. There are published bibliographies of some of the more important European and American cities. Books on London, for instance, are so numerous that there exists in the city of London a library devoted exclusively to works on that city. A similar volume of literature is available about Paris, Rome, and other centers of culture around which there has grown up an historical tradition which gives to the locality a world-wide human interest. There are a number of books on such cities as Moscow, the city of churches, which emphasize the fact that this metropolis has occupied a position of dominance in Russian life because of its spiritual leadership, which expresses itself institutionally in its magnificent cathedrals. There are other Meccas of this sort, the literature on which would occupy many pages.

The inclusion of such books as Augustus Hare's *Paris* and von Ende's *New York* in this list might well raise the question as to why these two rather unimportant works were included and others of a similar nature excluded. Their pertinence in this connection was thought to lie in the fact that they are typical of books on many cities which are intended as guides to tourists or represent accounts of travelers, which are not included in this bibliography, but which might prove of interest to the student dealing with the individualities and eccentricities of individual cities.

There has grown up in recent years a renewed interest in the variety and diversity of American cities. Many such books have appeared, often in series including several cities, which give more than a traveler's account, and actually succeed in entering into the spirit of the city. Grace King's volume on New Orleans is perhaps the best, if not the most representative, of these American volumes.

III. TYPES OF CITIES

Each city, like every other object in nature, is, in a sense, unique. A scientific study of the city presupposes, however, that a study of a number of cities will reveal certain classes or types, the members of which have certain common characteristics which mark them off from other types. There are, obviously, many criteria, on the basis of any one of which cities might be classified and distinguished from each other. Certain fundamental types appear in the literature of the subject of which the sociologist may profitably take note.

1. One of the very first characteristics that we observe about a city is its age. The difference between European and American cities in this respect is so obvious as to be inescapable. The cities of Western Europe, when compared with some of those of the Orient, again show their relative youth. A detailed study of the city reveals this important conservative influence of the early experiences of a city. Streets, walls, names, and the tradition that has grown up through centuries of existence leave their indelible impress upon the city as we find it today. Experienced observers are able to distinguish cities belonging to one historical period from those of another by their appearance, just as they are able to differentiate between the cities of adjoining countries. These differences show themselves not only in a dominant type of architecture, but also in general atmosphere, the mode of life of the inhabitants, and the activities that find expression in the life of the people.

Fleure, Herbert John. "Some Types of Cities in Temperate Europe," *Geog. Rev.*, X, No. 6 (1920), 357–74.
Traces the historical influences on the character of cities. (II; III, 2, 3, 5, 6.)

———. *Human Geography in Western Europe: A Study in Appreciation* (London, 1919). (III.)

Fraser, E. "Our Foreign Cities," *Sat. Eve. Post*, CXCVI (August 25, 1923), 14–15.
The background of its inhabitants gives the city its dominant atmosphere. (V, 3; VII, 2, 3.)

Gamble, Sidney D. *Peking: A Social Study* (New York, 1921).
A survey of an oriental city. Incidentally reveals a strange variety of the modern city. (II, III, 4, 6; IV, 3; V, VI; VII; VIII; IX, 3.)

Hanslik, Erwin. *Biala: eine deutsche Stadt in Galizien* (Wien: Teschen und Leipzig, 1909).
The persistence of a historical type in a changing environment. (III, 6.)

Homburg, F. "Names of Cities," *Jour. Geog.*, XV (September, 1916), 17–23.

Rhodes, Harrison. *American Towns and People* (New York, 1920).

Uhde-Bernays, Herman. *Rothenburg of der Tauber* (Leipzig, 1922).
One of a series of volumes on "cities of culture." The persistence of the historical influences on the atmosphere of cities. (III, 6.)

2. The means of communication that are in use at any given period in history determine the location of human settlements. For this reason the dominant location of the ancient and medieval city was on the seacoast or near a navigable body of water. The founding and the development of cities still depends on their location with reference to the means of communication in use and the consequent accessibility of the region. The coming of the railroads made large inland cities possible. Settlements located favorably along the seacoast or along an important river or lake enjoy a natural advantage which has an important bearing on their growth. Location is an important competitive element which produces fundamental types.

Faris, J. T. "The Heart of the Middle West," *Travel*, XLII (December, 1923), 30–34.

Geddes, Patrick. "Cities, and the Soils They Grow From." *Survey Graphic* (April, 1925), pp. 40–44.
A rather philosophical conception of the city as related to the natural environment. Suggestions concerning geotechnics, afforestation, and regional development. (III, 2, 3; V, 5.)

Jefferson, Mark. "Some Considerations on the Geographical Provinces of the United States," *Ann. of the Ass. of Amer. Geographers*, VII (1917), 3–15.
Develops the theory that the country as a whole can be divided into provinces according to location on seacoast, inland lake, river, etc., and that the cities of each province are characterized by factors arising out of their location. (III, 3, 4; IV, 1, 6.)

Mercier, Marcel. *La Civilisation Urbaine au Mzab: Étude de Sociologie Africaine* (Alger, 1922).

The study of an African city in a desert region, whose immediate site is determined by water supply and transportation routes. The directions and the limitation of the social activities of the community are dictated by the environment. (III, 1, 6; IV, 1, 6; V, 1; VI; VII, 2; IX, 1.)

Ratzel, Friedrich. "Die geographische Lage der grossen Städte," in volume *"Die Grossstadt,"* edited by Th. Petermann, Dresden, 1903.

A thoroughgoing consideration of the location types of cities by one of the earliest and most competent students of the subject. Offers the theory, also held by Cooley (C. H. Cooley, *The Theory of Transportation*) that cities arise at the end of a route of transportation, or at a juncture of several such routes, or at the point where one route of transportation joins another; where, for instance, a land transportation route ends and a waterway begins. Ratzel also gives one of the earliest and soundest geographical definitions of the city: "A permanent condensation (or dense settlement) of human beings and human habitations covering a considerable area and situated in the midst (or at the juncture) of several routes of transportation." (I, II, III, 1, 3, 4, 5, 6; IV, 1; V, 5; VII, 2.)

Ridgley, Douglas C. "Geographic Principles in the Study of Cities," *Jour. of Geog.*, XXIV (February, 1925), 66–78.

A reiteration of Cooley's theory: "Population and wealth tend to collect wherever there is a break in transportation." (I, 1; VII, 1, 2.)

Wright, Henry C. *The American City: An Outline of Its Development and Functions* (Chicago, 1916).

Chapter i outlines the location of cities and classifies them according to their purpose. The rest of the book is taken up with government, finance, administrative problems, such as health, police, education, housing, zoning, and the effect of the city on the citizens. (III, 3, 4; V, 4, 5; VI; VII, 2; IX.)

3. A classification in use especially among the geographers is that arising from differences in site. It is important to distinguish between the general situation of a city, i.e., its location with reference to the surrounding territory and the means of communication with other centers of population and resources, and its immediate local setting which influences its structure and growth and brings with it certain other more deep-seated consequences.

Biermann, Charles. "Situation et Site de Lausanne," *Bull. Soc. Neuchateloise de Geog.*, XXV (1916), 122–49. Reviewed in *Geog. Rev.*, VI (1918), 285.

Distinguishes between general location and immediate site as factors determining the character of the city. Emphasizes the limitations imposed on the modern city by its medieval defensive system. (III, 1, 2; VI, 3.)

Brunhes, Jean. *Human Geography: An Attempt at a Positive Classification, Principles and Examples.* Translated by T. C. LeCompte (Chicago and New York, 1920).

The most comprehensive and basic work in human geography at the present time available. Discusses the city as a form of occupation of the soil. Describes the principles and gives many illustrations of the effect of location on the growth and the character of cities. (I, 1; II, 2, 3; III; IV; VII, 1, 2.)

King, C. F. "Striking Characteristics of Certain Cities," *Jour. School Geog.,* IV (1900), 201–7, 301–8, 370–91. (III, 1, 2, 4, 6.)

Semple, Ellen C. "Some Geographical Causes Determining the Location of Cities," *Jour. School Geog.,* I (1897), 225–31.

Smith, Joseph Russell. *Human Geography: Teachers' Manual* (Philadelphia and Chicago, 1922).

4. Cities may be classified according to the functions they characteristically perform in national or world economy. The competitive process tends to operate between cities as well as within cities, so as to give each city a rôle defining its status in the world-community. The capital city has certain features which distinguish it from a commercial and industrial city. The railroad city is fundamentally different from a resort city, from the religious Mecca, the university seat, and the international port. Even within these classes we find further specialization. Thus, we have a steel city, a film city, an automobile city, a rubber city, and a tool city. The ecological process on a national and world-wide scale is not sufficiently well known at the present time to permit of any definite system of classification, but that there is a strong tendency toward functional specialization between cities as entities is no longer open to doubt.

Cornish, Vaughan. *The Great Capitals: An Historical Geography* (London, 1922).

A study of the variations within the type of city serving as a political center. A work which has given a great deal of impetus to the study of functional types of cities. (III, 1.)

"F.O.B. Detroit," *Outlook,* III (1915), 980–86.

A sample of the industrial type of city which is built around the production of a single product—the automobile. (IV, 6; IX, 1.)

Homburg, F. "Capital Cities," *Jour. Geog.*, XIX (January, 1920), 8–15.

Kellogg, Paul U. (editor). *The Pittsburgh District* (New York, 1914).

Introductory volume of the *Pittsburgh Survey*, one of the most comprehensive studies of an industrial, urban area. Contains material bearing on many phases of city structure and city life. (V; VI; VII; VIII; IX, 1, 3.)

Kenngott, George F. *The Record of a City: A Social Survey of Lowell, Massachusetts* (New York, 1912).

A cross-section of a typical manufacturing city. (V; VI; VII; VIII; IX, 1, 3.)

McLean, Francis H., Todd, Robert E., and Sanborn, Frank B. *The Report of the Lawrence Survey* (Lawrence, Massachusetts, 1917). (V; VI; VII; VIII; IX, 1, 3.)

"The Right of the Community to Exist," *Living Age*, CIII (October 4, 1919), 46–48.

Roberts, Peter. *Anthracite Coal Communities* (New York, 1904).

A study of mining communities in the United States. (V; VI; VII; VIII; IX, 1, 3.)

Steele, Rufus. "In the Sun-Spot," *Sunset*, XXXIV (1915), 690–99.

A study of Los Angeles, the city of moving pictures. (IV, 6; IX, 1.)

Semple, Ellen. "Some Geographical Causes Determining the Location of Cities," *Jour. School Geog.*, I (1897), 225–31.

———. *Influences of Geographic Environment, on the Basis of Ratzel's System of Anthropogeography* (New York, 1911).

A comprehensive work dealing with the factors in the natural environment in relation to the settlement and the activity of man. (III, 2, 3.)

Tower, W. S. "Geography of American Cities," *Bull. Amer. Geog. Soc.*, XXXVII (1905), 577–88.

Distinguishes between industrial, commercial, political, and social centers and suggests that cities might combine several of these functions. Gives examples of each type, pointing out their distinctive characteristics. (III, 2, 3.)

Wood, Arthur Evans. *Some Unsolved Problems of a University Town* (Philadelphia, 1920.)

A study of housing, public health, and dependency in Princeton, New Jersey. (VI, 10; VII, 5.)

In the current periodical literature one can find numerous articles dealing with the various functional types of cities of the present day. The *National Geographic Magazine* has many numbers which are devoted to individual cities from this standpoint.

5. The town, the city, and the metropolis are genetically related concepts which represent three successive stages of an ever widening zone of interrelationships and influences. The town represents a local aggregation which is intimately bound up with a rather narrow surrounding rural periphery. It is the product of limited means of communication and constitutes a more or less self-sustaining economic unit. The city is a more highly specialized unit and, as a result, is a part of a wider interrelated area, while the metropolis tends to become a cosmopolitan unit based upon a relatively high degree of development of the means of communication. The differences between these three urban types is not only expressed in terms of number of inhabitants and area of occupation, but also in social organization and in attitudes. There is a tendency to divide the United States up into provinces according to the zone of influence of the greater metropolitan units dominating the surrounding territory and dependent upon it.

Cottrell, E. A. "Limited Town-Meetings in Massachusetts," *Nat. Mun. Rev.*, II (July, 1918), 433–34.
While dealing primarily with an administrative problem, points out one of the essential differences between town and city. (V, 3; VI, 7; IX, 3.)

Febvre, Lucien. *A Geographical Introduction to History*. Translated by E. G. Mountsford and T. H. Paxton (New York, 1925).
Contains a clear statement of the problems of human geography. Part III, chap. iii, on towns is suggestive. (I, 1; II; III.)

Gide, Charles. "L'habitation hors la ville," *Revue Economique Internationale* (January, 1925), 141–57.

Gilbert, Bernard. *Old England: A God's-Eye-View of a Village* (Boston, 1922).
A cross-section of village life and economy.

Gras, Norman S. B. "The Development of Metropolitan Economy in Europe and America," *Amer. Hist. Rev.*, XXVII (1921–22), 695–708.
Differentiates clearly between manorial, village, town, city, and metropolitan economy. (I, 4; II; III, 1; IV, 1, 2, 6; X, 1, 2.)

Lasker, B. "Unwalled Towns," *Survey*, XLIII (March 6, 1920), 675–80.

Lohman, K. B. "Small Town Problems," *Amer. City*, XXIII (July, 1920), 81.

Maine, Sir H. S. *Village Communities in the East and West* (7th ed.; London, 1913).

The most authoritative English study of the village. (II, 1, 2; III, 1; IV, 3; VI, 7; X, 2.)

McVey, Frank L. *The Making of a Town* (Chicago, 1913). (IV, 1, 2, 3; V, 4, 5; VI; VII, 1.)

Shine, Mary L. "Urban Land in the Middle Ages," in volume, *Urban Land Economics*, Institute for Research in Land Economics (Ann Arbor, Michigan, 1922).

Shows the transition from town to city life. Contains valuable collection of material on the medieval city. (I, 2, 4; II, 2, 3; III; V, 4, 5; VI; VII, 2, 5; IX, 1; X, 1, 2.)

Sims, Newell Leroy. *The Rural Community, Ancient and Modern* (New York, 1920). (II, 1, 2,; III, 1, 6; IV, 1; V, 3.)

Slosson, P. "Small-Townism," *Independent*, CVI (July 9, 1921), 106–7. (X, 2, 3.)

Wilson, Warren H. *Quaker Hill: A Sociological Study* (New York, 1907).

A picture of a community held together by religious and social bonds. Shows the transition from a primary to a secondary type of contact. (V, 3; VII, 2; IX, 3.)

6. The city may be the unplanned product of the interaction of successive generations with the environment, or it may be the result of intentional activity with a specific end in view. We hear of ancient cities springing up at the will of an emperor bent on glorifying his name. There are cities in America that are the premeditated product of individuals or corporations bent on creating an adjunct to a factory. There are capital cities in America owing their existence to the decisions of a legislature. The planned city differs from the "natural" city not only in its structural form but in its functional aspects and its capacity for growth. Probably no planned city can grow into a metropolis if it does not somehow find for itself an important function in world-economy and earn its place in the competitive process.

Aurousseau, M. "Urban Geography: A Study of German Towns," *Geog. Rev.*, XI (October, 1921), 614–16.

A review of a German work (Geisler, Walter, "Beiträge zur Stadtgeographie." *Zeitschrift der Gesellschaft für Erdkunde*, Nos. 8–10 [Berlin, 1920], 274–96). Shows the influence of the old town plan on the development of the modern city. (II, 2, 3; III.)

Bodine, H. E. "Study of Local History Teaches Value of City-Planning," *American City*, XXV (September, 1921), 241–45.

Cushing, C. P. "Rambler on the Standardized City," *Travel*, XXIX (July, 1917), 40.

Ely, Richard T. "Pullman: A Social Study," *Harper's New Monthly Magazine*, LXX (December, 1884), 453–65.
> While more of a general survey than a special study of the influence of the city plan upon the actual growth of the city, it does show some disharmonies arising out of the attempt to control a planned urban project in the face of growth and unexpected complications. (IV, 4; VII, 3; IX, 1.)

Ormiston, E. "Public Control of the Location of Towns," *Econ. Jour.*, XXVIII (December, 1918), 374–85.
> Shows some of the abortive attempts to establish towns in unfavorably situated environments. Suggests public control as a possible preventive measure, if based on thorough study of all factors involved in the possibilities for growth and development. (III, 2, 3, 4; IV, 6.)

Whitbeck, R. H. "Selected Cities of the United States," *Jour. Geog.*, XXI (September, 1922), 205–42.
> Contains several maps showing city structure.

The city-planning literature contains many instances of comparisons between planned cities and natural cities as well as examples of the effects of the city plan on the actual development of the city, and the opposite phenomenon—the effect of the natural development of the city on the city plan.

IV. THE CITY AND ITS HINTERLAND

Far from being an arbitrary clustering of people and buildings, the city is the nucleus of a wider zone of activity from which it draws its resources and over which it exerts its influence. The city and its hinterland represent two phases of the same mechanism which may be analyzed from various points of view.

1. Just as Galpin, in his *Social Anatomy of a Rural Community*, was able to determine the limits of the community by means of the area over which its trade routes extend, so the city may be delimited by the extent of its trading area. From the simpler area

around it the city gathers the raw materials, part of which are essential to sustain the life of its inhabitants, and another part of which are transformed by the technique of the city population into finished products which flow out again to the surrounding territory, sometimes over a relatively larger expanse than the region of their origin. From another point of view the city sends out its tentacles to the remotest corners of the world to gather those sources of supply which are not available in the immediate vicinity, only to retail them to its own population and the rural region about it. Again, the city might be regarded as the distributor of wealth, an important economic rôle which has become institutionalized in a complex financial system.

Chisholm, George G. "The Geographical Relation of the Market to the Seats of Industry," *Scott. Geog. Mag.*, *April*, 1910.

Galpin, C. J. "The Social Anatomy of an Agricultural Community," Agricultural Experiment Station of the University of Wisconsin, *Research Bulletin 34* (Madison, Wisconsin, 1915).
Deals primarily with trade routes of an agricultural area, but throws considerable light on the urban trade area. (V, 2; X, 2.)

Levainville, Jacques. "Caen: Notes sur l'évolution de la fonction urbaine," *La Vie Urbaine*, V (1923), 223–78.
Through its emphasis on the economic functions of the city this study makes clear the significance of the trade areas.

Newspapers, business houses, and mail-order houses in particular have published numerous discussions and graphic statements of their circulation or their trade relations with the surrounding territory. Such documents are to be found in numerous specialized trade and commercial journals. In addition there are government reports and publications of chambers of commerce bearing on this question.

2. One of the outstanding prerequisites of any city is a local transportation system which makes possible ready access of the population living in diverse sections to their places of work, the

centers of trade, of culture, and of other social activities. The city consists of not merely a continuous densely populated and built up area, but of suburbs and outlying regions which by means of rapid transit are within easy reach of urban activities. This area has been termed the commuting area. Although the inhabitants of this larger area of settlement may not be under the same taxing, policing, and governing authorities as the inhabitants of the city proper, they think of themselves as part of the same metropolis and actively participate in its life.

Edel, Edmund. *Neu Berlin*, volume L in "Grossstadt Dokumente Series," edited by Hans Ostwald, Berlin, 1905.
Discusses the changes brought about by recent growth in the city of Berlin, with emphasis on the recently built-up suburbs. (VII, 1, 2, 4.)

Lueken, E. "Vorstadtprobleme," *Schmollers Jahrb.*, XXXIX (1915), 1911–20.
Discussion of the governmental and technical problems brought about by the rise of the suburbs. (IV, 3; V, 1; VI.)

Wright, Henry C. "Rapid Transit in Relation to the Housing Problem," in *Proceedings of the Second National Conference on City Planning* (Rochester, 1910), pp. 125–35.
Considers the possibility of distributing the urban population in the suburbs by building up a rapid transit system. (VI, 2, 3, 10.)

3. That part of the inhabitants of a given metropolitan area who actually are under the same administrative machinery may constitute only a relatively small part of the inhabitants of the metropolitan district as a whole. The size of the administrative unit tends to lag behind the size of the metropolis proper. Suburbs are incorporated gradually, and changes in charters and legal organization often do not keep pace with the rapid expansion of the district. The city of London proper is only a relatively small part of metropolitan London. As a result of such anomalous situations many difficulties occur in interpreting statistical data compiled by governmental agencies.

Gross, Charles. *Bibliography of British Municipal History* (New York, 1897). (I, 2; VI, 7.)

Howe, Frederic C. *European Cities at Work* (New York, 1913).
    A general survey of the structure and the government of the European city. (II, 3; VI; VII, 1.)

————. *The British City: The Beginnings of Democracy* (New York, 1907). (II, 2, 3; VI.)

Kales, Albert M. *Unpopular Government in the United States* (Chicago, 1914).
    A discussion of the administrative problems of the city, emphasizing the anomalous situations brought about by legal restrictions in the face of urban development. (VI, 7; X, 1, 2.)

Maxey, C. C. "Political Integration of Metropolitan Communities," *National Munic. Rev.*, XI (August, 1922), 229–53. (IV, 2; VI, 7.)

Wilcox, Delos F. *The American City: A Problem in Democracy* (New York, 1906).
    A work dealing mainly with the administration of the city. Chapter i, "Democracy and City Life in America," chapter ii on "The Street," and v on "The Control of Leisure" are suggestive. (VI; VII, 5.)

4. One of the latest phases of city growth is the development of satellite cities. These are generally industrial units growing up outside the boundaries of the administrative city, which, however, are dependent upon the city proper for their existence. Often they become incorporated into the city proper after the city has inundated them, and thus lose their identity. The location of such satellites may exert a determining influence upon the direction of the city's growth. These satellites become culturally a part of the city long before they are actually incorporated into it.

Taylor, Graham Romeyn. *Satellite Cities: A Study of Industrial Suburbs* (New York and London, 1915).
    The most comprehensive study of its kind. (III, 4; VII, 2; IX, 1.)

Wright, R. "Satellite Cities," *Bellman*, XXV (November 16, 1918), 551–52.

5. The city has come to be recognized as the center of culture. Innovations in social life and in ideas gravitate from the city to the country. Through its newspapers, theaters, schools, and museums, through its traveling salesmen and mail-order houses, through its large representation in the legislatures, and through many other

points of contact with the inhabitants of the rural periphery about it, the city diffuses its culture over a large area. The city is in this respect an important civilizing agent.

Desmond, S. "America's City Civilization: The Natural Divisions of the United States," *Century*, CVIII (August, 1924), 548–55.

Holds that America is creating a new type of city civilization of a decentralized type. Several outstanding American cities are described as cultural entities and as exerting a dominating influence over a large rural area, thus suggesting the emergence of cultural provinces. (III, 1, 2, 3; IX, 2.)

Petermann, Theodor. "Die geistige Bedeutung der Grossstädte," in the volume, *Die Grossstadt* (Dresden, 1903).

One of the best concise statements on the cultural significance of the city from the standpoint of the rural periphery. (IV, 6; IX, 1, 2; X, 1, 2, 3.)

Wells, Joseph. *Oxford and Oxford Life* (London, 1899).

An example of a cultural type of city from the functional standpoint, and its influence. (II, 2, 3; III, 4.)

There are a number of studies of cities as cultural centers. The city of Moscow has often been described as the city of churches, for instance, and as such has exercised an influence over the life of Russia all out of proportion to its function in other respects. Similar studies are available of Rome, Venice, Dresden, and a number of others.

6. With the advent of modern methods of communication the whole world has been transformed into a single mechanism of which a country or a city is merely an integral part. The specialization of function, which has been a concomitant of city growth, has created a state of interdependence of world-wide proportions. Fluctuations in the price of wheat on the Chicago Grain Exchange reverberate to the remotest part of the globe, and a new invention anywhere will soon have to be reckoned with at points far from its origin. The city has become a highly sensitive unit in this complex mechanism, and in turn acts as a transmitter of such stimulation as it receives to a local area. This is as true of economic and political as it is of social and intellectual life.

Baer, M. *Der internationale Mädchenhandel*, Vol. XXXVII in "Grossstadt Dokumente" (Berlin, 1905).
    Shows that the large city is the center of the world white-slave traffic. (III, 4; VII, 5; IX, 4.)

Bernhard, Georg. *Berliner Banken*, Vol. VIII in "Grossstadt Dokumente" (Berlin, 1905).
    While primarily a study of Berlin banks, shows the large city as the center of the economic life of the world. (III, 4; V, 1; IX, 1, 4.)

Jefferson, Mark. "Distribution of British Cities and the Empire," *Geog. Rev.*, IV (November, 1917), 387–94.
    "English cities are unique in that they have taken the whole world for their countryside. . . . . The conception of the British empire as the direct result of English trade in English manufactures, which in turn are largely a response to English treasures in coal and iron, is strongly reenforced by the distribution of her great cities." (III, 4; VI, 8.)

Olden, Balder. *Der Hamburger Hafen*, Vol. XLVI in "Grossstadt Dokumente" (Berlin, 1905).
    The influence of world-commerce on the city. (III, 3, 4; IV, 4; V, 1; IX, 1, 4.)

Penck, Albrecht. *Der Hafen von New York*, Vol. IV of the collection, "Meereskunde" (Berlin, 1910).
    An excellent view of the traffic in the harbor of New York. (III, 2, 3, 4.)

Zimmern, Helen. *Hansa Towns* (New York, 1895).
    An historical example of a typical function of cities in world-economy. (I, 2; II, 2.)

V. THE ECOLOGICAL ORGANIZATION OF THE CITY

Just as the city as a whole is influenced in its position, function, and growth by competitive factors which are not the result of the design of anyone, so the city has an internal organization which may be termed an ecological organization, by which we mean the spatial distribution of population and institutions and the temporal sequence of structure and function following from the operation of selective, distributive, and competitive forces tending to produce typical results wherever they are at work. Every city tends to take on a structural and functional pattern determined by the ecological factors that are operative. The internal ecological organization of a city permits of more intensive study and accurate analysis than the ecology of the city from the external standpoint. For the latter phase of the subject we will have to rely on further investigations of the economists, the geographers, and the statisticians. The facts of the local groupings of the population that arise as a result of ecological factors are, however, readily accessible to the sociologist.

1. Plant ecologists have been accustomed to use the expression "natural area" to refer to well-defined spatial units having their own peculiar characteristics. In human ecology the term "natural area" is just as applicable to groupings according to selective and cultural characteristics. Land values are an important index to the boundaries of these local areas. Streets, rivers, railroad properties, street-car lines, and other distinctive marks or barriers tend to serve as dividing lines between the natural areas within the city.

Addams, Jane. *A New Conscience and an Ancient Evil* (New York, 1912).
A discussion of vice and the vice district in Chicago. (V, 4; VI, 6.)

Anderson, Nels. *The Hobo: The Sociology of the Homeless Man* (Chicago, 1923).
The study of a typical deteriorated area in the city where the homeless men congregate. (VII, 5; IX, 4.)

Bab, Julius. *Die Berliner Bohème*, Vol. II in "Grosstadt Dokumente" (Berlin, 1905).
An intimate study of a natural area which has developed an exotic atmosphere as a result of the social isolation of its members and their peculiar personalities. At the same time furnishes an excellent history of a local community and is a unique contribution to the mentality of city life. (V, 3; VII, 2; IX, 2, 3, 4.)

Booth, Charles. *Life and Labor of the People of London* (London, 1892).
The most comprehensive study of London in existence. Especially interesting in this connection for its description of the natural areas of that city. Volume V, on East London, offers a wealth of insight into city life. These volumes cover almost every phase of city life and should be cross-referenced with most of the categories suggested in this outline.

Brown, Junius Henri. *The Great Metropolis: A mirror of New York* (Hartford, 1869).
Gives a view of New York at about the middle of the nineteenth century. Is of interest for a comparative study of the city then, and now from the point of view of its natural divisions. (VII, 2; IX, 1.)

Denison, John Hopkins. *Beside the Bowery* (New York, 1914). (VII, 2.)

Dietrich, Richard. *Lebeweltnächte der Friedrichstadt,* Vol. XXX in "Grossstadt Dokumente" (Berlin, 1905).

A view of Berlin's bright- light area. (VI, 6; VII, 2, 5; IX.)

Goldmark, Pauline. *West-Side Studies* (New York, 1914).

Historical and social investigations of local urban areas, especially from the point of view of social welfare and pathology. (V, 2, 3; VI; VII, 2, 5; VIII; IX, 1.)

Harper, Charles George. *Queer Things about London; Strange Nooks and Corners of the Greatest City in the World* (Philadelphia, 1924). (II, 3; V, 2, 3; VI, 3, 5, 8, 10.)

Kirwan, Daniel Joseph. *Palace and Hovel, or Phases of London Life; Being Personal Observations of an American in London* (Hartford, 1870). (II, 3; VI; VII, 2; IX, 1, 4.)

Ostwald, Hans O. A. *Dunkle Winkel in Berlin,* Vol. I in "Grossstadt Dokumente" (Berlin, 1905).

A description of the more obscure areas in Berlin, particularly those of the underworld. (II, 3; VII, 2; IX, 2, 3, 4.)

Scharrelmann, Heinrich. *Die Grossstadt; Spaziergänge in die Grossstadt Hamburg,* 1921.

Sketches of city areas encountered in a walk about the city.

Seligman, Edwin R. A. (editor). *The Social Evil, with Special Reference to Conditions Existing in the City of New York* (New York and London, 1912).

The vice area of a large city. Typical of a number of surveys of moral areas in the larger cities of the United States. Compare, for instance, with the report of the Illinois investigation, *The Social Evil in Chicago.* (VII, 2, 5; IX, 1.)

Smith, F. Berkley. *The Real Latin Quarter* (New York, 1901). (V, 3; VII, 2; IX, 2, 3, 4.)

Strunsky, Simeon. *Belzhazzar Court, or, Village Life in New York City* (New York, 1914). (V, 2, 3; VII, 2; IX, 2, 3, 4.)

Timbs, John. *Curiosities of London* (London, 1868). (IX, 1, 4.)

Werthauer, Johannes. *Moabitrium,* Vol. XXXI of the "Grossstadt Dokumente" (Berlin, 1905).

A report of a personal investigation of the rooming-house area of Berlin. (VII, 2, 4; IX, 2, 3, 4.)

Woods, Robert A. *The City Wilderness: A Settlement Study of South End, Boston* (Boston and New York, 1898).

One of a number of similar studies viewing the city and its slums from the standpoint of the settlement worker. (V, 2, 3; VI; VII, 5.)

Young, Erle Fiske. "The Social Base Map," *Jour. App. Sociol.*, IX (January-February, 1925) 202–6.
A graphic device for the study of natural areas. (VII, 2.)

2. The neighborhood is typically the product of the village and the small town. Its distinguishing characteristics are close proximity, co-operation, intimate social contact, and strong feeling of social consciousness. While in the modern city we still find people living in close physical proximity to each other, there is neither close co-operation nor intimate contact, acquaintanceship, and group consciousness accompanying this spatial nearness. The neighborhood has come to mean a small, homogeneous geographic section of the city, rather than a self-sufficing, co-operative, and self-conscious group of the population.

Daniels, John. *America via the Neighborhood* (New York, 1920). (V, 3; IX, 3.)

Felton, Ralph E. *Serving the Neighborhood* (New York, 1920). (V, 3; VI, 1.)

Jones, Thomas Jesse. *The Sociology of a New York City Block*, "Columbia University Studies in History, Economics, and Public Law," Vol. XXI (New York, 1904).
A minute cross-section of a congested urban block. (VI; VII, 2, 4, 5; VIII; IX, i, 3.)

McKenzie, R. D. *The Neighborhood: A Study of Local Life in Columbus, Ohio* (Chicago, 1923).
An excellent study of local groupings. (V, 1, 3; VII, 1, 2, 4, 5.)

Perry, Clarence A. "The Relation of Neighborhood Forces to the Larger Community: Planning a City Neighborhood from the Social Point of View," *Proceedings of the National Conference of Social Work* (Chicago, 1924), pp. 415–21. (V, 2, 3; VII, 5.)

White, Bouck. *The Free City: A Book of Neighborhood* (New York, 1919).
A fantastic, sentimental picture of what city life might become if the author's views of social organization were a reality. (V, 3, 5; IX, 1, 2, 3.)

Williams, James M. *Our Rural Heritage; the Social Psychology of Rural Development* (New York, 1925).
A book which has as its subject matter the analysis of rural life in New York State up to about the middle of the last century. Chapter iii deals with the distinction between neighborhood and community. (V, 3; X, 1, 2, 3.)

3. The local community and the neighborhood in a simple form of society are synonymous terms. In the city, however, where specialization has gone very far, the grouping of the population is more nearly by occupation and income than by kinship or common tradition. Nevertheless, in the large American city, in particular, we find many local communities made up of immigrant groups which retain a more or less strong sense of unity, expressing itself in close proximity and, what is more important, in separate and common social institutions and highly effective communal control. These communities may live in relative isolation from each other or from the native communities. The location of these communities is determined by competition, which can finally be expressed in terms of land values and rentals. But these immigrant communities, too, are in a constant process of change, as the economic condition of the inhabitants changes or as the areas in which they are located change.

Besant, Walter. *East London* (London, 1912).
    A remarkable account of an isolated community in a metropolis. (V, 1; VII, 2; IX, 1, 2, 3, 4.)

Buchner, Eberhard. *Sekten und Sektierer in Berlin*, Vol. VI in "Grossstadt Dokumente" (Berlin, 1904).
    An intimate account of the habitat of the many obscure religious sects that congregate in local communities in the large city. (VII, 2; IX, 2, 3, 4.)

Burke, Thomas. *Twinkletoes: A Tale of Chinatown* (London, 1917).
    A romantic account of London's Chinatown. (VII, 2.)

Daniels, John. *In Freedom's Birthplace* (Boston and New York, 1914).
    The Negro community in Boston. (VII, 2.)

Dreiser, Theodore. *The Color of a Great City* (New York, 1923).
    The various aspects of city life by an observer with keen insight and rare literary genius. (IX, 2, 4.)

Dunn, Arthur W. *The Community and the Citizen* (Boston, 1909).
    An elementary textbook in civics. Gives a simple presentation of the concept community. (V, 3, 2; I 4; II, 3; IV, 3; VI.)

Eldridge, Seba. *Problems of Community Life: An Outline of Applied Sociology* (New York, 1915).
    A sociological textbook dealing with the various phases of community organization and disorganization. (V, 2, 4, 5; VI, VII, 5; VIII; IX, 3.)

Hebble, Charles Ray, and Goodwin, Frank P. *The Citizens Book* (Cincinnati, 1916).
  Discusses the foundations of community life, its cultural activities, business interests, governmental activities, and gives suggestions on the future city. (VI, 7; IX, 3.)

Jenks, A. E. "Ethnic Census in Minneapolis," *Amer. Jour. Sociol.*, XVII (1912), 776–82.
  The ethnic groupings in a large city.

Jewish Community of New York City: The Jewish Communal Register of New York City (New York, 1917–18).
  A collection of studies on the organization, size, distribution, history, and activities of the New York Jewish Community. (VII, 2, 3, 4, 5; IX, 3, 4.)

Katcher, Leopold (pseudonym, "Spektator"). *Berliner Klubs*, Vol. XXV in "Grosstadt Dokumente" (Berlin, 1905).
  An inside view of club life in Berlin. (VI, 6; IX, 1, 2, 3, 4.)

Lucas, Edw. V. *The Friendly Town: A Little Book for the Urbane* (New York, 1906). (V, 1; IX, 2, 3.)

Maciver, R. M. *Community; a Sociological Study, Being an Attempt to Set Out the Nature and Fundamental Laws of Social Life* (London, 1917).
  Distinguishes between natural areas and communities, showing how occupational and cultural groupings enter into the political process. (IV, 3; V, 1, 2, 4; VI, 7.)

Maurice, Arthur Bartlett. *The New York of the Novelists* (New York, 1916).
  The New York as seen through the eyes of literary men.

Park, Robert E., and Miller, H. A. *Old-World Traits Transplanted* (New York, 1921).
  A study of immigrant communities. (VII, 2, 5; IX, 3, 4.)

Sears, C. H. "The Clash of Contending Forces in Great Cities," *Biblical World*, XLVIII (October, 1916), 224–31. (VII, 5; IX, 1, 3.)

Symposium, "The Greatest Negro Community in the World," *Survey Graphic*, LIII (March 1, 1925), No. 11.
  A collection of articles on the Negro community in Harlem, New York. (VII, 2, 3; IX, 1, 3, 4; X 1.)

Williams, Fred V. *The Hop-Heads: Personal Experiences among the Users of "Dope" in the San Francisco Underworld* (San Francisco, 1920). (VII, 2; IX, 3, 4.)

4. The city may be graphically depicted in terms of a series of concentric circles, representing the different zones or typical areas

of settlement. At the center we find the business district, where land values are high. Surrounding this there is an area of deterioration, where the slums tend to locate themselves. Then follows an area of workmen's homes, followed in turn by the middle-class apartment section, and finally by the upper-class residential area. Land values, general appearance, and function divide these areas off from each other. These differences in structure and use get themselves incorporated in law in the form of zoning ordnances. This is an attempt, in the face of the growth of the city, to control the ecological forces that are at work.

Cheney, C. H. "Removing Social Barriers by Zoning," *Survey*, XLIV (May, 1922), 275–78. (V, 1, 5; VII, 2.)

Eberstadt, Rudolph. *Handbuch des Wohnungswesens und der Wohnungsfrage* (4th ed.; Jena, 1910).
An encyclopedic work on housing, city-zoning, and planning. (VI, 1, 2, 3, 6, 7, 8, 9, 10; VII.)

Kern, Robert R. *The Supercity: A Planned Physical Equipment for City Life* (Washington, D.C., 1924).
A planned model city with co-operative services of many sorts, with zoning as an important feature. (V, 5; VI.)

Wuttke, R. *Die deutschen Städte* (2 vols.; Leipzig, 1904).
A collection of articles on various technical phases of city life. Article 4, "Die Baupolizei," by Oberbaukommissar Gruner, is a discussion of the public regulation of buildings and the function of zoning and building codes in the modern city. (VI; VII, 3; VII, 1, 2.)

In addition there are available reports of zoning commissions of the various cities and numerous articles in magazines dealing with the administrative aspects of city life, such as *The American City*, in which digests, criticisms, and discussions of these zoning devices may be found.

5. The needs of communal life impose upon the city a certain degree of order which sometimes expresses itself in a city plan which is an attempt to predict and to guide the physical structure of the city. The older European cities appear more like haphazard, un-

planned products of individualistic enterprise than the American cities with their checkerboard form. And yet, most European cities were built according to some preconceived plan which attempted to take account of the needs of the community and the limitations of the environment. There is a tendency, however, for the city to run counter to the plan which was laid out for it, as is seen, for instance, in the problems of city-planning of the city of Washington. The fact is that the city is a dynamic mechanism which cannot be controlled in advance unless the conditions entering into its genesis and its growth are fully known. City-planning, which has grown into a highly technical profession, is coming to be more concerned with studying the problems of a changing institution, with city growth, and the forces operating in city life than with the creation of artistic schemes of city structure. On the one hand the importance of devising a scheme of wholesome, orderly existence in the city is being recognized, on the other hand, the limitations of any attempt to make the city conform to an artificial plan impresses itself upon the experience of the technicians engaged in this work.

Agache, Auburtin and Redont. *Comment reconstruire nos cités destruites*, reviewed in *Scott. Geog. Mag.*, XXXIII, 348–52, and *Annales de Geog.*, January, 1917, by F. Schrader.
   A criticism of suggested plans for the reconstruction of cities in the French devastated area. (III, 6.)

American Institute of Architects. *City-Planning Progress in the United States* (New York, 1917).

Bartlett, Dana W. *The Better City: A Sociological Study of a Modern City* (Los Angeles, 1907). (III, 6.)

English Catalogue, "International Cities and Town-Planning Exhibition, Gothenburg, Sweden, 1923."
   A comprehensive summary of the town-planning movement. A work to be consulted by all students of the subject. (II, 3; V, 4.)

Geddes, P. *Cities in Evolution: An Introduction to the Town-Planning Movement and the Study of Civics* (London, 1915).
   An introductory statement by the foremost authority in England. (II; III; IV, 2; V, 4; VI, 3, 5, 6, 9; VII, 1, 2.)

Haverfield, F. J. *Ancient Town Planning* (Oxford, 1913). (II, 1; III, 6.)

Hughes, W. R. *New Town: A Proposal in Agricultural, Industrial, Educational, Civic, and Social Reconstruction* (London, 1919).

Lewis, Nelson P. *The Planning of the Modern City: A Review of the Principles Governing City-Planning* (New York, 1916).

Mulvihill, F. J. "Distribution of Population Graphically Represented as a Basis for City-Planning," *American City*, XX (February, 1919), 159–61. (VII, 2.)

Purdom, C. B. *The Garden City* (London, 1913). (IV, 6.)

Roberts, Kate L. *The City Beautiful: A Study of Town-Planning and Municipal Art* (New York, 1916). (VI, 3, 5, 6.)

Sennett, A. R. *Garden Cities in Theory and Practice* (2 vols.; London, 1905). (III, 6.)

Stote, A. "Ideal American City," *McBride's*, XCVII (April, 1916), 89–99.

Symposium. "Regional Planning," *Survey Graphic*, May 1, 1925.
   Contains a series of suggestive articles on various aspects of city growth and city-planning. (V, 5; VII, 1, 2, 3; III, 6.)

Tout, T. F. *Medieval Town-Planning* (London, 1907). (II, 2; III, 6.)

Triggs, H. Inigo. *Town Planning* (London, 1909).

VI. THE CITY AS A PHYSICAL MECHANISM

The aggregation of large numbers of human beings within a restricted area, as is represented by the modern city, makes possible, and at the same time makes imperative, the communal effort to satisfy certain essential needs of all the inhabitants. The manner in which these needs are met has become institutionalized. The facilities which have been created to meet these needs make up the physical structure of the city as a social mechanism.

1. The need for uninterrupted water supply, fuel, and light have brought it about that the means of satisfying these wants are either in the hands of the city as a corporate body, or, if in private hands, are controlled and regulated by the city government. These public utilities are of interest to the sociologist only in so far as they have a bearing on group life and call forth attitudes, sentiments, and behav-

ior which influences the group. These factors may have an important relation to the ecological organization of the city, and may furnish indexes to the selective and distributive processes which result in the grouping of the population. The lighting of the city may have a direct bearing on the crime of the city, the water supply, on the health, etc. The regulation of public utilities may become issues at elections and call forth factionalism, thus bringing into play the social groupings in the community.

Fassett, Charles M. *Assets of the Ideal City* (New York, 1922).
 A brief statement of various structural aspects of the city, with a bibliography. (V, 4, 5; VI.)

Grahn, E. "Die städtischen Wasserwerke," in Wuttke, *Die Deutschen Städte* (Leipzig, 1904), pp. 301–44.
 A statement of the water-supply problem in German cities.

Höffner, C. "Die Gaswerke," in Wuttke, *Die Deutschen Städte* (Leipzig, 1904), pp. 198–238.
 A statement of the evolution and present status of the technique of gas supply in the modern city.

Jephson, H. L. *The Sanitary Evolution of London* (London, 1907). (VI.)

Kübler, Wilhelm. "Über städtische Elektrizitätswerke," in Wuttke, *Die Deutschen Städte*, pp. 239–300.
 An account of the municipal electricity works in German cities.

Most books on the modern city contain a chapter on public utilities, and a great many technical journals and municipal reports are accessible giving detailed accounts of various aspects of both the technical, the administrative, and the functional sides of the public utility situation.

2. One of the most characteristic features of city life is the high degree of intercommunication. This is made possible by technical devices, such as the telephone, street cars, and the automobile. While the sociologist has no intrinsic interest in these technical devices, they become an object of study as factors entering, for instance, into the problem of mobility of the city population.

D'Avenel, G. le Vicomte. *Le Mécanisme de la Vie moderne* (3 vols.; Paris, 1922).
Among many other aspects of the city as a physical mechanism, has a chapter on publicity, urban transportation, and communication. This work has gone through many editions and is written in a popular style. (VI; IX, 1.)

Harris, Emerson Pitt. *The Community Newspaper* (New York, 1923). (IX, 3.)

Kingsbury, J. E. *The Telephone and Telephone Exchanges: Their Invention and Development* (London and New York, 1915).

Lewis, H. M., and Goodrich, E. P. *Highway Traffic in New York and Its Environs* (New York, 1924).
The results of a study embodied in a report for the Committee on a Regional Plan for New York and its Environs. (IV, 2; V, 4, 5; VI, 2; VII, 2, 4.)

Park, Robert E. *The Immigrant Press and Its Control* (New York, 1922).
A study of the organization and the influence of the press in the immigrant communities of the large city (IX, 3.)

The municipal transportation and communication question has developed a large literature which is to be found in many separate works on the telephone, telegraph, radio, street-car systems, busses, automobile, mail service, newspaper, and railways as well as in municipal reports, technical and administrative journals, and textbooks on the city.

3. The existence of streets, pavement, alleys, sewers, and other devices of the same sort that characterize the city as a physical mechanism influence the behavior of the person and the group, and as such are of interest to the sociologist.

Hirschfeld, Magnus. *Die Gurgel Berlins*, Vol. XLI in "Grossstadt Dokumente" (Berlin, 1905).
A study of the main street of Berlin from the standpoint of its effect on the individual and as a revelation of city life. (VI, 2; VII, 2, 4.)

Quaife, Milo Milton. *Chicago's Highways, Old and New* (Chicago, 1923).
The changes wrought in the character of the city as viewed from the point of view of the streets. (VI, 2; VII, 1, 2.)

Whipple, G. C. "Economical and Sanitary Problems of American Cities," *American City* (February, 1921), p. 112. (VI.)

4. The many devices in the realm of public safety and welfare which are the characteristic product of the city, such as fire depart-

ment, police, health inspection, and the manifold activities of the social agencies concern the sociologist as typical expressions of group life in the city environment.

Addams, Jane. *Twenty Years at Hull House; With Autobiographical Notes* (New York, 1910).
> City life as seen in a typical social agency—the social settlement. (V, 2, 3; VII, 5.)

Assessor (pseudonym). *Die Berliner Polizei*, Vol. XXXIV in "Grossstadt Dokumente" (Berlin, 1905).
> A personal account of the police force of the modern city. (IX, 1.)

Anonymous. *Berliner Gerichte*, Vol. XXIV in "Grossstadt Dokumente" (Berlin, 1905).
> Daily experiences in a typical city court.

Carbaugh, H. C. *Human Welfare Work in Chicago* (Chicago, 1917).
> A brief account of the various specialized social agencies operating in the large city. (VII, 5; IX, 1.)

Fitzpatrick, Edward A. *Interrelationships of Hospital and Community*, reprint from *Modern Hospital*, February, 1925. Pamphlet.
> A sketch of the possible place and nature of a health agency in a modern urban community.

Fosdick, Raymond, and Associates. *Criminal Justice in Cleveland*, directed and edited by Roscoe Pound and Felix Frankfurter (Cleveland, 1922). (VI, 7.)

Fosdick, Raymond B. *European Police Systems* (New York, 1915).
———. *American Police Systems* (New York, 1920).

Harrison, Shelby M. *Public Employment Offices; Their Purpose, Structure, and Method* (New York, 1924). (IX, 1.)

Richmond, Mary E. *The Good Neighbor in the Modern City* (Philadelphia and London, 1913).
> Suggestions to the layman about the social agencies and their work in the large modern city. (V, 2, VII, 5.)

Wilson, Warren H. *The Evolution of the Country Community: A Study in Religious Sociology* (Boston, New York, Chicago, 1912).
> Gives types of organizations and institutions. (V, 3; X, 2.)

In almost every large city the number of social agencies and public institutions is so large and their work so varied that directories of these agencies have been made available. In addition, reports and surveys of many cities are at hand, and the periodical literature is tremendous.

5. The cultural needs of the community find expression in the city in the form of schools, theaters, museums, parks, monuments, and other public enterprises. They exert an influence extending beyond the boundaries of the city itself, and may be regarded as agencies for the definition of the person's wishes. They are indicative of the level of social life which the community has achieved.

Carroll, Charles E. *The Community Survey in Relation to Church Efficiency* (New York, 1915).
  Typical of studies bearing on the place of religious and cultural agencies in city life. (X, 2.)
  For a basic statement of the problem of education in the modern city, compare Dewey, John, *Democracy and Education* (New York, 1916).

Moore, E. C. "Provision for the Education of the City Child," *School and Society*, III (February 19, 1916), 265–72.

Phelan, J. J. *Motion Pictures as a Phase of Commercialized Amusement in Toledo, Ohio* (Toledo, Ohio, 1919).

Tews, Johannes. *Berliner Lehrer*, Vol. XX in "Grossstadt Dokumente" (Berlin, 1905).
  An intimate study of a professional group in the large city. (IX, 1.)

Trawick, Arcadius McSwain. *The City Church and Its Social Mission* (New York, 1913).

Turszinsky, Walter. *Berliner Theater*, Vol. XXIX of "Grossstadt Dokumente" (Berlin, 1905). (III, 4; V, 1; VI, 6.)

Ward, Edward J. *The Social Center* (New York and London, 1915). (VI, 6; VII, 5.)

6. The leisure-time activities which the city produces are so intimately connected with the life of the people that they furnish clues as to the pathology or disorganization typical of city life. The dance hall, the movie, the amusement park, the back-yard or vacant lot improvised playground, and the many other forms of public,

commercialized, or improvised recreation facilities are phases of group life which cannot escape the sociologist.

Arndt, Arno. *Berliner Sport*, Vol. X in "Grossstadt Dokumente" (Berlin, 1905).
Describes various specialized, institutionalized, and commercialized forms of sport life in Berlin. (IX, 2, 4.)

Bowman, LeRoy E., and Lambin, Maria Ward. "Evidences of Social Relations as Seen in Types of New York City Dance Halls," *Jour. Social Forces*, III (January, 1925), 286–91. (IX, 2, 3, 4.)

Buchner, Eberhard. *Berliner Variétés und Tingeltangel*, Vol. XXII in "Grossstadt Dokumente" (Berlin, 1905).
Analysis of various types of the variété, cabaret, and burlesque, and the development of these institutions in the city. (IX, 1, 3, 4.)

Günther, Viktor. *Petersbourg s'amuse*, Vol. XXXII in "Grossstadt Dokumente" (Berlin, 1905).
The recreational activities of the Russian capital. (III, 4; V, 1; IX, 2.)

Herschmann, Otto. *Wiener Sport*, Vol. XII in "Grossstadt Dokumente" (Berlin, 1905).
Describes the recreational activities of the dominant population groups in Vienna. (IX, 4.)

Ostwald, H. O. A. *Berliner Kaffeehäuser*, Vol. VII in "Grossstadt Dokumente" (Berlin, 1905).
Human behavior in the coffee-houses of Berlin. (IX, 1, 4.)
———. *Berliner Tanzlokale*, Vol. IV in "Grossstadt Dokumente" (Berlin, 1905).
Intimate glimpses of the diverse types of dance halls and their habitués. (V, 2, 3; VII, 5; IX, 1, 4.)

Phelan, John J. *Pool, Billiards, and Bowling Alleys as a Phase of Commercialized Amusement in Toledo* (Toledo, 1919). (VII, 5).

Rhodes, H. "City Summers," *Harper's*, CXXXI (June, 1915), 2–15.
The seasonal aspects of city recreation.

7. The city government shows, perhaps more clearly than many other phases of city life, the extent to which the city has revolutionized social life and has changed the habits and attitudes of the people. In the city government we can see the various local, national, cultural, and interest groups attempting to exert their

influence. In the city we see the political boss as a typical product of an anomalous situation. Here we find such phenomena as non-voting, the clash between local and occupational groups, and many other disharmonies between the needs of the people and the institutions that are present to satisfy them.

Bruere, Henry. *The New City Government* (New York, 1913).
A study of the commission form of government in cities.

Capes, William Parr. *The Modern City and Its Government* (New York, 1922).

Clerk (pseudonym). *Berliner Beamte*, Vol. XLIII in "Grossstadt Dokumente" (Berlin, 1905).
A study of the types of civil servants developed by modern city government. (IX, 1, 2, 4.)

Cleveland, Frederick A. *Chapters on Municipal Administration and Accounting* (New York, 1909 and 1915).

Cummin, G. C. "Will the City-Manager Form of Government Fit All Cities—Large Cities—Machine-Controlled Cities?" *National Municipal Rev.*, VII (May, 1918), 276–81.

Ely, Richard T. *The Coming City* (New York, 1902).
An address taking up some of the problems connected with the government, public interest in administration, and corruption in the modern American city. (VII, 5.)

Gilbert, Arthur Benson. *American Cities: Their Methods of Business* (New York, 1918).

Goodnow, Frank J. *City Government in the United States* (New York, 1904 and 1909).

Hill, Howard C. *Community Life and Civic Problems* (New York, 1922).
An elementary textbook for community civics classes. (V, 3; VI.)

McKenzie, R. D. "Community Forces: A Study of the Non-Partisan Municipal Elections in Seattle," *Journal of Social Forces* (January, March, May, 1924).
A study of the relation between local groupings and political attitudes. (IV, 3; V, 1, 2, 3; VII, 5; IX, 3.)

Munro, W. B. *Municipal Government and Administration* (New York, 1923). (II, 3; IV, 3; VII, 1.)

———. *The Government of American Cities* (3d ed.; New York, 1921).
A standard textbook on city government in the United States. By the same author, a companion volume, *The Government of European Cities*. (VI, 7; IV, 3.)

Odum, Howard W. *Community and Government: A Manual of Discussion and Study of the Newer Ideals of Citizenship* (Chapel Hill, North Carolina, 1921).

Steffens, Lincoln. *The Shame of the Cities* (New York, 1907).
An exposure of corruption in city governments. (VII, 5.)

Toulmin, Harry A. *The City Manager: A New Profession* (New York, 1915). (IX, 1.)

Weber, G. A. *Organized Efforts for the Improvement of Methods of Administration in the United States* (New York and London, 1919).

Weyl, Walter E. "The Brand of the City," *Harper's*, CXXX (April, 1915), 769–75.

Wilcox, Delos F. *Great Cities in America: Their Problems and Their Government* (New York, 1910). (IV, 3; VI; VII, 1, 5.)

Zueblin, Charles. *A Decade of Civic Development* (Chicago, 1905).
A discussion of the state of American city civilization at the beginning of the twentieth century. (V, 4, 5; VI; VII, 1; VIII, 1.)

8. The complexity, specialization, and dependence of the city are seen clearly in the methods by which the city gets its food supply and other vital necessities for the existence of the population. The food trains, milk trains, cattle trains, the miles of refrigerator cars and coal cars that daily enter the large city, the warehouses and the stores, the countless delivery wagons that line the streets—all these are evidence of what a tremendously complex and efficient organization has grown up to meet the urgent wants, the desires for subsistence and for luxury of our millions of city-dwellers. Here too we sometimes see examples of what anxiety and what calamity might result from the slightest interruption or dislocation in the methods of supplying the city with these varied specialties. The department store and the chain store are characteristic city institutions, corresponding to the grouping of the city population.

Colze, Leo. *Berliner Warenhäuser*, Vol. XLVII in "Grossstadt Dokumente" (Berlin, 1905).
Berlin stores. (III, 4; IV, 1; V, 1; IX, 1.)

Loeb, Moritz. *Berliner Konfektionen*, Vol. XV in "Grossstadt Dokumente" (Berlin, 1905).
Ready-made clothing establishments. (V, 1, 4; IX, 1.)

Parker, Horatio Newton. *City Milk Supply* (New York, 1917). (IV, 1.)

Shideler, E. H. "The Business Center as an Institution," *Jour. Appl. Sociol.*,
IX (March, April, 1925), 269–75.
An outline of the local trade center in the urban community and its significance in
city life. (IV, 1; V, 1 2, 3; VII, 1, 2.)

9. One of the latest phases of city development is the direct
result of the invention of a new technique of building. Steel construction has made possible the skyscraper, the elevated railroad,
and the subway, and thus introduced a new dimension into city
growth. This new technique has made possible a density, per unit
of ground surface, which has given the city an entirely new complexion. The full effects of this new invention are still not fully known.

Holborn, I. B. S. "The City: The Outer Expression of an Inner Self," *Art
World*, III (December, 1917), 217–21. (III, 1; IX, 2.)

Mumford, Lewis. *Sticks and Stones: A Study of American Civilization* (New
York, 1925).
An evaluation and critique of the architectural aspects of American cities and their
cultural significance. (V, 5; VI, 9; X, 2.)

Nichols, C. M. (editor). *Studies on Building-Height Limitations in Large Cities*
(Chicago, 1923).
Written from the point of view of the real-estate profession.

Schumacher, Fritz. "Architektonische Aufgaben der Städte," in Wuttke, *Die
Deutschen Städte*, pp. 47–66.
Discussion of the changing needs and methods in urban construction.

The literature on the significance of the steel-construction technique is still very small. The professional engineers and architects
have contributed some to their journals, but the interpretation of
their contributions is still to be made.

10. Land values are the chief determining influence in the
segregation of local areas and in the determination of the uses to
which an area is to be put. Land values also determine more
specifically the type of building that is to be erected in a given area
—whether it shall be a tenement house, an office building, a factory,

or a single dwelling—what buildings shall be razed, and what buildings are to be repaired. The technique of determining city land values has developed into a highly specialized and well-paid profession. Land values are so potent a selective factor that the human ecologist will find in them a very accurate index to many phases of city life.

Aronovici, Carol. *Housing and the Housing Problem* (Chicago, 1921).
    A study of the relation between rent, income, and housing.

Arner, G. B. L. "Urban Land Economics," in volume, *Urban Land Economics*, Institute for Research in Land Economics (Ann Arbor, Michigan, 1922).
    Gives a summary of land values in New York City and an outline of the subject. (VII, 1, 2.)

George, W. L. *Labor and Housing at Port Sunlight* (London, 1909). (III, 4, 6; V, 4, 5; IX, 1.)

"Housing and Town Planning," *Ann. Amer. Acad.*, LI (January, 1914), 1–264.
    An excellent collection of authoritative articles on housing, city planning, city land values, transportation, and government. (III, 6; IV, 1, 2, 3; V; VII; VIII.)

Hull House Maps and Papers (New York, 1895).
    A presentation of nationalities and wages in a congested district of Chicago together with comments and essays on problems growing out of the social conditions. (VII, 2, 3, 4, 5; IX, 3.)

Hunter, Robert. *Tenement Conditions in Chicago: Report by the Investigating Committee of the City Homes Association* (Chicago, 1901). (VII, 5.)

Hurd, Richard M. *Principles of City Land Values* (New York, 1924).
    Land valuation on the basis of city growth. Shows that the coming of the automobile, making available large tracts for residential purposes, the radio, and other devices for intercommunication have not materially changed the general principles of city growth. Contains maps and photographs showing foot-front values for various cities and land utilization. (VII, 1, 4; VI, 2.)

Morehouse, E. W., and Ely, R. T. *Elements of Land Economics* (New York, 1924).
    An introduction to land valuation. Chapter vi, on urban land utilization. (VII, 1, 2; X, 2.)

McMichael, Stanley L., and Bingham, Robert F. *City Growth and Values* (Cleveland, 1923).
    An authoritative statement. (VII, 1.)

Olcott, George C. *Olcott's Land Value Maps* (annually, Chicago, 1909–25).
Valuations of Chicago real estate.

Pratt, Edward Ewing. *Industrial Causes of Congestion of Population in New York City* (New York, 1911).
Contains an excellent bibliography. (III, 4; V, 1, 2, 4, 5; VI, 2, 3; VII, 1, 2, 3, 4, 5.)

Reeve, Sidney A. "Congestion in Cities," *Geog. Rev.*, III (1917), 278–93.
Regards congestion as a growing menace to public health and social stability, and analyzes the causes and suggests remedies. (V, 4, 5; VI; VII, 1, 2, 5; VIII 1.)

Riis, Jacob A. *How the Other Half Lives: Studies among the Tenements of New York* (New York, 1890 and 1914).
This together with his other book, *The Battle with the Slum* (New York, 1892), has done much to call public attention to the tenement problem of the large American city and to invite remedial legislation. (V, 1, 2, 4, 5; VII, 1, 2, 5.)

Schumacher, F. "Probleme der Grossstadt," *Deutsche Rundschau für Geog.*, CXXC (July 5, 1919), 66–81, 262–85, 416–29. (V; VI, VII; VIII.)

Smythe, William Ellsworth. *City Homes on Country Lanes: Philosophy and Practice of the Home-in-a-Garden* (New York, 1921). (V, 5.)

Stella, A. *"The Effects of Urban Congestion on Italian Women and Children,"* *Medical Record*, LXXIII (New York, 1908), 722–32. (V, 1, 3; VIII, 1.)

Südekum, Albert. *Grossstädtisches Wohnungselend*, Vol. XLV in "Grossstadt Dokumente" (Berlin, 1905).
A description of a typical tenement area in the European city and its effects on human behavior. (VII, 5; IX, 3.)

Veiller, Lawrence. "The Housing Problem in America," *Ann. Amer. Academy*, XXV (1905), 248–75.
In this article, as well as in his later works (for instance, *Housing Reform* (New York, 1910), the writer, who has been regarded as one of the foremost housing students in America, outlines some of the social consequences of bad housing in the modern city and questions the adequacy of democratic form of government in the slum areas. (V; IX, 3.)

VII. THE GROWTH OF THE CITY

The growth of the city has been described as the outstanding characteristic of modern civilization. The sociologist is interested in the processes underlying this phenomenon.

1. One of the most obvious phases of this growth is the addition in numbers and the expansion in area of the city. This has been

accurately measured by the statisticians and geographers. The typical process of expansion is from the core of the city outward toward the periphery. While ample materials for such studies of processes exist, their interpretation and analysis is yet to be undertaken. In the process of growth the city tends to become empty, as concerns habitations, at the center. This phenomenon is referred to as "city-building."

Ballard, W. J. "Our Twenty-nine Largest Cities, *Jour. Educ.*, XXCIII (April 27, 1916), 468.

Bassett, E. M. "Distribution of Population in Cities," *American City*, XIII (July, 1915), 7–8.

Bernhard, H. "Die Entvölkerung des Landes," *Deutsche Rundschau für Geog.*, XXXVII (1914–15), 563–67.

Of twenty-one countries examined, all showed an increase in urban population between 1880–1910, in most cases far exceeding the natural increase in population, and a decrease in percentage of rural population. (VII, 3; VIII, 1; X, 2.)

Brown, Robert M. "City Growth and City Advertising" (Abstract of paper read at 1921 Conference of American Geographers), *Ann. Assoc. Amer. Geog.*, XII (1922), 155.

A discussion of the causes of growth of American cities with an analysis of the one hundred cities showing the largest gains since 1910. Classification as to type of advertising campaigns used.

Bushee, F. A. "The Growth of Population of Boston," *Pub. Amer. Statistical Assoc.*, VI (1899), 239–74. (VIII, 3.)

City-Building: A Citation of Methods in Use in More Than One Hundred Cities for the Solution of Important Problems in the Progressive Growth of the American Municipality (Cincinnati, 1913). (V, 4, 5; VI; VII, 5.)

"City Growth by Dead Reckoning," *Literary Digest*, XXCII (August 9, 1924), 12.

Fawcett, C. B. "British Conurbations in 1921," *Sociol. Rev.*, XIV (April, 1922), 111–22.

Feather, W. A. "Cities That Make Good," *Forum*, LVII (May, 1917), 623–28.

Gregory, W. M. "Growth of the Cities of Washington," *Jour. Geog.*, XIV (May, 1916), 348–53. (VII, 3.)

"How Big Should a City Be?" *Literary Digest*, LI (August 28, 1915), 399–400.

James, Edmund J. "The Growth of Great Cities," *Ann. Amer. Academy*, XIII (1899), 1–30. (VII, 2, 3.)

Traces the growth of the cities and the genesis of the problems connected with it.

Jefferson, Mark. "Great Cities of the United States in 1920," *Geog. Rev.*, XI (July, 1921), 437–41.

Martell, P. "Die Bevölkerungsentwicklung der Stadt Berlin," *Allgemeines Statistisches Archiv*, X (1917), 207–15. (VII, 3; VIII, 1.)

Püschel, Alfred. *Das Anwachsen der Deutschen Städte in der Zeit der mittelalterlichen Kolonialbewegung* (Berlin, 1910).

Contains fifteen city plans. Traces the growth of cities in the medieval period and the changes in city structure. (II, 2; VII, 2.)

Ridgley, D. C. "Sixty-eight Cities of the United States in 1920," *Jour. Geog.*, XX (February, 1921), 75–79.

One of a series of postcensus-report analyses of the growth of the urban population.

Roth, Lawrence V. "The Growth of American Cities," *Geog. Rev.*, V (May, 1918), 384–98.

Holds that the growth of the cities of the United States has passed through four periods, each of which in its turn was the response to the commercial and industrial development of a new geographical region. Distinguishes between site and situation in city growth, and is here concerned mainly with general situation as a contributory influence. (III, 2, 3, 4.)

Sedlaczek. "Die Bevölkerungszunahme der Grossstädte im XIX Jahrhundert und deren Ursachen," *Report of the Eighth International Congress of Hygiene and Demography* (Budapest, 1894). (VII, 3; VIII, 1; X, 1.)

United States Bureau of the Census. *A Century of Population Growth* (Washington, 1909). (VII, 3; VIII; X, 2.)

United States Bureau of the Census. *Population: Fourteenth Census of the United States* (3 vols.; Washington, 1920). (VII, 3; VIII, 1, 2, IX; 1, X, 2.)

Van Cleef, E. "How Big Is Your Town?" *American City*, XVII (November, 1917), 471–73.

Weber, Adna Ferrin. *The Growth of Cities in the Nineteenth Century: A Study in Statistics*, "Columbia University Studies in History, Economics, and Public Law" (New York, 1899).

Besides being the most important book on the growth of the city from a statistical standpoint, it contains many other features of great value to the student of the city, especially of the influence of the urban environment on the population. (VII, 2, 3; VIII.)

"Why Cities Grow," *Literary Digest*, LVIII (August 17, 1918), 22–23.

Zahn, F. "Die Volkszählung von 1900 und die Grossstadtfrage," *Jahrbuch für Nationalokonomie und Statistik*, XXCI (1903), 191–215. (VII, 3.)

2. Every addition in numbers and expansion of the city area is accompanied by the redistribution and re-allocation of the whole population. Some elements are given a new locus, while others shift but little as a result of the stimulus incident to the arrival of new-comers. This redistribution of the city population has become a constantly operating process in view of the constant growth of the city either through natural increase of the population or through migration from without.

Allison, Thomas W. "Population Movements in Chicago," *Jour. of Social Forces*, II (May, 1924), 529–33. (V, 1, 3; VII, 4.)

Aurousseau, M. "Distribution of Population: A Constructive Problem," *Geog. Rev.*, XI (October, 1921), 568–75.
"Density concerns itself with the number of people per unit of area; distribution deals with the comparative study of density from area to area; and arrangement considers the way in which people are grouped. Grouping is the fundamental concept . . . ." (I, 1; IV, 1; X, 2.)

Bushee, F. A. "Ethnic Factors in the Population of Boston," *Pub. Amer. Statistical Assoc.*, Vol. IV, No. 2, pp. 307–477. (V, 1, 2, 3.)

Douglas, H. Paul. *The Suburban Trend* (New York, 1925).
Traces the movement toward decentralization in the larger American urban communities. (VII, 2, 1, 4; IV, 2; III, 5; V, 4.)

Hirschfeld, Magnus. *Berlins drittes Geschlecht*, Vol. III in "Grossstadt Dokumente" (Berlin, 1905).
A study of the homosexuals in Berlin as a sample of the grouping of population in the large city. (V, 1, 3; VII, 5.)

Hooker, G. E. "City-Planning and Political Areas," *Nat. Mun. Rev.*, VI (May, 1917), 337–45. (IV, 3; V, 1, 4, 5; VI, 7.)

The London Society. *The London of the Future* (New York and London, 1921).
An excellent view of the processes bringing about the allocation of the population and the trend of growth of the city from the core pressing outward toward the periphery. (II, 3; III, 1, 5, 6; IV; V; VI; VII; VIII, 1, 2, 3; IX, 1, 2, 3, 4.)

Ripley, W. Z. "Racial Geography of Europe," *Popular Science Monthly*, LII (1898), 591–608; XIV, "Urban Problems." See also his "Races of Europe," chap. xx, on "Ethnic Stratification and Urban Selection." (V, 3.)

Salten, Felix. *Wiener Adel*, Vol. XIV in "Grossstadt Dokumente" (Berlin, 1905).

Shows the local grouping of the nobility in the large European city. (IX, 4.)

Schmid, Herman. *City bildung und Bevölkerungsverteilung in Grossstädten: Ein Beitrag zur Entwicklungsgeschichte des modernen Städtewesens* (München, 1909).

Shows that the normal process of growth of the city is by emptying at the center, and redistributing its population around the periphery. (Compare Mark Jefferson, "The Anthropography of Some Great Cities: A Study in Distribution of Population," *Bull. Amer. Geog. Soc.*, XLI (1909), 537–66. (VII, 4, 5.)

Williams, James M. *An American Town: A Sociological Study* (New York, 1906).

Primarily an analysis of an American community from a socio-psychological standpoint. Contains some interesting facts on growth and distribution of population. (III, 5; V, 1, 2, 3; IX, 1, 3.)

Winter, Max. *Im unterirdischen Wien*, Vol. XIII in "Grossstadt Dokumente" (Berlin, 1905).

A description of Vienna, showing the processes of segregation, allocation, and communication at work in the city population. (V, 1; VI, 4, 6; VII, 5; IX, 3, 4.)

3. During the latter part of the nineteenth century the expressions, "the flight from the country," and "the drift to the city" began to be heard. The rapid increase in population of the cities was found to be due not to natural increase, i.e., excess of births over deaths, but to migration from the surrounding rural area. In America the rapid increase in the size of the cities was due chiefly to an increasing stream of European immigrants who avoided the farm but were attracted to the urban environment. Population statisticians have been alert to discover whether this process is continuing or whether a change is taking place. Improvements in rural life and conscious efforts to control the movement of population have been observed as to their possible effect on the rural-urban population equilibrium.

Ashby, A. W. "Population and the Land," *Edinburgh Rev.*, CCXXIV (1916), 321–39. (X, 1, 2.)

Ballod, C. "Sterblichkeit und Fortpflanzung der Stadtbevölkerung," *Jahrbuch für Nationalökonomie und Statistik*, XXXIII (1909), 521–41. (VIII, 1, 3.)

Bauer, L. *Der Zug nach der Stadt* (Stuttgart, 1904). Reviewed in *Archiv f. Rassen u. Gesellschaftsbiologie*, II, 300. (VII, 1.)

Beusch, P. *Wanderungen und Stadtkultur: eine bevolkerungspolitische und sozialethische Studie* (München-Gladbach, 1916).

Böckh, R. "Der Anteil der örtlichen Bewegung an der Zunahme der Bevölkerung der Grossstädte," *Congress Intern. d'Hygiène et de Démographie* (Budapest, 1894). (VII, 1.)

Bowley, A. L. "Births and Population in Great Britain," *Econ. Jour.*, XXXIV (June, 1924), 188–92. (VII, 1; VIII, 1.)

Bryce, P. H. "Effects upon Public Health and Natural Prosperity from Rural Depopulation and Abnormal Increase of Cities," *Amer. Jour. Public Health*, New York, V, 48–56. (VIII; X, 1, 2.)

Cacheux, E. "Influence des grandes villes sur la dépopulation," *Rev. Philanthrop.* Paris, XXXVII (1916), 513–18. (VIII; X, 1.)

Dickerman, G. S. "The Drift to the Cities," *Atlantic Monthly*, CXI (1913), 349–53. (IX, 2; X, 1, 2.)

Dittmann, P. *Die Bevölkerungsbewegung der deutschen Grossstädte seit der Gründung des deutschen Reiches* (Bamberg, 1912). (VII, 1.)

Groves, E. R. "Urban Complex: A Study of the Psychological Aspects of the Urban Drift," *Sociol. Rev.*, XII (1920), 73–81. (IX, 2; X, 2.)

Hecke, W. "Volksvermehrung, Binnenwanderung, und Umgangssprache in den österreichischen Alpenländern und Südländern," *Statist. Monatsschr.*, XXXIX (1913), 323–92. (VIII, 1. 3; X, 2.)

Hoaglund, H. E. "The Movement of Rural Population in Illinois," *Jour. Pol. Econ.*, XX (1912), 913–27.

Mayr, G. von. *Die Bevölkerung der Grossstädte*, in "Die Grossstadt" (Dresden, 1903).
  One of the best statements of the problem. (VII, 1, 2; VIII, 1, 2, 3.)

Prinzing, Dr. F. "Die Bevölkerungsentwicklung Stockholms, 1721–1920," *Jahrbuch für Nationalökonomie und Statistik*, XLVII (1924), 87–93.
  An excellent case study of the situation in a modern European city. (VII, 1; X, 1, 2.)

———. "Einheimische und Zugezogene in den Grossstädten," *Zeitschr. für Sozialwiss.*, VII (Berlin, 1904), 660–67.

Ravenstein, E. G. "The Laws of Migration," *Jour. Royal Statist. Soc.*, XLVIII (1885), 167–227. (X, 2.)

Spencer, A. G. "Changing Population of Our Large Cities," *Kindergarten Primary Mag.*, XXIII (1910), 65–71.

Steinhart, A. *Untersuchung zur Gebürtigkeit der deutschen Grossstadtbevölkerung, Entwicklung, und Ursachen,* "Rechts und Staatswissenschaftliche Studien," Heft 45 (Berlin, 1912). (VIII, 1; X, 2.)

Voss, W. "Städtische Kleinsiedlung," *Archiv für exacte Wirtschaftsforschung,* IX (1919), 377–412.

Weisstein, G. "Sind die Städte wirklich Menschenverzehrer?" *Deutsche Städte Ztg.* (1905), pp. 153–54.

4. The mobility of a city population incident to city growth is reflected in the increased number of contacts, changes of movement, changes in appearance, and atmosphere of specific areas due to succession of population groups, and in differences in land values. Mobility implies not mere movement, but fresh stimulation, an increase in number and intensity of stimulants, and a tendency to respond more readily to new stimulation. The process by which the city absorbs and incorporates its own offspring or foreign elements into its life, and what becomes of them, may be referred to as the metabolism of city life. Mobility is an index of metabolism.

Bercovici, Konrad. *Around the World in New York* (New York, 1924).
Discusses the local communities and the sifting process in the large city. (VII, 1, 2; IX, 3; V, 1, 2, 3.)

Digby, E. "The Extinction of the Londoner," *Contemp. Rev.*, London, XXCVI (1904), 115–26. (VII, 2, 3; VIII, 1; IX, 2, 3.)

Herzfeld, Elsa G. *Family Monographs; The History of Twenty-four Families Living in the Middle West Side of New York City* (New York, 1905).
Examples of extreme mobility (tendency to migrate) in the tenement district. (VII, 5.)

Meuriot, P. "Les Migrations internes dans quelques grandes villes," *Jour. Soc. Stat.*, Paris, L (1909), 390. (V, 1; VII, 2.)

Prinzing, F. "Die Bevölkerungsbewegung in Paris und Berlin," *Zeitschr. für Soziale Medizin,* Leipzig, III (1908), 99–120.

212 THE CITY

Stephany, H. "Der Einfluss des Berufes und der Sozialstellung auf die Be-völkerungsbewegung der Grossstädte nachgewiesen an Königsberg i. *Pr.,*" *Königsb. Statist.*, No. 13, 1912. (VII, 2, 3.)

Weleminsky, F. "Über Akklimatisation in Grossstädten," *Archiv für Hygiene,* XXXVI (1899), 66–126. (VII, 3, 5; VIII, 1.)

Woods, Robert A. *Americans in Process: A Settlement Study, North- and West-End Boston* (Boston, 1902). (VII, 2; V, 3; IX, 3.)
Typical of a number of settlement studies giving a view of the effect of the city on its foreign population.

5. City growth may be thought of as a process of disorganization and reorganization. Growth always involves these processes to some extent, but when the city grows rapidly we see the disorganization assuming proportions which may be regarded as pathological. Crime, suicide, divorce, are some of the behavior problems in which social disorganization, when viewed from the personal side, expresses itself. The disappearance of the neighborhood and the local community with its personal forms of control is one of the immediate causal elements in this process.

Addams, Jane. *The Spirit of Youth and the City Streets* (New York, 1909). (V, 1, 2, 3; IX, 3; X, 2.)

Bader, Emil. *Wiener Verbrecher*, Vol. XVI, "Grossstadt Dokumente" (Berlin, 1905). (VI, 4; VII, 5; IX, 4.)

Bonne, G. "Über die Notwendigkeit einer systematischen Dezentralisation unserer Grossstädte in hygienischer, sozialer, und volkswirtschaftlicher Beziehung," *Monatschr. für soz. Med.*, I (Jena, 1904), 369, 425, 490. (V, 5; VIII.)

Buschan, G. H. *Geschlecht und Verbrechen*, Vol. XLVIII, "Grossstadt Doku-mente" (Berlin, 1905).
Some observations on the natural history of the city population. Very fragmentary. (VIII, 2; IX, 3, 4.)

Chalmers, Thomas. *The Christian and Civic Economy of Large Towns* (Glasgow, 1918). (IV, 5; VII; VIII, 1, 4.)

Classen, W. F. *Grossstadt Heimat: Beobachtungen zur Naturgeschichte des Grossstadtvolkes* (Hamburg, 1906).

Classen, W. *Das stadtegeborene Geschlecht und seine Zukunft* (Leipzig, 1914).

Henderson, C. R. "Industry and City Life and the Family," *Amer. Jour. Sociol.*, XIV, 668. (VIII, 1, 2, 3.)

Lasson, Alfred. *Gefährdete und verwahrloste Jugend*, Vol. XLIX, "Grossstadt Dokumente" (Berlin, 1905).
The dangers confronting youth in the city and juvenile delinquency. (IX, 4.)

Marcuse, Max. *Uneheliche Mütter*, Vol. XXVII in "Grossstadt Dokumente" (Berlin, 1905). (VIII, 1, 3; IX, 3.)
Illegitimacy in Berlin. Types of unmarried mothers.

Ostwald, H. O. A. *Das Berliner Spielertum*, Vol. XXXV in "Grossstadt Dokumente" (Berlin, 1905). (VI, 6; IX, 4.)
Gambling in the city.

———. *Zuhältertum in Berlin*, Vol. V, "Grossstadt Dokumente" (Berlin, 1905).
Panderers and their victims in the city. (IX, 1, 4.)

Schuchard, Ernst. *Sechs Monate Arbeitshaus*, Vol. XXXIII in "Grossstadt Dokumente" (Berlin, 1905).
Six months' experiences in the workhouse of the city, where the opportunity to observe social disorganization is great. (VI, 4; IX, 3, 4.)

Sears, Charles H. *The Redemption of the City* (Philadelphia, 1911).

Sharp, Geo. W. *City Life and Its Amelioration* (Boston, 1915).

Steiner, Jesse F. "Theories of Community Organization," *Jour. Social Forces*, III (November, 1924), 30–37. (V; VIII, 3.)

———. "A Critique of the Community Movement," *Jour. App. Sociol.*, IX (November-December, 1924), 108.
Problems of social control in relation to community organization and disorganization. (V; VIII, 3.)

Stelze, Charles. *Christianity's Storm Center: A Study of the Modern City* (New York and Chicago, 1907).

Strong, Josiah. *The Challenge of the City* (New York, 1907).
From a religious and moral standpoint. (X, 1, 2.)

Thomas, W. I., and Znaniecki, Florian. *The Polish Peasant in Europe and America*, Vol. V, "Organization and Disorganization in America" (Boston, 1920). (V, 3; VII, 2.)

"The Tragedy of Great Cities," *Outlook*, CXXVI (1920), 749–50.

Werthauer, Johannes. *Sittlichkeitsdelikte der Grossstadt*, Vol. XL in "Grossstadt Dokumente" (Berlin, 1905).
A collection of typical city delinquencies of the sex type. (V, 4; IX, 4.)

VIII. EUGENICS OF THE CITY

Considerable literature has grown up recently dealing with the biological aspects of city life. Detailed studies as to the effect of city life on the human stock remain to be made. On the basis of the material now available, however, fruitful avenues of research are opened, and certain tentative conclusions may be entertained.

1. The changes incident to city life in the birth, death, and marriage rates of the population are noticeable on the basis of statistics. These phenomena permit of sociological interpretation and analysis. The difference between the urban and the rural span of life offers a similar problem to the investigator. The proportions of the human scrap-heap and its social consequences in the city have been recognized as an important phase of urban existence.

Bailey, W. B. *Modern Social Conditions: A Statistical Study of Birth, Marriage, Divorce, Death, Disease, Suicide, Immigration, etc., with Special Reference to the United States* (New York, 1906). (VII, 5; VIII.)

Bajla, E. "Come si distribuiscono topograficamente le malattee contagiose negli aggregati urbani," *Attualita Med. Milano*, V (1916), 542–46.
The local distribution of contagious diseases in the urban area.

Barron, S. B. "Town life as a Cause of Degeneracy," *Pop. Sci. Mo.*, XXXIV (1888–89), 324–30. (X, 2.)

Billings, J. S. "The Mortality Rates of Baltimore; Life Table for Baltimore; Mortality in Different Wards; Causes of Disease," *Baltimore Med. Jour.*, X (1883–84), 487–89. (V, 1.)

"Biological Influences of City Life," *Literary Digest*, LII (February, 1916), 371–72.

"Birth- and Death-Rates in American Cities," *Amer. City*, XVI (1917), 195–99.

Bleicher, H. "Über die Eigentümlichkeiten der städtischen Natalitäts- und Mortalitätsverhältnisse," *Intern. Kongr.* für Hygiene und Demographie (Budapest, 1894). (VIII, 3.)
The peculiarities of urban birth and death rates.

Dublin, Louis I. "The Significance of the Declining Birth-Rate," *Science,* (new series), XLVII, 201–10.

Fehlinger, Hans. "De l'influence biologique de la civilization urbaine," *Scientia,* X (1911), 421–34. (VIII, 3.)

Guilfoy, W. H. *The Influence of Nationality upon the Mortality of a Community, with Special Reference to the City of New York,* "Department of Health of New York City Monograph Series 18," 1919. (V, 1, 2, 3.)

———. *An Analysis of the Mortality Returns of the Sanitary Areas of the Borough of Manhattan for the Year 1915,* "Department of Health of New York City Monograph Series 15," 1916.

Hammond, L. J., and Gray, C. H. "The Relation of the Foreign Population to the Mortality and Morbidity Rate of Philadelphia," *Bull. Amer. Acad. of Med.,* XIV (1913), 113–29. (V, 1.)

Harmon, G. E. "A Comparison of the Relative Healthfulness of Certain Cities in the United States, Based upon the Study of Their Vital Statistics," *Publ. Amer. Statist. Assoc.,* XV (Boston, 1916), 157–74.

Holmes, Samuel J. *A Bibliography of Eugenics,* "University of California Publications in Zoölogy," Vol. XXV, Berkeley, California, 1924.
Contains a chapter on "Urban Selection and the Influence of Industrial Development on Racial Heredity." Has served as a source of many references listed in this bibliography. (VIII.)

Love, A. G., and Davenport, C. B. "Immunity of City-Bred Recruits," *Arch. Med. Intern.,* XXIV (1919), 129–53.

Macpherson, J. "Urban Selection and Mental Health," *Rev. of Neurol. and Psychiatry,*" I (1903), 65–73. (VII, 2, 5; IX, 2, 3, 4; X, 3.)

Meinshausen: "Die Zunahme der Körpergrösse des deutschen Volkes vor dem Kriege; ihre Ursachen und Bedeutung für die Wiederherstellung der deutschen Volkskraft," *Archiv für Hygiene und Demographie,* XIV (1921), 28–72.
Points out degeneration of urban youth. (VII, 3; X, 3.)

Pieper, E. "Über die Verbreitung der Geschlechtskrankheiten nach Stadt und Land mit besonderer Berücksichtigung der Verhältnisse der Stadt Rostock und des Staates Mecklenburg," *Arch. für Soz. Hygiene und Demographie,* XIV (1923), 148–87. (X, 2.)

Sarker, S. L. "The Comparative Mortality of the Towns of the Nadia District," *Indian Med. Gaz.,* LII (Calcutta, 1917), 58–60.

Walford, C. "On the Number of Violent Deaths from Accident, Negligence, Violence, and Misadventure in the United Kingdom and Some Other Countries," *Jour. Royal Stat. Soc.*, XLIV (1881), 444–521.
Number of violent deaths in cities greater than rural region. (X, 2.)

Weber, L. W. "Grossstadt und Nerven," *Deutsche Rundschau*, CLXXVII (December, 1918), 391–407. (IX, 2, 4.)

Weiberg, W. "Zur Frage nach der Häufigkeit der Syphilis in der Grossstadt," *Arch. Rass. und Gesellsch. Biol.*, Vol. XI, 1914; 3 articles.

Whipple, G. C. *Vital Statistics: An Introduction to Demography* (New York, 1923). (VII, 1; VIII, 2, 3; IX, 2.)

2. The relative differences in the age and sex groups, in the city as over against the country, and in the various areas in the city are indicative of fundamental processes tending to produce typical results.

Baker, J. E. "City Life and Male Mortality," *Publ. Amer. Statist. Assoc.*, XI (1908), 133–49. (VIII, 1.)

Böckh, R. "Sterbetafeln C (für Grossstädte); Die fünfzig Berliner Sterbetafeln," *Bericht über 14ten Intern. Kongr. Hygiene*, III (Berlin, 1908), 1078–87. (V, 1, 2, 3, 4; VIII, 1.)

Heron, David. *On the Relation of Fertility in Man to Social Status and on the Changes in This Relation That Have Taken Place during the Last Fifty Years* (London, 1906). (VII, 1, 5; VIII, 1.)

Röse, C. "Die Grossstadt als Grab der Bevölkerung," *Aerztliche Rundschau*, XV (München, 1905), 257–61. (VII, 3; VIII, 1.)

3. Whether the conditions of city life have an influence on the fecundity of women and the size of the family is an aspect of city life inviting accurate study, attempts at which have already been made.

Haurbeck, L. "Der Wille zur Mutterschaft in Stadt und Land," *Deutsche Landwirtsch. Presse.*, XI (1915), 12. (VIII, 1, 2; X, 2.)

Kühner, F. "Stadt und Bevölkerungspolitik," *Städte-Zeit*, XIV (1917), 306.

Lewis, C. F., and J. N. *Natality and Fecundity: A Contribution to National Demography* (Edinburgh, 1906).
Based on statistics in the Scottish birth register of 1855. (VIII, 1, 2.)

Manschke, R. "Innere Einflüsse der Bevölkerungswanderungen auf die Geburtenzahl," *Zeitschr. für Sozialwiss.*, *neue Folge*, VII (1916), 100–115, 161–74. (VII, 3; VIII, 1, 2; X, 2.)

Morgan, J. E. *The Danger of Deterioration of Race from the Too Rapid Increase of Great Cities* (London, 1866). (VII, 1, 3; VIII, 1.)

Prinzing, F. "Eheliche und uneheliche Fruchtbarkeit und Aufwuchsziffer in Stadt und Land in Preussen," *Deutsche Med. Wochenschrift*, XLIV (1918), 351–54. (VIII, 1; X, 4.)

Theilhaber, F. A. *Das sterile Berlin* (Berlin, 1913). (VIII, 1, 2.)

Thompson, Warren S. "Race Suicide in the United States," *Sci. Mo.*, V, 22–35, 154–65, 258–69. (VIII, 1; X, 2.)

"Urban Sterilization," *Jour. Hered.*, VIII (1917), 268–69. (VIII, 1.)

IX. HUMAN NATURE AND CITY LIFE

The city is remaking human nature and each city is producing its own type of personality. These influences of city life are of prime interest to the sociologist. The materials bearing on this question are not primarily those collected by the scientist, but by the artist. It requires insight and imagination to perceive and to describe these deep-seated changes which are being wrought in the nature of man himself.

1. The division of labor and the fine specialization of occupations and professions that is so distinctly characteristic of city life has brought into existence a new mode of thought and new habits and attitudes which have transformed man in a few generations. The city man tends to think less in terms of locality than he does in terms of occupation. In a sense he has become an adjunct of the machine which he operates and the tools he uses. His interests are organized around his occupation, and his status and mode of life is determined by it.

Bahre, Walter. *Meine Klienten*. Vol. XLII in "Grossstadt Dokumente" (Berlin, 1905).
  Specialization and professional types and classes as seen from a lawyer's office. (IX, 4.)

Benario, Leo. *Die Wucherer und ihre Opfer*, Vol. XXXVIII in "Grossstadt Dokumente." (IX, 3, 4.)

The profession of money-lending in the large city and the behavior patterns that this professional group exhibits. (IX, 3, 4.)

Burke, Thomas. *The London Spy: A Book of Town Travels* (New York, 1922). (II, 3; V, 1, 2, 3; IX.)

Donovan, Frances. *The Woman Who Waits* (Boston, 1920).

The impressions and occupational experiences of a waitress in Chicago. (IX, 2, 3.)

Hammond, J. L., and Barbara. *The Skilled Labourer, 1760–1832* (London, 1919).

The emergence of occupational types in the course of industrial evolution. (III, 4; IV, 6.)

Hammond, J. L., and Barbara. *The Town Labourer, 1760–1832: The New Civilization* (London, 1917). (II, 3; III, 4; IV, 6; IX, 2, 3; X, 2.)

Hyan, Hans. *Schwere Jungen*, Vol. XXVIII in "Grossstadt Dokumente" (Berlin, 1905)

Describes the life of an occupational group—the pugilists—in the large city (Berlin). (V, 1, 3; VI, 6; IX, 4.)

Mayhew, Henry. *London Labour and London Poor: A Cyclopaedia of the Condition and Earnings of Those That Will Work, Those That Cannot Work, and Those That Will Not Work* (London, 1861–62), 4 vols.

A description of occupational types created by city specialization. (II, 3; VII, 5; IX, 4.)

Noack, Victor. *Was ein Berliner Musikant erlebte*, Vol. XIX in "Grossstadt Dokumente" (Berlin, 1905).

The experiences of a Berlin musician in his occupational life. Showing the evolution of an occupational type, with many highly specialized subtypes. (IX; X, 2.)

Roe, Clifford. *Panders and Their White Slaves* (New York and Chicago, 1910). (V, 1; VII, 5.)

Rowntree, B. Seebohm, and Lasker, Bruno. *Unemployment: A Social Study* (London, 1911).

Simkhovitch, Mary K. *The City Worker's World in America* (New York, 1917). (V, 1, 2, 3; VI, 10; VII, 2, 5.)

Solenberger, Alice W. *One Thousand Homeless Men: A Study of Original Records* (New York, 1914).

What a social agency's records reveal about occupational careers in the city. (VI, 4; VII, 4, 5; VIII, 1.)

Veblen, Thorstein. *The Instinct of Workmanship, and the State of the Industrial Arts* (New York, 1914).
Showing the development of the specialization of labor and its effect on human behavior. (IX, 2.)

Werthauer, Johannes. *Berliner Schwindel*, Vol. XXI in "Grossstadt Dokumente" (Berlin, 1905).
Showing the extent to which fraud has become a technical profession. (VII, 5; IX, 2, 4.)

Weidner, Albert. *Aus den Tiefen der Berliner Arbeiterbewegung*, Vol. IX, in "Grossstadt Dokumente" (Berlin, 1905).
The significance of the labor movement in the large city. (V, 1, 4; VII, 5; IX, 2, 3, 4.)

2. There is a city mentality which is clearly differentiated from the rural mind. The city man thinks in mechanistic terms, in rational terms, while the rustic thinks in naturalistic, magical terms. Not only does this difference exist between city and country, it exists also between city and city, and between one area of the city and another. Each city and each part of the city furnishes a distinct social world to its inhabitants, which they incorporate in their personality whether they will or no.

Carleton, Will. *City Ballads, City Festivals, and City Legends* (London, 1907). (X, 2.)

Grant, James. *Lights and Shadows of London Life* (London, 1842).
Giving a view of the picturesque aspects of the modern city.

———. *The Great Metropolis* (London, 1836). (III, 5; IV, 6; V, 3; IX.)

Marpillero, G. "Saggio di psicologia dell'urbanismo," *Revista Italiana di Sociologia*, XII (1908), 599–626.

Morgan, Anna. *My Chicago* (Chicago, 1918).
A city from the standpoint of the social aristocracy. (V, 3.)

Seiler, C. Linn. City Values. "An Analysis of the Social Status and Possibilities of American City Life" (University of Pennsylvania, Ph.D. Thesis, 1912).

Simmel, G. *Die Grossstädte und das Geistesleben*, in "Die Grossstadt" (Dresden, 1903).
The most important single article on the city from the sociological standpoint.

Sombart, Werner. *The Jews and Modern Capitalism,* translated from the German by M. Epstein (London and New York, 1913).
The best study of a city people and the influence of city life on their mentality. (IX, 1, 4; X, 3.)

Spengler, Oswald. *Der Untergang des Abendlandes: Umrisse einer Morphologie der Weltgeschichte,* Vol. II (München, 1922), chap. II, "Städte und Völker," pp. 100–224. (II; VII, 1, 5; IX, 1.)

Winter, Max. *Das Goldene Wiener Herz,* Vol. XI in "Grossstadt Dokumente" (Berlin, 1905).
A study of the financial nexus in city life. (IX, 4.)

Woolston, H. "The Urban Habit of Mind," *Amer. Jour. Sociol.,* XVII, 602 ff.

3. The medium through which man is influenced and modified in the city is the intricate system of communication. The urban system of communication takes on a special form. It is not typically the primary, but the secondary, contact that it produces. The public opinion that is built up in the city and the morale and *ésprit de corps* growing out of it relies on such typical media as the newspaper rather than the gossip monger; the telephone and the mails rather than the town meeting. The characteristic urban social unit is the occupational group rather than the geographical area.

Chicago Commission on Race Relations. *The Negro in Chicago* (Chicago, 1922).
A study growing out of the Chicago race riots, showing the growth of public opinion and the behavior of crowds and mobs in the city. (V, 1, 3; VII, 2.)

Follett, Mary P. *The New State: Group Organization the Solution of Popular Government* (New York, 1918).
Analyzes the conditions under which public opinion of today is formed and suggests local organization as a possible way out. (V, 3; VII, 5; IX, 1.)

Howe, Frederic C. "The City as a Socializing Agency," *Amer. Jour. Sociol.,* XVII, 509 ff. (VII, 5.)

————. *The City: The Hope of Democracy* (New York, 1905).
Has chapters on the new city civilization, the causes of political corruption, and gives a general description of city life, showing in particular the problems of public opinion it creates. (V; VI; VII, 1, 2.)

Park, Robert E. "The Immigrant Community and the Immigrant Press," *American Review,* III (March-April, 1925), 143–52. (V, 3.)

Triton (pseudonym). *Der Hamburger "Junge Mann,"* Vol. XXXIX in "Grossstadt Dokumente."

Shows the effect of the city and the contacts it makes possible on the development of an *ésprit de corps* and a type. In this case the young office clerks of Hamburg are shown to be a product of the international character of the port of Hamburg. (IV, 6; IX, 1, 2, 4.)

4. The final product of the city environment is found in the new types of personality which it engenders. Here the latent energies and capacities of individuals find expression and locate themselves within the range of a favorable milieu. This possibility of segregating one's self from the crowd develops and accentuates what there is of individuality in the human personality. The city gives an opportunity to men to practice their specialty vocationally and develop it to the utmost degree. It provides also the stimulus and the conditions which tend to bring out those temperamental and psychological qualities within the individual through the multiple behavior patterns which it tolerates.

Hammer, Wilhelm. *Zehn Lebensläufe Berliner Kontrollmädchen,* Vol. XVIII in "Grossstadt Dokumente."

The life-history of ten Berlin prostitutes with a suggested classification of types. (VI, 4; IX, 1.)

Deutsch-German, Alfred (pseudonym). *Wiener Mädel,* Vol. XVII in "Grossstadt Dokumente" (Berlin, 1905).

An intimate study of the types of girls to be found in the large city. (IX, 2, 3.)

Flagg, James M. *City People. A Book of Illustrations* (New York, 1909).

Freimark, Hans. *Moderne Geistesbeschwörer und Wahrheitssucher,* Vol. XXXVI in "Grossstadt Dokumente" (Berlin, 1905).

Fortune-tellers and persons in the "occult fields" in the modern city. A study of magical vestiges in city mentality. (IX, 1, 2.)

Hapgood, Hutchins. *Types from City Streets* (New York, 1910).

———. *The Spirit of the Ghetto* (New York and London, 1909).

An intimate study of life in the New York Jewish quarter with a graphic presentation of personality types. (V, 2.)

Hecht, Ben. *A Thousand and One Afternoons in Chicago* (Chicago, 1922).

Journalistic sketches of Chicago scenes, experiences, and types. (V, 3; IX.)

Mackenzie, C. "City People," *McClure's*, XLVII (August, 1916), 22.

Markey, Gene. *Men About Town: A Book of Fifty-eight Caricatures* (Chicago, 1924).

Mensch, Ella (pseudonym). *Bilderstürmer in der Berliner Frauenbewegung.* Types found in the feminist movement of Berlin. (IX, 2, 3.)

X. THE CITY AND THE COUNTRY

The city and the country represent two opposite poles in modern civilization. The difference between the two is not merely one of degree, but of kind. Each has its own peculiar type of interests, of social organization, and of humanity. These two worlds are in part antagonistic and in part complementary to each other. The one influences the life of the other, but they are by no means equally matched. The analysis of these differences, antagonisms, and interacting forces has not passed even the descriptive stage.

1. The ancient city was regarded as a parasitic growth. It dominated the country by skill and by force, but contributed little to its welfare. The modern city, too, is often regarded as a superfluous burden which the rural sections are carrying. This view of the matter is fast passing away, however, as the city extends its influence, not by force, but by fulfilling a set of functions upon which the rural population has become dependent. The economists have been especially concerned with the antagonistic interests which the city and the country have presented. These antagonisms have come to play a political rôle which influences local, national, and international affairs.

Bookwalter, J. W. *Rural Versus Urban; Their Conflict and Its Causes: A Study of the Conditions Affecting Their Natural and Artificial Relation* (New York, 1911). (X, 2.)

Damaschke, Adolf. *Die Bodenreform: Grundsätzliches und Geschichtliches zur Erkenntnis der sozialen Not* (19th ed.; Jena, 1922). (VI, 10.)

Reibmayr, A. "Die wichtigsten biologischen Ursachen der heutigen Landflucht," *Arch. für Rass. und Gesellsch. Biol.*, VII (1911), 349–76.
Decrease in rural population of Germany. Shows also unfavorable effects of alcohol, venereal disease, and other factors on population of city, and the effects of the city on the country. (VII, 2, 5; VIII, 1.)

Ross, E. A. "Folk Depletion as a Cause of Rural Decline," *Publ. Amer. Sociol. Soc.*, XI (1917), 21–30. (VII, 3; VIII, 1, 3; X, 2.)

Roxby, P. M. *Rural Depopulation in England During the Nineteenth Century and After*, LXXI (1912), 174–90. (VIII, 3.)

"Rural Depopulation in Germany," *Scient. Amer. Suppl.*, LXVIII (1908), 243. (VII, 3.)

Smith, J. Russell. *North America: Its People and Resources, Development, and the Prospects of the Continent as an Agricultural, Industrial, and Commercial Area* (New York, 1925).
One of the best geographical discussions of the relation between country and city. (I, 1, 4; III, 2, 3, 4.)

Vandervelde, E. *L'exode rural et le retour aux champs* (Paris, 1903). (VIII, 3.)

Waltemath. "Der Kampf gegen die Landflucht und die Slawisierung des platten Landes," *Archiv für Innere Kolonisation*, IX (1916–18), 12.

2. As a result of city life new forms of social organization have been developed which are foreign to the country. The family, the neighborhood, the community, the state have become transformed by city needs into new institutions with a different organization and with a different set of functions. The social processes that characterize rural life do not apply in the city. A new moral order has developed which is fast breaking down the precedents of an earlier epoch of civilization.

Bowley, A. L. "Rural Population in England and Wales: A Study of the Change of Density, Occupations, and Ages," *Jour. Royal Stat. Soc.*, LXXVII (1914), 597–645. (VII, 2; VIII, 2.)

Brunner, Edmund de S. *Churches of Distinction in Town and Country* (New York, 1923). (VI, 5.)

Busbey, L. W. "Wicked Town and Moral Country," *Unpop. Rev.*, X (October, 1918), 376–92. (X, 3.)

Cook, O. F. "City and Country, Effects of Human Environments on the Progress of Civilization," *Jour. Hered.*, XIV (1921), 253–59.

Galpin, Charles J. *Rural Life* (New York, 1918).
One of the best analyses of rural life available, and of great value as a basis for comparison between city life and country life. (IV, 1, 2, 5; V, 1, 2, 3; X, 1, 3.)

Gillette, J. M. *Rural Sociology* (New York, 1922). (IV; V, 1, 2; VI, 8; X, 1, 3.)

Groves, E. R. "Psychic Causes of Rural Migration," *Amer. Jour. Sociol.*, XXI (1916), 623–27. (IV, 5; VII, 3; X, 1, 3.)

Jastrow, J. "Die Städtegmeinschaft in ihren kulturellen Beziehungen," *Zeitschr. für Sozialwiss.*, X (1907), 42–51.
Indicates institutions to which urban life has given impetus.

Morse, H. N. *The Social Survey in Town and Country Areas* (New York, 1925).

Peattie, Roderick. "The Isolation of the Lower St. Lawrence Valley," *Geog. Rev.*, V (February, 1918), 102–18.
An excellent study of provincialism as a result of isolation. (IV, 5.)

Prinzing, F. "Die Totgeburten in Stadt und Land," *Deutsche Med. Wochenschr.*, XLIII (1917), 180–81.
The number of still births indicates the technique available in city and country. (VIII, 1.)

Sanderson, Dwight. *The Farmer and His Community* (New York, 1922). (V, 1, 2, 3.)

Smith, Arthur H. *Village Life in China: A Study in Sociology* (New York, Chicago, and Toronto, 1899).
The oriental village and its place in social organization.

Thurnwald, R. "Stadt and Land im Lebensprozess der Rasse," *Arch. für Rass. und Gesellsch. Biol.*, I (1904), 550–74, 840–84.
Contains excellent bibliography. (VII, 3; VIII, 1, 3.)

Tucker, R. S., and McCombs, C. E. "Is the Country Healthier Than the Town?" *Nat. Mun. Rev.*, XII (June, 1923), 291–95. (VIII, 1.)

Welton, T. A. "Note on Urban and Rural Variations According to the English Census of 1911," *Jour. Royal Stat. Soc.*, LXXVI (1913), 304–17. (VII, 3; VIII; X, 1.)

3. The rustic and the urbanite not only show certain fundamental differences in personality, but the variations found in the city far exceed the country, and the rate at which new types are constantly being created in the city far exceeds that of the country. The rural man still is to a great extent the product of the nature which surrounds him, while the urbanite has become a part of the machine with which he works, and has developed as many different

species as there are techniques to which he is devoted. The attitudes, the sentiments, the life organization of the city man are as different from the country man as those of the civilized man are from the primitive. As the city extends its influence over the country the rural man is also being remade, and ultimately the differences between the two may become extinguished.

Anthony, Joseph. "The Unsophisticated City Boy," *Century*, CIX (November, 1924), 123–28. (VII, 5.)

Coudenhove-Kalergi, H. "The New Nobility," *Century*, CIX (November, 1924), 3–6.
A concise analysis of the outstanding differences in the personality of the rustic and the urbanite. (IX, 1, 2, 3, 4; X, 1, 2.)

Humphrey, Z. "City People and Country Folk," *Country Life*, XXXVII (January, 1920), 35–37.

McDowall, Arthur. "Townsman and the Country," *London Mercury*, VIII (August, 1923), 405–13. (IV, 5; IX, 2; X, 1, 2.)

Myers, C. S. "Note on the Relative Variability of Modern and Ancient and of Rural and Urban Peoples," *Man*, VI (London, 1906), 24–26.
An anthropological study. (VIII.)

Vuillenmier, J. F. "A comparative Study of New York City and Country Criminals," *Jour. Crim. Law and Criminol.*, XI (1921), 528–50. (VII, 5; IX, 2.)

XI. THE STUDY OF THE CITY

Attempts to understand the city and city life have resulted in two types of studies. On the one hand there are the investigations into special phases of the subject, and on the other are a number of systematic, generally co-operative, scientific approaches to the city as a whole. The increased attention which the city has been receiving at the hands of various types of experts has brought into existence a number of organizations and institutions which regularly occupy themselves with the collection of information relating to the city. This has given rise to a number of technical journals which are of great importance to the student of the city.

1. There are available at the present time a number of fairly exhaustive systematic studies of various cities. In most instances they represent the combined efforts of many students, extending over a period of years, to explore the realms of urban life in diverse parts of the world, generally with a definite objective in view. Only a few of such studies have been listed under this category.

Booth, Charles. *Life and Labor of the People of London* (16 vols.; London, 1892).
   Attempts to describe the people of London "as they exist in London under the influence of education, religion, and administration." Required seventeen years for its completion. Contains a wealth of information about the city and city life.

Gamble, Sidney D. *Peking: A Social Survey* (New York, 1921).

Harrison, Shelby M. *Social Conditions in an American City: A Summary of the Findings of the Springfield Survey* (New York, 1920).

Johnson, Clarence Richard. *Constantinople Today, or the Pathfinder Survey of Constantinople: A Study in Oriental Social Life* (New York and London, 1923).

Kellogg, Paul U. (editor). *The Pittsburgh Survey* (6 vols.; New York, 1914).

Kenngott, George F. *The Record of a City: A Social Survey of Lowell, Massachusetts* (New York, 1912).

Ostwald, Hans O. A. "Grossstadt Dokumente," (Berlin, 1905).
   A series of fifty volumes by various authors giving accounts of personal experience and investigation in the local communities and among various groupings and personality types in the city of Berlin and in some other large cities of Europe.

Rowntree, B. Seebohm. *Poverty: A Study of Town Life* (London, 1901).

Rowntree, B. S., and Lasker, Bruno. *Unemployment: A Social Study* (London, 1911).

2. The social survey is not only a technique which has been employed to study the urban community, but has grown into a movement of considerable proportions. From another standpoint the social survey may also be regarded as a means of control. Many of the "surveys" are merely single investigations of administration, housing, justice, education, recreation, in urban and rural communities, carried on by the group itself or by some outside experts called

in for the purpose. Others are highly integrated studies of the community in all its phases. There is a tendency at the present time for systematic social research to take the place of the social survey in the study of community life. The latter emphasizes diagnosis and treatment, while the former strives to develop methods of disinterested research into various aspects of city life.

Aronovici, Carol. *The Social Survey* (New York, 1916).

Burns, Allen T. "Organization of Community Forces," *Proceedings of Nat. Con. Charities and Corrections, 1916*, pp. 62–78.

Elmer, Manuel C. "Social Surveys of Urban Communities," Ph.D. Thesis, University of Chicago (Menasha, Wisconsin, 1914).
Considers the social survey up to 1914 and outlines the scope and methods of the urban community survey. Also his "Technique of the Social Surveys" (Lawrence, Kansas, 1917).

Kellogg, P. U., Harrison, S. M., and Palmer, George T. *The Social Survey Proceedings of the Academy of Political Science in the City of New York*, Vol. II (July, 1912), 475–544.
"The Social Survey and Its Further Development," *Publ. Amer. Statist. Assoc.*, 1915.

3. While there are many periodicals which contain departments devoted to the urban community, such as the *Survey*, the *Journal of Social Forces*, and a number of others, the following are listed as typical of periodicals exclusively concerned with various phases of the study of the city.

The American City (monthly), New York. Now in its thirty-second volume.

American Municipalities (monthly), Marshalltown, Iowa. Now in its forty-ninth volume.

Municipal and County Engineering (monthly), since 1890. Indianapolis, Indiana.

The Municipal Journal and Public Works Engineer (weekly). Now in its thirty-fourth year. London.

The National Municipal Review (monthly), published by the National Municipal League. Now in its fourteenth volume. New York.

Die Städte-Zeit. In its fourteenth volume in 1917.

Der Städtebau. Monatsschrift für die künstlerische Ausgestaltung der Städte nach ihren wirtschaftlichen, gesundheitlichen, und sozialen Grundsätzen (monthly), since 1904. Berlin.

The Town-Planning Review. The journal of the department of civic design of the school of Architecture. University of Liverpool. Now in its eleventh volume. Liverpool.

La Vie Urbaine. Volume VII in 1924.

LOUIS WIRTH

INDEXES

SUBJECT INDEX

Age, the *New York*, 139

Areas: natural, 6, 50–51, 54, 77, 188; of vice and poverty, 55; "bright light," 56; local trade, 67; commuting, 184; of deterioration, 193

Attitudes: sentiments and interests, 16, 22; and money, 17

Automobiles: and community growth, 70; and vice, 107

Bohemia, 150

Chain stores, characteristic of city, 202

Chicago: Little Sicily, 10, 56; the Gold Coast, 10; regional planning association of, 48; the Loop, 51; the Ghetto, 56; population of, 60; land values in, 61; occupations in, 57; ecological forces in, 147; Black Belt of, 147

Church, the, and city life, 24

Cities: classified by functions, 178; satellite, 185; as cultural centers, 186; systematic studies of, 226

City, the: A product of nature, 1–2; an ecological unit, 2; natural habitat of civilized man, 2; population of, 5, 6, 8; and human nature, 4, 46, 63; and the division of labor, 14; and primary relations, 23; vice and crime in, 25; and secondary relations, 26; and intellectual life, 30; crusades in, 33; and politics, 34; advertising in, 37; a melting-pot, 40; rewards eccentricity, 41; growth of, 47; population groups, 47; expansion of, 49; age groups in, 47; aggregation, 48; defined, 165, 169; statistics of, 167; and economic development, 168; natural history of, 170; bibliographies of, 174; types of, 175; relation to town and metropolis, 180; and ecological organization, 187, 196; as a physical mechanism, 195; and politics, 201; growth of population in, 208–9, 212; as a parasitic growth, 222

City-building, 206

City life: biological aspects of, 214; and the new moral order, 223

City man, the, life-organization of, 225

City mentality, 219

Colonies: immigrant, 26; and second generation, 28

Communication: mechanism of, 29, 197; and the newspaper, 39; and social contagion, 45

Community: defined, 64, 115, 144; and human nature, 65; four types of, 66; agricultural, 68; skeletal structure of, 73; and moral codes, 105–6; and the delinquent, 111; local, 114, 191; measure of efficiency, 118; institutions of, 199

Community-center associations, 117

Community organizations, 114

Competition, and the struggle for space, 63, 64, 71

Conurbation, 49

Crisis: financial, 21; defined, 27; positive law, 28

Cultural areas. *See* Bohemia, Ghetto, Gold Coast

Culture, city-born, 2; urban life and, 3; and political organization, 116–17; and the local community, 145–46

Dance hall, public, and the neighborhood, 151

Delinquency triangle, the, 152

Department store, characteristic city institution, 202

Division of labor, the, and new modes of thought, 217

Ecological organization, of the city, 2, 115

Ecology: human, 2, 63, 145; succession, 50, 75; centralization, 51; climax, 68, 77; culmination, 71; invasion, 72, 74, 76

Economic organization, 116

231

INDEX TO AUTHORS